JERUSALEM
architecture

JERUSALEM
architecture

David Kroyanker

Introduction by
Teddy Kollek

Editor: Ralph Mandel
Graphic design: Marc Walter, Paris
Photolithography: Colourscan, Singapore
Printing and binding: EBS—Editoriale Bortolazzi—Stei, Verona

Published in 1994 by
Tauris Parke Books
45 Bloomsbury Square
London WC1A 2HY

All rights reserved. Except for brief quotations in a review,
this book, or any part thereof, may not be reproduced in any form
without permission in writing from the publisher.

A CIP record for this book is available from the British Library

ISBN: 1-85043-873-0

Contents

— 7 —
Introduction
Teddy Kollek

— 11 —
Three Thousand Years of History and Urban Development
Ralph Mandel

— 19 —
The Old City: Urban Structure and Texture
Dense and Introspective Architecture

— 27 —
The Old City from 1000 BC Through the Ottoman Empire
A Study of Remnants

— 85 —
The Old City in Modern Times
Preservation and Reconstruction

— 101 —
Jewish, Arab, and European Christian Building in the New City
Architecture with Ethnic Identity

— 143 —
Building a New Jerusalem: The British Mandate
The Emergence of New Architectural Styles and Technologies

— 169 —
Modern Architecture: 1948-1993
From the International to the Neo-Oriental Style

— 201 —
Epilogue
Stone: The Unifying Element

— 202 —
Bibliography

— 203 —
Glossary

— 206 —
Index

— 209 —
Chronology

— 210 —
Acknowledgments

Introduction

Teddy Kollek

1. The Old City, contained within the historic walls, meets New Jerusalem outside the walls, built since the middle of the 19th century.

Jerusalem is a city like no other. Three thousand years of history have fashioned a living museum of varied and intriguing architectural forms. The vast span of periods and styles has created a truly unique physical entity. Perhaps nowhere else is it possible to see such a wide range of building types and technologies in such a limited area.

Jerusalem as imagined across the centuries by untold millions around the world—a Utopian holy city, a shimmering vision of towers and battlements—has often been depicted in art and literature. But only rarely did the image derive from personal observation, a situation that foisted on the city an element of the unreal. Of course Jerusalem is a sacred, historically resonant city, but it is also the living, dynamic place where over half a million people, of different faiths and nationalities, go about their everyday pursuits. It is a city that finds itself coping with an array of problems—political, religious, economic, and social, as well as urban and architectural.

Jerusalem's physical pattern, both inside and outside the fortified ramparts, is forged by a panoply of architectural modes, which together express the distinctive character of the religious and national communities that have ruled the city or made it their home. Above all, each of the three great monotheistic faiths has been instrumental in shaping the Jerusalem landscape. Architectural, ethnic, and religious features identify a building as Jewish, Christian, or Muslim. The physical imprint left by so many peoples—Turks, Germans, Russians, French, English, Armenians, Ethiopians, Greeks, and Italians—is evident in the structure of the city's neighborhoods as well as in the design of individual houses and institutional buildings. Yet, in some way, perhaps because of the pervasive use of Jerusalem stone, these diverse elements blend into a cosmopolitan tapestry of which the eye never tires.

Jerusalem is one city, but the history of building in Jerusalem falls naturally into two major sections: the Old City inside the 16th-century walls, its origins lying three millennia in the past; and the New City, outside the walls, which began to develop less than a century and a half ago.

Encircling the Old City is a rampart more than four centuries old. Compressed within lies an astonishing variety of structures both ancient and modern. They date all the way back to the artificial platform on the Temple Mount/Haram al-Sharif, built by King Herod in the 1st century BC, and forward through early mosques and Muslim shrines, medieval Crusader churches, Mamluk buildings for everyday and sacred use, and 19th-century European Christian edifices. Finally, they also embrace the generation-long project, undertaken after 1967, to rebuild the Jewish Quarter and restore the city walls and gates.

Urban development in the New City is best considered as a five-tiered process of periods and their related architectural styles. First, there are the traditional Jewish neighborhoods that began to rise in the mid-19th century. They mark the beginning of organized Jewish settlement outside the Old City walls. Next, there is Arab construction, both the rural variety, a feature around Jerusalem for countless

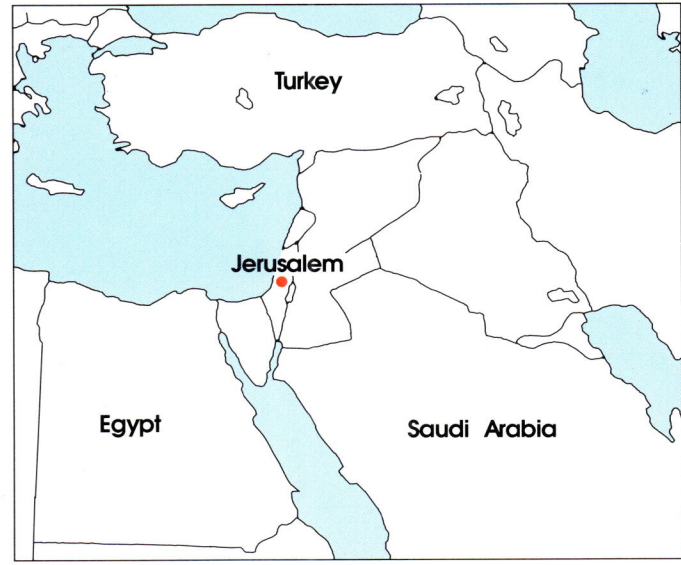

generations, and the urban, which comprises neighborhoods and buildings erected by Arab Muslims and Christians outside the walls since the second half of the 19th century. As this book makes clear, Muslim culture has had a great impact on Jerusalem; deep-rooted aspirations derive from the Muslim vision of the city as a realm of sanctity. Indeed, the Arabic name for Jerusalem, "al-Quds," means "the holy place."

The third tier of New City development, international in character, consists of European Christian buildings erected from 1860 to 1918. These are monumental edifices—sponsored by the Germans, French, Russians, English, Greek Orthodox, and Italians for religious and other purposes—which continue to play a preponderant role in determining the city's physical character.

The two remaining tiers are bound up with the expansion of Jerusalem in the modern era. During the period of the British Mandate (1918-48), the Jewish community initiated a series of garden neighborhoods, which in some cases bordered on affluent neighborhoods then being established by Jerusalem's Arab population. The period also saw the construction of significant British public buildings and of Jewish institutions for the "state-in-the making." After 1948, when Jerusalem was proclaimed by the newly formed State of Israel as its capital, government building quite naturally became a dominant factor. Large-scale public-housing projects and many new neighborhoods arose, in an ongoing process marked by striking urban and design developments.

Beginning in June 1967, when the physical and official barriers that had divided Jerusalem for nineteen years came down, we witnessed a torrent of feeling, which even now erupts whenever decisions must be taken regarding the preservation of the city's authentic character. There are few places on earth where, within a relatively small area, buildings, sites, and indeed entire city quarters pack such an emotional charge for so many people around the world. Sometimes it seems as if we were under observation through a magnifying glass by the whole international community.

Jerusalem is not only a city of holiness, bristling with minarets, church towers, and domed synagogues; it is equally a city of residential complexes, commercial quarters, traffic jams, parking lots, and industrial zones. Here, the overwhelming problem in urban planning is how to strike a judicious balance between the development needs of a modern city and the preservation of its historical heritage. Acknowledging this responsibility, we are frequently obliged to moderate aspirations toward urban development and thus ensure that a particular plan meets the stringent criteria we have set ourselves for the safeguarding of Jerusalem and its image.

In the early 1970s, contentious public debate still raged over the merits of demolition and redevelopment versus those of preservation and restoration. What drove many of these controversies, some of which became quite acrimonious, was an absence of what we needed—consciousness, knowledge, sensitivity—to understand the city's unparalleled physical values.

There are no objective criteria by which to choose between preservation and demolition, or to determine the relative value of neighborhoods and buildings. Arguments for salvaging the given evolve from a diversity of sources—nostalgic, national, religious, historical, architectural, and ethnographic. By contrast, opponents of conservation insist that the very attempt to redeem the old serves primarily to confer an aura of near sanctity on buildings and sites that are merely run-down, all the while that it avoids coming to terms with the ravages of time. According to this view, preservationists are ultra-conservatives who lack vision and a sense of progress. Moreover, they would put a stop to development by fostering nostalgia and sentimentality for every stylized window or interesting staircase, by evoking "the good old days," which in reality were not invariably all that good. Thus, say the antipreservationists, new construction should prevail over renovation or revitalization, because it is politically more dramatic, financially less costly, and bureaucratically more efficient.

In the past, one sometimes had the impression that the preservation-averse had the upper hand, thanks to a dearth of basic knowledge about the significance of urban and architectural values. Clearly, there was a need for tools that would permit everyone to gain a better and more detailed understanding of urban texture, which in turn would assist the planning authorities and the City Council in their examination of building proposals, allowing them to make better-informed judgments about the implications of conserving or renovating or razing buildings and other sites. The lessons of the past can be learned by a careful study of the elements that make up the urban texture and architectural styles of Jerusalem in each of the city's periods, and that knowledge contributes to the development of new ideas and standards with which to fashion a future image.

Perhaps the exclusive contribution of *Jerusalem Architecture*—a contribution that distinguishes the book from all other works on the city—is its illustration program, which includes commissioned line drawings. These provide a telling record of how certain buildings looked in their prime, before age and neglect left them in a state of disrepair. They capture the look as well of edifices that cannot be photographed owing to their close integration into the fabric of the city, which leaves the camera without enough space to produce a reasonable facsimile. Even so, the most meaningful details of buildings can be captured on film, and this has been done with great success. The resulting combination of line drawings and photographs makes the book unique among publications on Jerusalem.

For many years, research and publication on Jerusalem's urban and architectural image across the ages lagged behind studies focusing on its history, religious sects, archaeology, communities, and politics. To rectify this situation, the Jerusalem Municipality, the Jerusalem Foundation, and the Jerusalem Institute for Israel Studies, with the support and help of others, joined together in a prolonged effort. This program enlisted architect David Kroyanker to prepare a comprehensive history of architecture, physical planning, and development in Jerusalem.

We supported this major endeavor because it is crucial to our appreciation of the city's architectural heritage. We were convinced that a thorough survey, presented to the public in a manner both aesthetically impressive and professionally accurate, would enhance awareness of Jerusalem's architectural values, and therefore of the importance of renovation and preservation alongside modern urban development.

The present book—*Jerusalem Architecture*—summarizes some twenty years of research, much of it published in Hebrew, and gives everyone who loves Jerusalem, particularly nonspecialists, access to the history of the city's architecture in all its manifold styles. Now all those fascinated by our city can explore its remarkable pattern of construction, a pattern made up of neighborhoods, quarters, compounds, and individual edifices. As we discover the clusters of space, texture, building technology, environmental design, architectural objects, scale, and color, the complete townscape begins to assume shape and form. Gradually, Jerusalem, old and new, reveals itself, in both grandeur and modest, human dimension, from the monumentality of its sacred temples to the privacy of its residential courtyards, from the overall structure of its twisting alleys and lanes to its ethnographical elements. The concise explanations, enhanced by striking graphic presentation, make available to the untrained eye physical values heretofore known only to specialists, in part because many architectural wonders have long been concealed behind high walls and padlocked gates.

In closing, let me acknowledge a special debt of gratitude to my friend Alexis Gregory, who devoted himself to this project with great love and unflagging energy. His efforts have been critical to the book's realization. *Jerusalem Architecture* presents to an international audience a little-known but enthralling and vital aspect of the timeless city of Jerusalem.

Three Thousand Years of History and Urban Development

Ralph Mandel

Jerusalem is a city of contradictions: ancient and new, heavenly and earthly, spiritual and material. And although traditionally its name means "foundation of peace," Jerusalem has probably known more strife than tranquility since King David captured it from the Jebusites and made it the capital of his united monarchy some three thousand years ago. Sacred since the 7th century to three faiths, the city is a monumental creation, its great man-made stone edifices grafted onto a primeval rock-strewn, ravine-lacerated terrain. The imposing structures proclaim the relationship of their builders—tribes, religious communities, nations—to the city's natural, and supernatural, surroundings. But more mundane considerations have also played a part, and in yet another contradiction, grandeur of construction sprang from pettiness of motive. Thus, political rivalries, personal feuds, and overweening egos have produced architectural statements as potently geared to eternity as those designed to raise humanity to the realm of the spiritual.

The city itself—the "Old City," that is, which was Jerusalem until the mid-19th century, just yesterday in terms of its history—stands on an elevated plateau. "Jerusalem is emphatically a mountain city," wrote its quintessential explorer Sir Charles Wilson in his four-volume work *Picturesque Palestine* (1880-84). "Surrounded on all sides by limestone hills ... and only approached by rough mountain roads, its position is one of great natural strength." Moreover, continued Wilson, "we may infer from the well-known words of the Psalmist, 'As the mountains are round about Jerusalem, so the Lord is round about his people,' that importance was attached to the hills as a barrier or protection against hostile attack."

Yet, as barriers, those hills, like the walls erected around the city at different times in its history, proved permeable. Jerusalem has been a coveted prize for conquerors down through the ages, even though in purely strategic terms it was unimportant, remote and dependent on the hinterland for most of its physical needs. The progenitor of the Jerusalem mystique was King David (r. 1004-965 BC), who built and fortified the "City of David" and laid the groundwork for expansion. We are told that King David initiated some monumental construction (such as the "House of the Mighty Men" [Nehemiah 3:16] and "David's Tower" [Song of Songs 4:4]), and in an act of vast symbolic import he brought the Jews' sacred Ark of the Covenant to the town. Jerusalem's status as a spiritual and political center—initially of the Jewish people, later of Christianity and Islam—was sealed during the reign of David's son, King Solomon (965-928 BC), who built the First Temple, sanctuary for the Holy Ark, and the adjacent royal palace, together forming what archaeologist B. Mazar called the "acropolis of Jerusalem." An enormous project, the complex took twenty years to complete and involved the labors of skilled artisans brought especially from Phoenicia—just as other construction enterprises in later centuries would bring craftsmen from overseas who possessed skills lost or unknown to the indigenous population.

Solomon initiated considerable public building, with the result that Jerusalem thrust northward from the City of David to encompass the Ophel area and, above it, the elevated platform of the Temple Mount. Prefiguring later eras, Jerusalem's markets made the city an important factor in the international commerce of the time. Another major builder of

1. "Absalom's Tomb," a Hellenistic burial monument in the Kidron Valley, below the Old City, dating from the 1st century BC, bears Classical motifs carved into the local Jerusalem stone.

2. The City of David: The initial stage of Jerusalem, around 1000 BC. Diorama at Tower of David Museum of the History of Jerusalem.

3. Jerusalem during King Hezekiah's reign (c. 701 BC), when the Siloam tunnel was hewn in order to ensure the city's water supply in case of a siege. Cross-section reconstruction at Tower of David Museum of the History of Jerusalem.

1. This large subterranean hall beneath the Temple Mount, known as "Solomon's Stables," was built originally by King Herod as an infill support structure when he expanded the area of the Temple Mount. The present vault dates to the Fatimid Period in the 10th century. The Crusader Templar Knights used the structure as a stable.

the city was King Hezekiah (727-698 BC), famous for the construction of fortifications and towers, as well as for a tunnel dug beneath the city to the Siloam Pool, which provided a water supply for Jerusalem during a siege laid by King Sennacherib of Assyria in 701 BC. (Jerusalem's vulnerability to water sanctions extends into our own time.) This historical period ended with the capture of the city in 586 BC by King Nebuchadnezzar of Babylon, who destroyed the First Temple and exiled the Jews.

Across the ages, Jerusalem often felt the aftershock of the clash of armies and empires at a vast remove from the Land of Israel. In 538 BC, King Cyrus of Persia, having defeated the Babylonians, issued a proclamation allowing the Jewish exiles to return home. By 515 BC the Second Temple was standing, though it took decades more, under the leadership of Nehemiah, before the city ramparts could be restored, providing enough security to permit resettlement. Jerusalem regained its status as the spiritual and national center of the Jewish

164 BC. Increasing strife, both internecine and international, marked the independent reign of the Hasmoneans, which effectively ended with Jerusalem's conquest by the Roman General Pompey in 63 BC. In 40 BC the Roman Senate sent Herod, "King of Judea," to assume power in the city, and three years later his forces breached the city's walls, unleashing a general massacre of the population.

Despite this inauspicious beginning, it was during the reign of King Herod (37-4 BC) that Jerusalem achieved its greatest size and splendor in ancient times. Herod undertook two major building projects. In order to guard the city's most vulnerable side, the north (on the other three flanks the perimeter wall rises above deep valleys), Herod erected a great palace and fortress dominated by three towers. The base of the largest tower, called "Phasael," is today part of the structure popularly known as "David's Tower." Located in the Citadel of

2. The magnificent city built by King Herod. The royal palace and the three towers of his fortress are seen in the foreground, while the Temple Mount is in the background. Reconstruction drawing at Tower of David Museum of the History of Jerusalem.

people, and on the three pilgrimage festivals the city could barely contain the huge influx of celebrants from every part of the country.

The centuries that followed witnessed conquests by the Greeks under Alexander the Great (332 BC) and his successors, the Ptolemies of Egypt (301-198 BC), followed by the Syrian Seleucids, who banned the practice of Judaism and profaned the Holy Temple. Following a bitter fifteen-year revolt, led by Judah Maccabee, from the Hasmoneans, a priestly family, the Temple was rededicated in

the Old City, it is one of Jerusalem's best-known landmarks. Revealed here is a major pattern in the history of Jerusalem: the fusion of present with past through the medium of architecture, not only by the continuous use of a site (creating layers of construction) but also by the physical integration of earlier elements into new structures. The Phasael tower itself was built into the older Hasmonean wall, and the site of the complex subsequently became the camp of the Romans' Tenth Legion as well as, still later, a power base of the Crusaders,

1. The Ophel Archaeological Garden and the southern wall of the Temple Mount. The garden, a treasure trove of finds from the city's various eras, also contains the Hulda Gate and steps, the main entrance to the Temple Mount during the Second Temple Period.
2. Jerusalem during the Second Temple Period was a resplendent city with many public buildings. This 1:50 scale model is on display at the Holyland Hotel in New Jerusalem.
3. Façade of the model of Herod's Temple, viewed from the east. The reconstruction, by archaeologist Michael Avi-Yonah, is based on historical sources and archaeological evidence.

then the Mamluks, and finally the Ottomans. Today it forms part of the Museum of the History of Jerusalem.

Herod's second large-scale construction project focused on the Temple Mount. Its area would be doubled with the use of massive supporting walls made of huge blocks—including what is now the most sacred site in Judaism, the Western Wall (or "Wailing Wall")—and endowed with the basic shape that it still retains. To protect the Temple, Herod built the huge Antonia Fortress (named for Mark Antony) atop a steep hill of rock. As for the Temple itself, Josephus Flavius relates (*The Jewish War*, AD c. 75) that the King transformed it into "the most wonderful edifice ever seen or spoken of." However, following Herod's death, Judea became a mere Roman province, governed by procurators based in Caesarea rather than in Jerusalem. It was one of those procurators, Pontius Pilate (AD 26-36), who condemned Jesus to death. Jerusalem in this period was a large, thriving city, a great spiritual and economic center and a magnet for Jewish pilgrims and immigrants.

Still, the city was also hurtling toward ruin. Sporadic clashes with the Romans, intra-Jewish social and religious tensions, the actions of underground "freedom fighters" for whom the end justified the means, and a pervasive atmosphere of messianic expectations finally erupted into a revolt against the Romans in AD 66. Four years later the city was decimated by Titus, son of the Emperor Vespasian, who destroyed the Second Temple despite his father's injunction to let it stand. There was one more spasmodic Jewish attempt at independence—an uprising led by Shimon Bar-Kokhba in reaction to a decision by the Emperor Hadrian, following his visit to Jerusalem in AD 129, to rebuild the city as a full-fledged Roman town called Aelia Capitolina. But in AD 135 Jerusalem, which had been held by the rebels for three years, was retaken, whereupon Hadrian barred Jews from entering the city on pain of death. In terms of its layout, the Old City of today is still basically the Roman town built by Hadrian.

The Roman Period is traditionally said to have ended in 324. In a sense, though, it continued for another three centuries—but with a difference. The inauguration of Constantine, a convert to Christianity, as Roman Emperor in 330 launched the longest sustained period of Christian rule in Jerusalem. The most imposing of the many monumental Christian structures built in the city during the Byzantine Period (named for Byzantium, the ancient site of the Emperor's new capital, Constantinople) was the Church of the Holy Sepulcher. Consecrated in 335 and ever since the most important Christian building in Jerusalem, the Holy Sepulcher stands on the spot where Constantine's mother, the Empress Helena, reputedly found the True Cross when she visited the city in 326. Most of the original structure, as well as many other Byzantine edifices in the city, were destroyed when the Persians, in league with the Jews, took the city in 614, holding it for some fifteen years. The Byzantines returned triumphantly in 630 and, under the Patriarch Modestos, began to rebuild Jerusalem as a Christian center. The Jews were again banished from the city. But within a decade both Christians and Jews found themselves at the mercy of a new force, one that had burst onto the stage of history. Thus, in 638 Jerusalem fell to the Muslims under the Caliph Omar Ibn Khattab.

With the exception of brief interludes, the Old City of Jerusalem would remain under

4. Ancient burial monuments on the slopes of the Mount of Olives include Abasalom's Tomb (left), the rock-hewn tomb of the Sons of Hezir (center), and Zechariah's Tomb (right). Built during the Second Temple Period, these Hellenistic tombs belonged to prominent and wealthy Jews.

5. Hewn out of the rock in the 1st century AD, the Tomb of Zechariah is a cube-shaped 39-foot (12-meter) high structure. Along its four sides are stylized Ionic columns surmounted by an Egyptian-style cornice, crowned by a pyramid.

1. Aelia Capitolina, the city built by the Roman Emperor Hadrian. His statue is seen atop a column at the city's main gate (present-day Damascus Gate). Buildings depicted include Aphrodite's Temple, and Jupiter's Temple on the Temple Mount. Reconstruction drawing at Tower of David Museum of the History of Jerusalem.

Muslim control for nearly thirteen hundred years. In the Islamic hierarchy of sacred cities, Jerusalem ranks third, after Mecca and Medina. It was from Jerusalem that the Prophet Muhammad was said to have ascended to Heaven, and to commemorate this the Caliph Omar declared the Temple Mount—which in the intervening centuries had become a garbage dump—a holy precinct for Islam, the Haram al-Sharif, or "Noble Sanctuary." It was here that the magnificent Dome of the Rock, one of the wonders of world architecture, was built at the end of the 7th century, followed by the great Al-Aqsa Mosque. This first lengthy period of Muslim rule, under a succession of caliphates, lasted about four hundred and fifty years. It would end with the arrival of the European Crusaders, who took the city in the summer of 1099 and held it until 1187, then returned to prevail for one more brief moment in 1229-44.

A fearful massacre of the city's Jewish and Muslim inhabitants heralded the creation of the Crusaders' Kingdom of Jerusalem. As the name suggests, Jerusalem became the kingdom's capital, the first time the city was vested with that status since the Herodian era more than a thousand years earlier. Having depopulated the city by slaughter, the Crusaders offered various economic inducements to attract new—Christian—settlers, while also moving Christian Arab tribes to the city from Syria and Trans-Jordan. The decades of Crusader rule saw intense construction activity, much of it religious in character and associated with traditions concerning the life of Jesus, traditions that were being established in this period. For the first time, though hardly the final one, European architectural elements were imported into the city, most notably in the construction of churches, such as the rebuilt Church of the Holy Sepulcher. Although the Crusaders preferred to slaughter infidels, they spared buildings, converting many Muslim mosques and shrines into Christian churches—most notably the Dome of the Rock.

This trend was reversed following the capture of Jerusalem by Salah al-Din (Saladin) in 1187. Once again in control, Muslims converted Crusader churches into mosques or Islamic institutions of learning. Now it was the turn of Christians, other than those of the Eastern Orthodox sects, to be banned from the city. In 1219 the Muslims demolished the outer wall and other fortifications, perhaps to reduce the city's attractiveness as a secure vantage point for a possible new Crusader drive or to intimidate the Christians. The decline that ensued would be reversed during the Mamluk Period (1260-1517), whose imprint on Jerusalem is evident to this day. Mamluk construction, with its highly distinctive architecture, was largely devoted to religious buildings, though some

2. Byzantine Jerusalem was known for the Church of the Holy Sepulcher (built on the ruins of Aphrodite's Temple), the extended Cardo, and many churches. Reconstruction drawing at Tower of David Museum of the History of Jerusalem.

splendid markets were also built. It was left to Suleiman the Magnificent, whose forty-six-year rule of the Ottoman Empire began in 1520, three years after Palestine was captured by the Turks, to restore the city's fortifications.

Suleiman's splendid wall still surrounds the Old City. His engineers also repaired Jerusalem's water-supply system and built six fine drinking fountains, decorating the latter, in part, with elements taken from Crusader structures. Such "secondary use" of earlier materials would become another recurrent pattern in Jerusalem construction, which did much to invest the city with its celebrated atmosphere of living history. Moreover, the fusion of such diverse architectural elements produced a uniquely Jerusalem style of building, a blend of East and West.

By and large, however, the Ottomans' four centuries of rule (1517-1917) were a period of decline and stagnation in Jerusalem. Not until the waning years of Ottoman hegemony, in the second half of the 19th century, when European Great Power rivalries intensified and conditions in the Old City became insufferable, did Jerusalem begin to awaken from its torpor—and then the focus would fall outside the ramparts. The arrival of the British at the end of 1917 signaled Jerusalem's entry into the 20th century. The New City expanded by leaps and bounds under British tutelage, although in the political sphere the Christian rulers failed to stem the growing conflict between Jews and Arabs. In May 1948 the proclamation of the State of Israel by the Jewish community triggered a bitter war, which left Jerusalem divided, with the eastern city and its walled section under Jordanian rule. West Jerusalem became the capital city, this time of the new State of Israel, which launched another period of large-scale construction—of institutions for the fledgling state and housing for a huge influx of immigrants. However, it was the reunification of Jerusalem in the Six-Day War of June 1967 that ushered in an era of growth and construction unmatched in the city's millennia-long history. The era would be presided over by Mayor Teddy Kollek, whom history will surely record as one of Jerusalem's great builders.

Mayor Kollek said that he was engaged in a perpetual struggle against the unearthly, visionary image of Jerusalem. Yet, that romantic conception of the city, as a kind of transcendent Xanadu, is deeply engraved in the Western mind. The English mystical poet William Blake (1757-1827), whose writings contributed powerfully to the creation of the metaphysical image, encapsulated such feelings:

I give you the end of a golden string;
  Only wind it into a ball,
It will lead you in at Heaven's gate,
  Built in Jerusalem's wall.

3. Royal palaces stood south of the Haram al-Sharif (Temple Mount) and Al-Aqsa Mosque (shown with gray dome) during the Early Muslim Period, under the Umayyad Dynasty. These magnificent edifices were destroyed in an earthquake in 748. Reconstruction at Tower of David Museum of the History of Jerusalem.

The Old City:
Urban Structure and Texture
Dense and Introspective Architecture

The basic urban structure of the Old City is determined by the wall that surrounds it, by the main thoroughfares that bisect it, and by narrow, branch-off alleys. Its infrastructure is that of a Roman-Byzantine town, divided into four quarters by two intersecting linear main streets: the Cardo, running from Damascus Gate in the north to Zion Gate in the south; and the Decumanus, extending from Jaffa Gate in the west to the Gate of the Chain at the entrance to the Temple Mount in the east. The two main streets meet at the Market Junction, the hub of commercial life. The Roman-Byzantine Cardo was rebuilt by the Crusaders as their market, and the same axis remains the Old City's major commercial artery to this day.

The four sections created by the geometry of the main streets form the basis for the ethnic-religious quarters—Jewish, Muslim, Christian, and Armenian—that comprise the Old City in its present state. Actually, this division dates only from the early 19th century, when European researchers drew up the first modern survey maps of the city. It is not a "surgical" division, for there is some ethnic-religious spillover between the sections. Architecturally speaking, moreover, there are really five areas, the fifth being the Temple Mount, or Haram al-Sharif ("the Noble Sanctuary"). Indeed, the street grid of the Old City was also influenced by the Haram al-Sharif, and by its Christian religious—and architectural—"rival," the Church of the Holy Sepulcher. A dense network of streets runs from west to east toward the gates leading to the Haram al-Sharif. Following an east to west route from Lions' Gate (St. Stephen's Gate) to the Church of the Holy Sepulcher is the Via Dolorosa, the street along which Jesus was led to be crucified and now an important commercial thoroughfare with many branching streets.

Diverging from the primary arteries of the Cardo and Decumanus is a maze of streets and lanes, typical of a Middle Eastern town. Each street and alley fits into a clear hierarchy that underlies the structure of the urban system: main street, secondary lane, local passage, and so forth. Typically, the street grid in an Oriental town is irregular, its narrow lanes ramifying in all directions, often to a cul-de-sac, another characteristic Eastern element that adds a touch of mystery and surprise. The streets or lanes have a character and spirit all their own. Some bustle with the activity of open or covered bazaars and *suqs* ("markets"); others are quietly residential or, lined with

1. The gray-domed Al-Aqsa mosque and the gilded Dome of the Rock rise above the southern part of the Old City wall. On the ridge above is Mount Scopus, with the tower of Augusta Victoria Hospital (right) and the Hebrew University (left).
2. Roads from four directions lead to the Old City, which is located at the geographic center of Jerusalem's municipal boundaries.

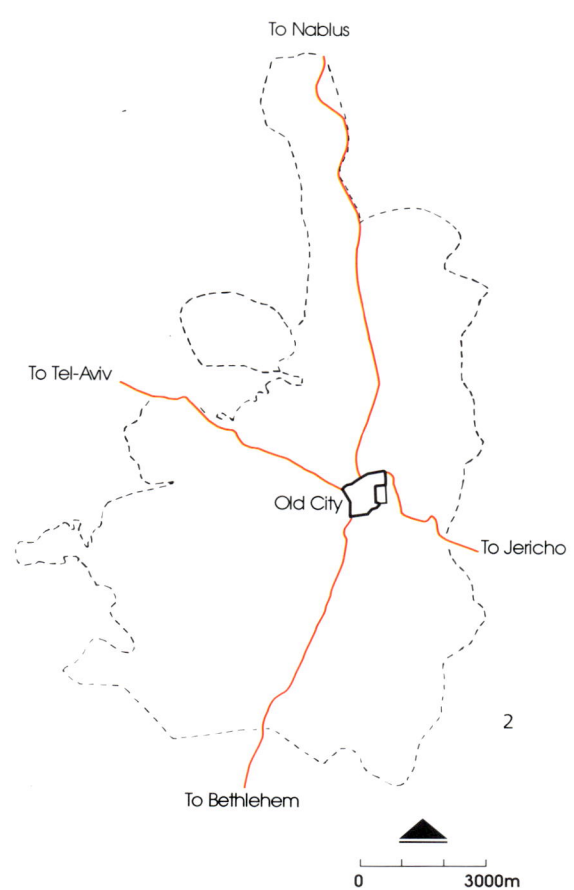

2

1. Picturesque narrow alleyways form the basic urban structure of the Old City.
2. The urban pattern of the Old City is determined by the proportion between the built-up areas (in black) and their negative, the open areas (in white). Prominent open areas are the Temple Mount and the adjacent Western Wall plaza.
3. Archaeological finds, mainly from the Hasmonean Period (2nd century BC), were unearthed in the 1970s along the southern side of the Old City wall.

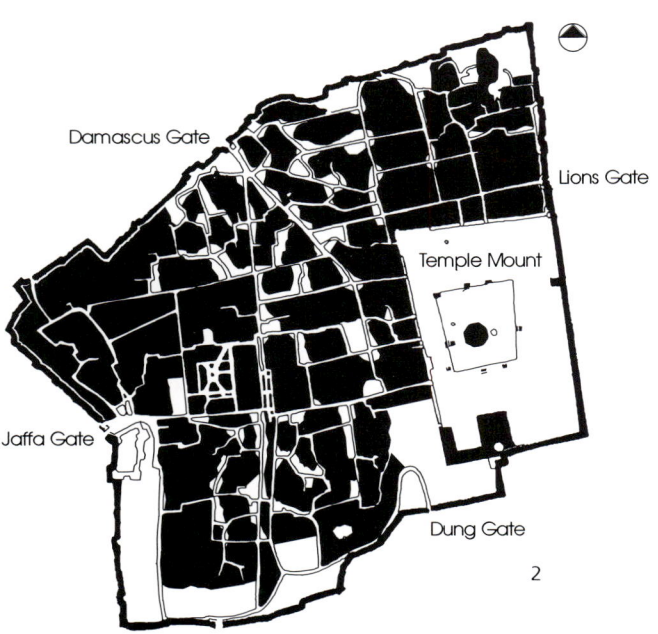

religious structures, exude an air of tranquil grandeur. Many are a mix of residential and commercial buildings.

Enclosed within a monumental, 16th-century wall, the Old City cannot escape its past. Tradition and heritage are as crucial as religion and government in shaping a historic city. To understand the continuing genesis of Jerusalem across millennia, we need to be aware of the Old City's symbols, given material form through architecture. Memory and commemoration are crucial parameters of the image. From the standpoint of architecture, history, or religion, the two most important buildings are the Christians' Church of the Holy Sepulcher (founded in the 4th century) and the Muslims' Dome of the Rock (dedicated in 691) on the Haram al-Sharif. These are structures of *memoria*, perpetuating an event and a place that are fundamental to religion and tradition. Their analogous symbolic role is reflected, again, in their layout.

The basilica, or prayer hall, of the Church of the Holy Sepulcher stands directly adjacent to the rotunda, its memorial structure. The same physical affinity, functionally and architecturally, exists on the Haram al-Sharif between Al-Aqsa Mosque, the place of prayer, and the Dome of the Rock, the commemorative shrine. Although physically separate, these two buildings are spiritually linked. The *memoria* structures—the Dome of the Rock and the rotunda in the Church of the Holy Sepulcher—symbolize God; the prayer structures—Al-Aqsa and the basilica—symbolize the people. Both shrines are concentrically built with the memorial site—grave, rock—at the center. Each structure—one round, one octagonal—is crowned by a vast, high dome, which dramatizes its importance and stamps its physical presence on the Old City's urban pattern. Yet, for all their similarities—indeed, because of them—the two structures are in competition. Physically, the Dome of the Rock serves as a counterweight to the Church of the Holy Sepulcher, built centuries earlier.

The Muslim *memoria*-prayer complex occupies the dominant element of the built-up pattern inside the walls—the Haram al-Sharif. Unlike most European cities, the Old City of Jerusalem cannot boast large squares or plazas that set off and enhance monumental structures. Like most cities of the East, it has few piazzas. Jerusalem does possess two large sacred spaces: the Haram al-Sharif enclosure, covering a sixth of the Old City's area, and the Western Wall Plaza, just below. The Temple Mount is an artificial platform built by Herod the Great when he enlarged and renovated the Second Temple. In its present condition, established under the Muslims, the Temple Mount occupies a special status in the Old City's spatial hierarchy, determined not only by its religious and historic significance, but equally by its location, its size, and the remarkable architecture of its buildings. This urban distinction derives in large measure from the sharp contrast between the scale of the open area and the density of the surrounding buildings, from the dramatic passage out of dark, narrow alleys, cacophonous with commercial activity, to a vast, open, serene precinct bathed in light.

Looking down from the Temple Mount at the Western Wall Plaza, the holiest site of the Jewish people, one sees not the result of careful planning but, rather, the very opposite: the product of a snap political decision, made in June 1967 after Israel's capture of the Old City, to demolish the Moghrabi houses in front of the Western Wall and create a huge area for prayer and assembly. The old narrow space between the Western Wall and the adjacent low houses, a space that had served exclusively for prayer and communion—known for centuries as "the Jews' wailing place"—was supplanted by an undefined, indeterminate space. Proposals, submitted in the early 1970s, to redesign the plaza and improve its appearance, while also abetting its functional purpose, were all turned down, victims of emotions, politics, and religious sensitivities.

At the heart of the public-private dichotomy in the Old City is spatial shortage. In a walled city, space is, by definition, at a premium, and in Jerusalem its scarcity produced a singular architecture with an overriding mission: to exploit every inch of available space, and then to find ways to create more space. Nearly every structure is built at the street threshold; makeshift or other structures are crammed into courtyards, but at the price of reduced ventilation and light; overpass rooms connecting two buildings above the narrow streets, as well as oriels jutting into alleys, increase living or storage space but also heighten urban density. The high-density architecture and spatial deficit are also reflected in the use of roof space. Terraced building enables residents of each floor to utilize the roof of the apartment below as a porch or courtyard. Roof gardens, such as the one on Sisters of Zion Convent along the Via Dolorosa, respond to a yearning for greenery in zero-earth conditions. Barrel and pot gardens are popular for the same reason in the Muslim and Christian quarters alike.

Urban texture is in part created by open spaces, which function like a photographic negative of the surrounding built-up area, enabling the viewer to form a visual impression of the construction. In a city where density of history goes hand in hand with density of building, a "public open space" assumes a special meaning, for, by definition, it is accessible to the public. In this sense, the only public open spaces in the Old City are the modern squares built in the Jewish Quarter as part of the post-1967 reconstruction effort. However, these—Batei Mahseh Square, or the area next to the Hurvah Synagogue—are, again, compositions in stone, "hard" and bare, with few trees or "soft," tended green spaces. The only public space inside the walls that can be likened to a "green belt" is the 1.5-acre archaeological park and playground in the south of the Jewish Quarter. The planned "Market Junction Roof Promenade" above the covered markets in the heart of the Old City has been impeded by political constraints and ownership disputes. The well-kept archaeological garden in the Citadel is part of the museum there. Secluded behind high walls, like the delightful gardens of many religious institutions, it is open to the public only at fixed times. The National Park surrounding the Old City wall on the north, west, and south is partial compensation for the residents.

The stark contrast between the few green public spaces and the unrelenting stone façades, so crucial to the Old City's urban texture, is in some sense echoed in the powerful contrast between the sacred and profane

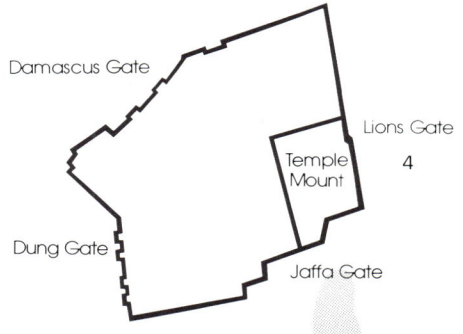

4. Jerusalem began as the City of David (1000 BC), which covered a small area south of the present day wall.

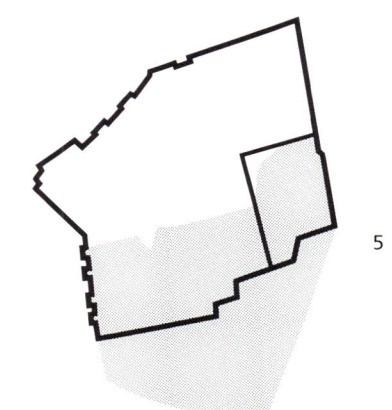

5. First Temple Period, 1000-586 BC.

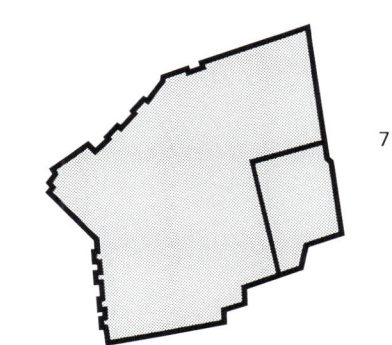

6. Second Temple Period (AD 70). The city at the height of its splendor.

7. Since the Ottoman Period (1517-present).

architecture—between monolithic religious structures that aspire to attain the transcendental in stone and the modest, earthly, human scale of private residences. Religious architecture did much to mold the city's character in the Crusader-Ayyubid Period, and the splendor of Mamluk building sprang from a desire to re-create Jerusalem in the image of a Muslim city. Throughout, there was massive construction to furnish believers and pilgrims with lodgings and other urban amenities. Hence the hospices and the monastery hostels, the public baths and the markets—all part of an architecture designed to serve the needs of Christian and Muslim pilgrims.

As for the Jews, during their centuries of exile following the destruction of the Second Temple, Jerusalem was the apple of their eye. "Next year in Jerusalem!" became the hope expressed every year at the Passover festival. But there were no mass pilgrimages of Jews from the diaspora. In the 19th century the few Jews who visited Jerusalem found lodgings mainly in residences of *kolels* (communities based on cities and countries of origin) or with friends and relatives.

Yet, with the exception of the brief Crusader and British Mandate periods, Jerusalem functioned as a capital solely under the Jews—in antiquity (from which only archaeological remains exist) and in the modern era (when Israel makes the New City its seat of government). Nonetheless, Old Jerusalem owes much of its architectural grandeur to

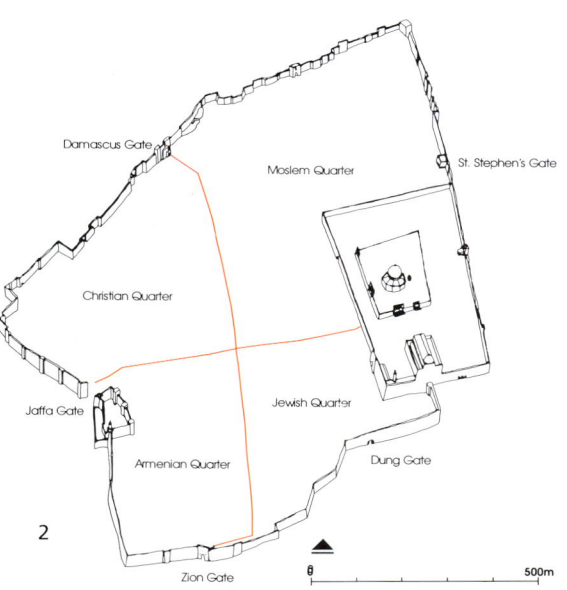

government support, both financial and administrative. Witness the 8th-century Umayyad palaces, the extensive Mamluk building, and the monumental projects of Suleiman the Magnificent.

The city's urban pattern reflects the role of architecture in interreligious and intercommunal struggles for influence and hegemony. Besides visual competition of the kind already described, Muslims turned churches into mosques, and Christians responded in kind. The 19th-century edifices built by Christian institutions in the Old City and then outside the walls were in part spurred by political and religious rivalries among the European Powers. In 1967 the Israeli government launched a huge twenty-year operation, investing vast resources to reconstruct the Jewish Quarter and solidify the Jewish national-political presence. Yet, the enterprise created, within the pattern of the Old City, a sharp contrast with the underdeveloped Muslim Quarter. This aspect of the urban scene is the architectural mirror of the Jewish-Arab struggle in and for Jerusalem.

Nevertheless, the architecture of the Jewish Quarter, to the degree that it is an attempt to translate past forms into modern terms, is also in part an emulation of what is probably the only vernacular style in the Old City: the houses of the Muslim Quarter. Owing to scarce means and nearly total dependence on local building materials, the construction methods employed by the Muslim inhabitants have changed little across the ages. This means that it is difficult to

1. The Old City's colorful roofscape. A mélange of domes, mosque minarets, church towers, gardens, water boilers, and solar heaters.
2. The Old City's urban and architectural texture is determined above all by the enclosing wall, the intersecting streets of the Cardo and the Decumanus, and the Temple Mount platform.

1. Kaleidoscopic pattern: Continuously shifting transitions back and forth from open to covered space and from light to shadow imbue the narrow lanes of the Old City with a colorful atmosphere.

identify periods of building in the Muslim Quarter with any exactness, but it also justifies taking the form and technology of Muslim courtyard residence as a reference point for comparison with construction in early periods. In essence, the housing found in the Muslim Quarter—small "box" structures with flat domes, thick walls, and narrow apertures, built haphazardly one above the other—is little different from that of a residential neighborhood in the ancient City of David.

Architectural continuity in the Old City has been achieved by builders in nearly every era by integrating stone remains from previous periods into new building. In other words, the "stones of destruction" from one age become the "stones of construction" for a succeeding age. There is also sound economics behind this, inasmuch as the use of cut and dressed stones simplifies building and lowers costs. After an earthquake in 1033 the Fatimid Caliph Al-Zahir repaired the ramparts with stones taken from churches he had destroyed. The Crusaders used Herodian stones to build the tower in the northwest corner of the city wall and to reinforce the Citadel. The richness of the Crusaders' own architecture later made their buildings favorite objects of plunder for the benefit of new construction, particularly that undertaken by the Ayyubids and Mamluks. Columns with stylized capitals and arches ornamented with "cushions" from Crusader times were especially coveted. Germany's Kaiser Wilhelm II, who considered himself the continuer of the Crusader heritage, asked architect Friedrich Adler to integrate into the Lutheran Church of the Redeemer (consecrated in 1898) the portal of the Crusader Church of Maria Latina, remains of which came to light during the erection of the new structure. Although such usage shows sensitivity to history and allows for physical continuity, the existence of stones from earlier eras presents another problem—like the uniform housing of the Muslim Quarter—for scholars seeking to establish the exact period of a building's construction.

Yet a third difficulty in this regard is the fact that a major part of the architecture in the Old City was influenced, in one way or another, by foreign styles, imported by Jerusalem's many conquerors. Few buildings are "pure" original creations. The most eclectic architecture in the Old City is that of the European Christian builders of the late 19th century, who adopted the various "Neo" styles then fashionable in Europe.

Post-1967 Israeli architecture created a contemporary "Neo" style that revived traditional Oriental forms through the utilization of state-of-the-art materials and techniques. Concurrently, though not unrelatedly, a Neo-Oriental style emerged in the construction of the new neighborhoods around Jerusalem after 1967. Most visitors to the Jewish Quarter have pronounced the attempt to adapt modern architecture to the historical fabric a success. Even those who would dispute that judgment appreciate the tremendous effort—in planning, financing, and organization—invested in the project.

A prodigious investment of the same sort went into Suleiman's monumental wall and gates, the 16th-century construction that has defined the Old City ever since, at the same time that it constitutes a most impressively beautiful example of fortification architecture from that period. Arab-Muslim building of all eras has indeed left its stamp on the Old City more than any other. The architecture of the Mamluk Period remains the most outstanding and significant in building with stone, from the standpoint of planning, design, and execution. Mamluk planners and builders forged a magnificent style, displaying extraordinary artistic and technical ability, while also making optimal use of different types and forms of stone, which they orchestrated in rich architectural compositions.

But one characteristic shared by virtually all types of Old City structures from every era is a propensity to inwardness. Even the expansive Temple Mount precinct is an internal plaza, cut off from the rest of the Old City by dense building in the north and west and by sections of the outer rampart in the south and east. The monasteries, the courtyard residences of the Muslim Quarter, and their modern counterparts in the Jewish Quarter all share the same trait. To understand the urban texture of the Old City, it is necessary to become acquainted with the development of the different architectural styles across the ages.

THE OLD CITY FROM 1000 BC
THROUGH THE OTTOMAN EMPIRE
A Study in Remnants

In the three thousand years since King David captured Jerusalem and made it his capital, the city has been ravaged by a series of conquerors, who then rebuilt it according to their own needs. As a result, different styles and forms of construction developed in Jerusalem, with each period contributing its share to the overall urban pattern, always in relation to what earlier generations had built. This book deals with townscape and with the architecture of extant complexes and structures, not with archaeological finds. Nevertheless, it will be useful to survey briefly several of the elements that not only shaped Jerusalem's urban pattern in ancient times but have also left their imprint on the city to this day.

During King David's reign Jerusalem was situated to the south of the present-day Old City wall. The city then gradually expanded northward. Under King Solomon (c. 950 BC) it included the fringes of the Temple Mount, as well as its surroundings, and continued, at the end of the First Temple Period, to push in the direction of the western hill. A remnant of the wall from that era was discovered in excavations carried out in the Jewish Quarter after 1967 and is known as the "broad wall." In the reign of King Agrippa I (AD c. 44), when the Third Wall began to rise, the city covered an area twice the size of today's Old City, although in the section included within the Third Wall, north of Damascus Gate, the urban pattern was not dense.

Many remnants have been unearthed from the Herodian era (37-4 BC). The reign of King Herod brought intense building on a monumental scale. The monarch's projects included the reinforcement of the city wall, a new water-supply system, lavish renovation of the

Second Temple, and, for the King himself, a magnificent palace with three adjacent towers. However, his major endeavor, which had a significant impact on the image of Jerusalem and its urban development in the course of succeeding generations, was the creation and expansion of the artificial platform of the Temple Mount, the largest in the Greco-Roman world. The same period also saw the construction of the supporting walls of the enlarged platform (one of which is the Western Wall, sacred to Judaism). However, no infill was allowed in the space between those walls and the natural slopes of Mount Moriah; instead, arches were constructed to stabilize the walls, and some of them form the structure known today as "Solomon's Stables," located beneath the Al-Aqsa Mosque.

During the Herodian Period, Jerusalem expanded toward the upper hill, today part of the Jewish Quarter. It was here that the city's aristocracy and *kohanim* ("priests") resided. The remnants of their luxurious dwellings, revealed during archaeological excavations, attest to building of a very high standard in a Hellenistic-Roman style. Other vestiges have been found outside the walls, notably burial crypts from the Second Temple Period whose façades are designed in a splendid Hellenistic manner.

1, 2. The two most important, impressive, and monumental urban and architectural elements in Jerusalem are the Temple Mount platform, dating from the Herodian era (1st century BC), and the Dome of the Rock, a Muslim shrine built in the 7th century AD.

3. The most significant buildings erected in the Early Muslim Period (638-1099) are (A) the Dome of the Rock and (B) the Al-Aqsa Mosque.

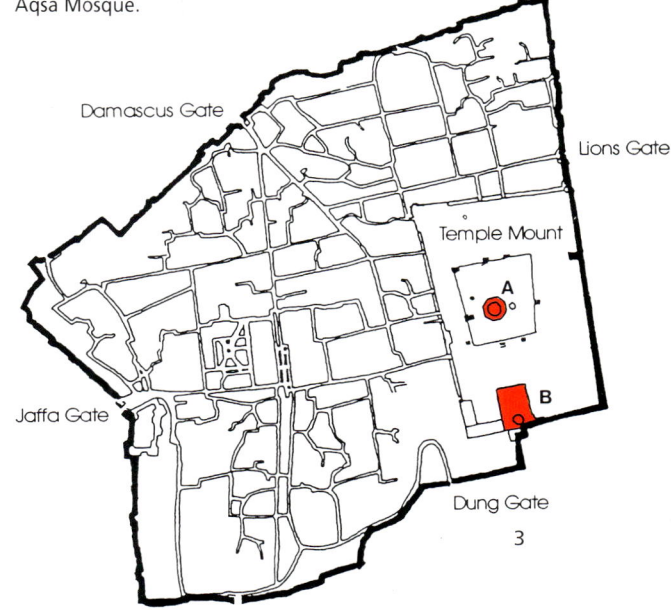

The five hundred years of the Roman Period (AD 135-324, when Jerusalem was known as Aelia Capitolina) and the succeeding Byzantine Period (324-638) gave the urban structure of Jerusalem its two main roads. The current boundaries of the Old City probably took shape toward the end of the Roman Period, although we know that in both the Byzantine Period and the Early Muslim Period Jerusalem was situated in areas south of the present-day city wall, including the areas of Mount Zion and the ancient City of David. Still, the vast majority of the complete structures that today comprise Jerusalem rose during the more than 1,350 years that began with the Muslim conquest in 638.

THE EARLY MUSLIM PERIOD: 638-1099
Monumental Religious Concepts

The creation of the Dome of the Rock alone would make this a significant period. Few structures survive from the era; thus, it is difficult to speak of a particular architectural style. But for thirteen hundred years the domed masterpiece on the Haram al-Sharif has been justly considered one of the architectural wonders of the world. Completed in 691, and largely unchanged since, it is the most magnificent and, architecturally speaking, the most important building in Jerusalem as well as the earliest complete example of Muslim architecture anywhere. Its influence on the Jerusalem cityscape is unsurpassed.

Under the Byzantines, Jerusalem had become a magnet for Christian pilgrims. The new rulers of the city, the Umayyads, the first Muslim dynasty, whose capital was Damascus, sought to proclaim Jerusalem's status in the Islamic world, doing so with all the energy of their conquering new faith, which had driven them to extend their vast caliphate from the approaches of India to Europe's Iberian Peninsula. Wise in the pursuit of their goals, they responded to the city's magnificent Byzantine churches, especially the Holy Sepulcher, and built the glorious Dome of the Rock. It is a shrine, not a mosque, that perpetuates and protects the holy rock believed to be the foundation stone of the world and the site where the Last Judgment will take place. A later Muslim tradition associated with the rock marks it as the place from which the Prophet Muhammad ascended to Heaven at the conclusion of his Night Journey.

On the the Haram al-Sharif's elevated platform stands the octagonal structure of the Dome of the Rock. Each of its outer sides is about 66 feet (20 meters) long, and it is topped by a towering dome 149 feet high (45 meters, equivalent to a modern-day 14-story building). In fact, there are really two independent domes: an outer, slightly elliptical one, covered with gilded sheets of aluminum; and an inner, spherical one, made of wood and richly

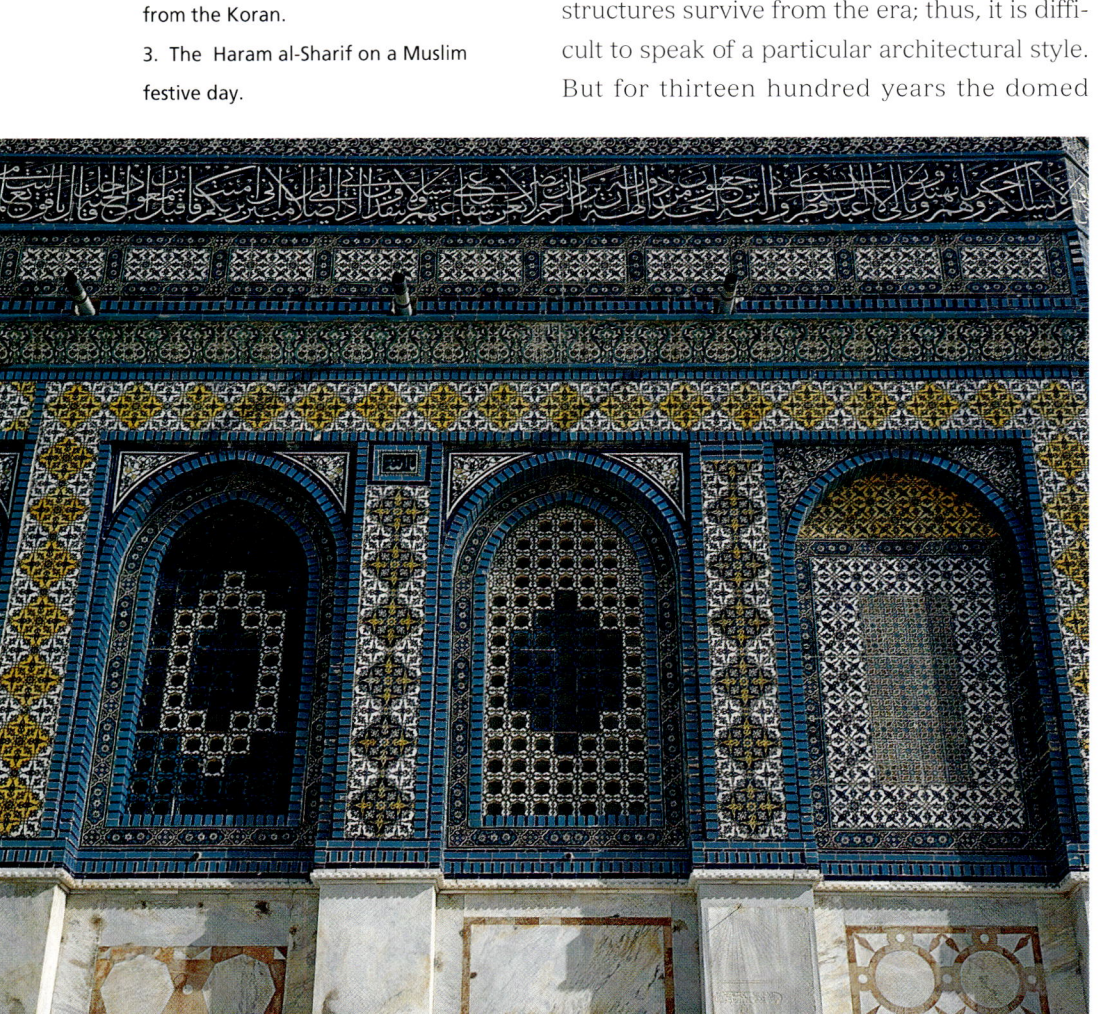

1. Glazed ceramic tiles on the exterior of the Dome of the Rock, installed by the 16th-century Ottoman ruler Suleiman the Magnificent, replaced the Umayyad mosaics. In the 20th century most of these were replaced by Armenian tiles.
2. The diverse decorative elements inside the Dome of the Rock include the first use of calligraphic motifs based on verses from the Koran.
3. The Haram al-Sharif on a Muslim festive day.

28

1, 2. The monumental 7th-century Dome of the Rock has the sacred rock at its center (2). The gilded dome is borne on a raised drum and punctuated with sixteen windows. Model (1) at Tower of David Museum of the History of Jerusalem.
3. Like gorgeous jewels, magnificent mosaics made of glass and gold, showing floral motifs, decorate the interior of the Dome of the Rock.

ornamented with stucco and arabesques. While the entire shrine protects the sacred rock, the exterior dome protects its more delicate interior counterpart from cracking under the effects of Jerusalem's sharp climatic fluctuations. Besides affording excellent insulation, the space between them, of a yard or more, is large enough for a person to enter for upkeep purposes.

Structurally, the dome, borne upon a drum punctuated with sixteen windows, is supported by four piers and twelve columns (three between each pier) that surround the sacred rock as closely as possible. A second, outer colonnade, octagonal in shape and required for support owing to the large space between the center and the exterior walls, consists of twenty-four arches springing from eight piers and sixteen columns. The beauty of the exterior is enhanced by marble panels and glazed ceramic tiles. Originally the structure was covered with gold and green glass mosaics, much like that on the interior. In the 16th century, the ravages of time led the Ottoman ruler Suleiman the Magnificent to face the building with Persian-style ceramic tiles. The present "Armenian" tiles were installed in the 20th century.

The Dome of the Rock owes its impact to more than innate prestige, self-confidence, and ostentatious religious statement. It is a paean to harmony, achieved architecturally by means of the nearly identical length of the octagon's sides, the height and diameter of the dome, and the balanced integration of the ornate exterior and interior designs, notwithstanding the diversity of materials.

Adjacent to this towering edifice, the Umayyads built the Dome of the Chain, seemingly a miniature version of the Dome of the Rock but one whose purpose remains unknown. It consists of two circular colonnades supporting a hexagonal drum topped with a small dome. The marble columns and the capitals were probably taken from the ruins of pre-Muslim structures.

Another structure generally attributed to the Umayyad Period (8th century), and one for which traditions exist in all three monotheistic faiths, is the Gate of Mercy, or Golden Gate. Now sealed, this portal is the only one on the

1. Modern plaster latticework with colored-glass insets. Western façade, Al-Aqsa Mosque.

2. Al-Aqsa Mosque was destroyed and rebuilt several times. The present-day main façade is from the Ayyubid Period (1187-1250). The seven arches of the front portico reflect the interior plan: a basilica with a central nave and three aisles on either side.
3. The southern and earliest part of Al-Aqsa Mosque (from the Umayyad Period, 8th century) borders on the Old City Wall.
4. Al-Aqsa Mosque. Worshippers direct their supplications toward the prayer niche (*mihrab*) in the southern wall (*gibla*), which faces the Saudi Arabian city of Mecca, Islam's holiest site.

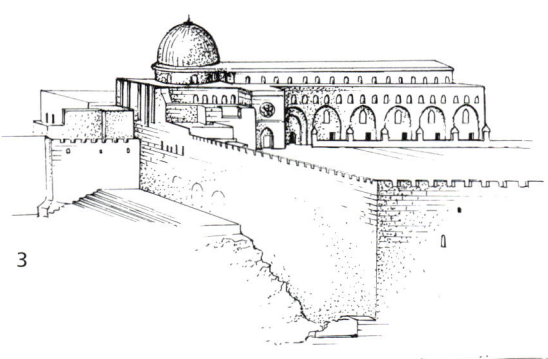

eastern wall of the Temple Mount. With its unique decorative features, the structure may commemorate the belief according to which Muhammad entered the Haram al-Sharif precinct from that juncture. Precise dating is virtually impossible owing to the gate's inclusion of elements from earlier periods.

The origins of Jerusalem's largest mosque, Al-Aqsa, the gray, lead-covered counterpoint to the Dome of the Rock, also probably lie in the Umayyad Period. The first Umayyad structure, built during the years 705-715, under Caliph Alwalid, at the southern extremity of the Haram al-Sharif (hence its name, meaning "the furthest point"), it was destroyed by an earthquake in 748, as were other major buildings. In its present form, Al-Aqsa probably dates from the 11th century, with important later additions made by the Crusaders and the Ayyubids.

The Umayyads also acknowledged the importance of Jerusalem—Islam's third holiest city, after Mecca and Medina—to both Judaism and Christianity. The dynasty annulled the Byzantine ban on Jewish settlement in the city, and by the late 7th century a Karaite community had already been established in the area of today's Jewish Quarter. The Christian-Byzantine character of the city's

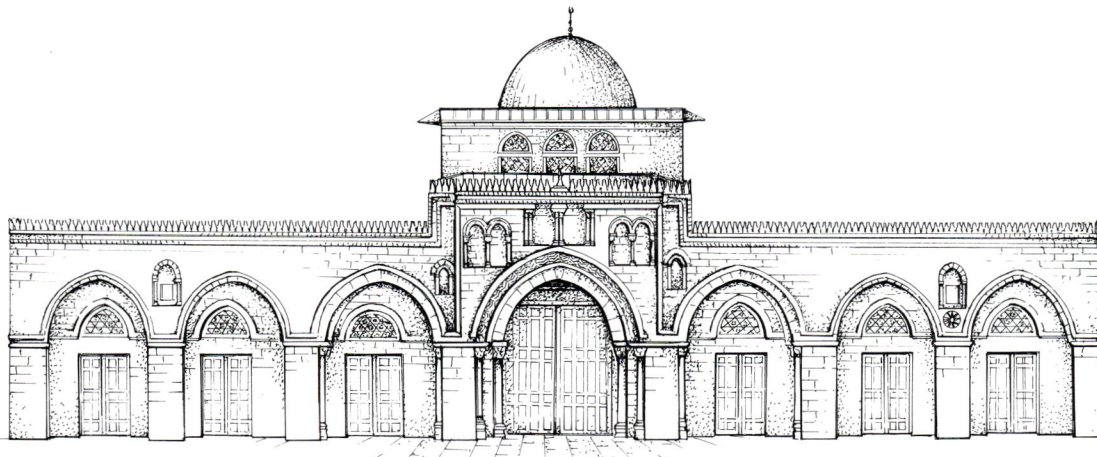

northwest section, particularly around the Church of the Holy Sepulcher, was maintained in the Early Muslim Period, thanks primarily to members of the Greek Orthodox community who inhabited the many monasteries built in Byzantine times. Yet, despite the great religious importance of Jerusalem, the Umayyads founded Ramlah on the coastal plain in 716 and designated it the administrative capital of Palestine. The Muslin dynasties that ruled Jerusalem over the next three centuries left no built heritage.

Marble columns with Corinthian capitals along the sides of Al-Aqsa Mosque (2) are a reconstruction of the original columns that supported the wooden beams of the 8th-century Umayyad building. A "zigzag" motif (4) decorates arches from the Ayyubid Period (1187-1250) on Al-Aqsa Mosque, an early Muslim house of worship, while the summer pulpit (5), built by the Mamluks in the 14th century and renovated in the 16th century under the Ottomans (3), contains elements in secondary use, notably the Byzantine Capital (1) and the dome, which is apparently a Crusader creation.

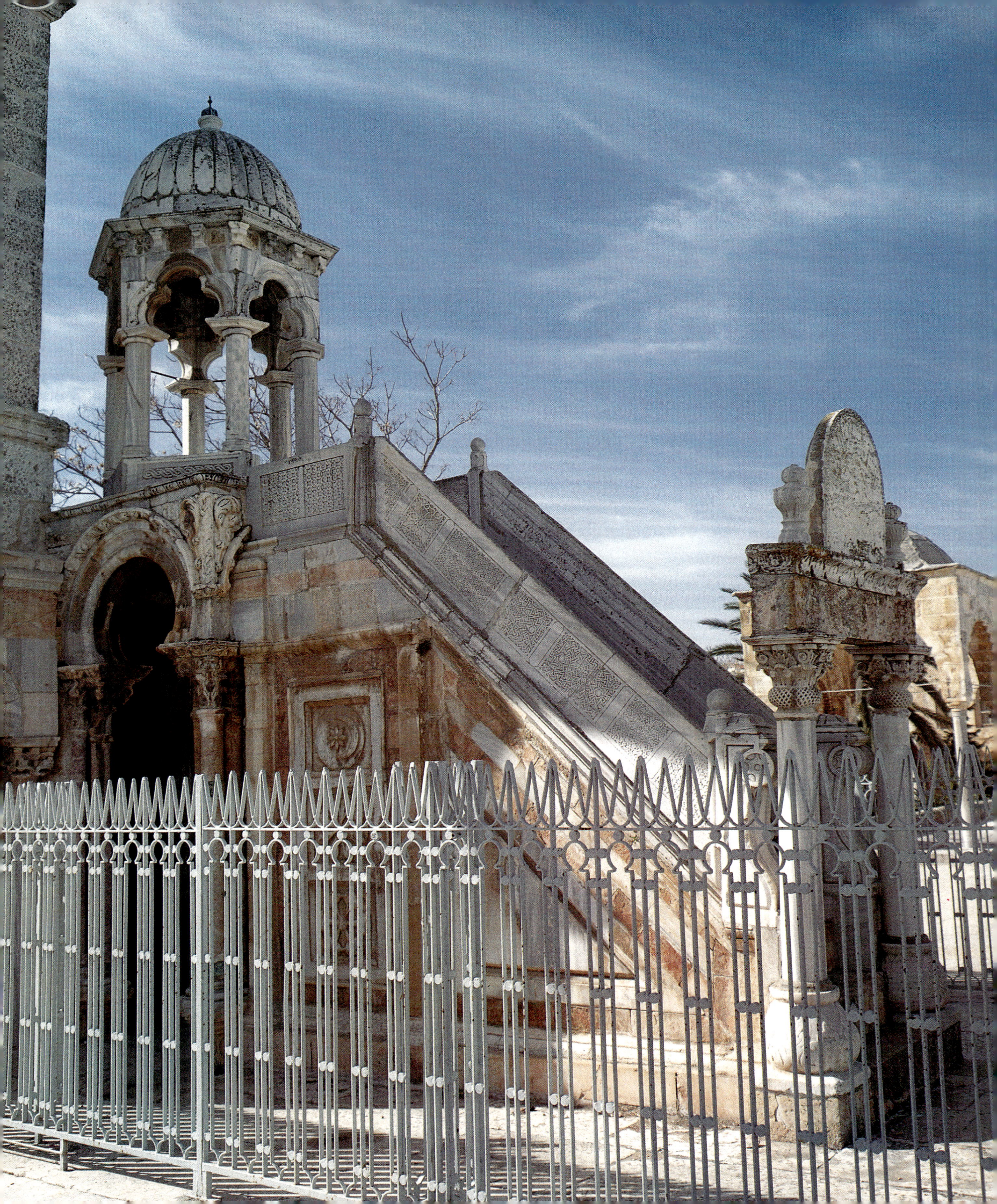

On the Haram al-Sharif (Temple Mount) are structures spanning the ages from the Early Muslim Period to the present. Among them are:

1. The Western *riwaq*, or arcade, dating from the Mamluk Period.

2. A prayer niche (*mihrab*) from the Ottoman Period. 3. An Ayyubid Period prayer niche with conchlike ornamentation, "cushions," and "zigzag" motifs, which are Crusader elements in secondary use, and (4) a typical commemorative structure from the early Ottoman Period.

THE CRUSADER PERIOD: 1099-1187
Local Romanesque

Architecturally, the Crusaders made their major contribution to Jerusalem in the realm of church construction; however, they also proved to be adept builders of military and public structures. Europeans who responded to Pope Urban II's call to liberate Jerusalem from the "infidels," the Crusaders ruled Jerusalem twice, in 1099-1187 and again in 1229-44. Nearly all their significant building took place in the earlier period.

The Crusaders' Kingdom of Jerusalem, with Jerusalem as its capital, was born in a bloodbath. Following their capture of the city after a five-week siege in the summer of 1099, the Crusaders systematically slaughtered the Muslim and Jewish inhabitants. To repopulate the ravaged city, the new rulers encouraged settlement by Eastern Christians from Syria and Trans-Jordan. Other new and permanent arrivals were Latin Christians (Franks) from Europe, who joined the ruling class, and members of the Greek Orthodox and Armenian communities. The large numbers of pilgrims who visited the city provided a major source of income, which helped finance large-scale construction projects. These included churches, chapels, and fortifications, but also buildings for the daily use of the growing population—hostels, hospitals, residential areas—as well as for administrative institutions now situated in the capital city.

Stunned by the splendor of the Muslim structures on the Temple Mount, the Crusaders left them intact but transformed the buildings into Christian shrines. The Dome of the Rock became Templum Domini ("Temple of the Lord"), while Al-Aqsa, renamed Templum Solomonis ("Temple of Solomon"), served as the headquarters of the Order of Templars. Other knightly orders also played an important role in the city's development. The Knights Hospitalers built their complex—church, monastery, hospital, hostel, and convent cloister—near the Holy Sepulcher (in the area known today as the Muristan).

Few of the approximately thirty Crusader churches built in Jerusalem, mainly in the period between 1125 and Saladin's victory in 1187, are still standing. (Many were converted into mosques, among them the Church of St. Agnes, today the Al-Maulawiyya Mosque.) The preferred architectural style was Romanesque, which, following its emergence in France, dominated European building from the 8th century to the 12th. In its European form, Romanesque church architecture was characterized by blocky masonry, round-headed arches, stone vaults, small apertures, massive, often elaborate capitals, and passages enriched by fantastically conceived figures, floral motifs, and geometric patterns. Also typical are a sculptured tympanum (the space between the lintel and arch above the portal) and relief-carved figures in the archivolts (ornamental bands carried about the tympanum) as well as on columns.

The two most important churches built in Jerusalem during the Crusader Period were the Church of the Holy Sepulcher and the Church of the Monastery of St. Anne. Both reflect a fusion of an imported Romanesque style and local architectural tradition deriving from Byzantine and Muslim construction. Crusader churches in Jerusalem, for example, had smaller windows than European churches, probably to keep the heat at bay and perhaps also for

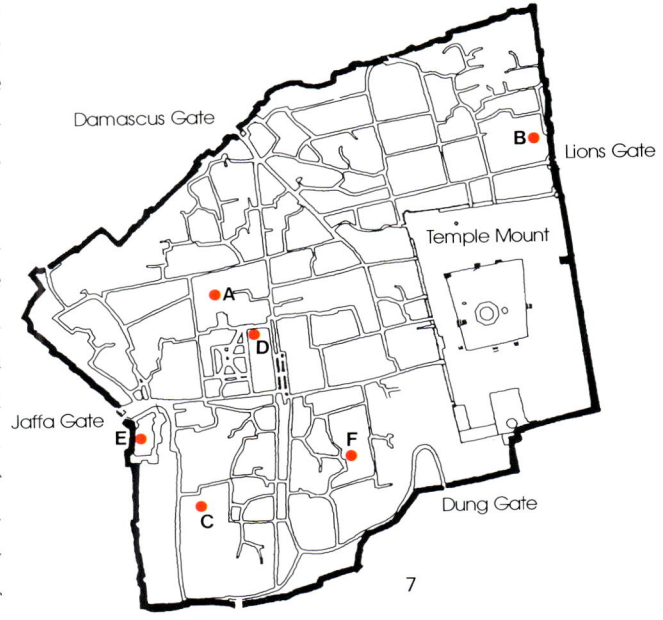

5, 6. Cross-section of the Church of the Holy Sepulcher in the mid-19th century.
7. The significant Crusader buildings:
A. Church of the Holy Sepulcher. B. Church of the Monastery of St. Anne. C. Cathedral of St. James.
D. Cloister, at the Church of the Redeemer.
E. The Citadel (Tower of David).
F. Church of St. Mary of the German Knights.

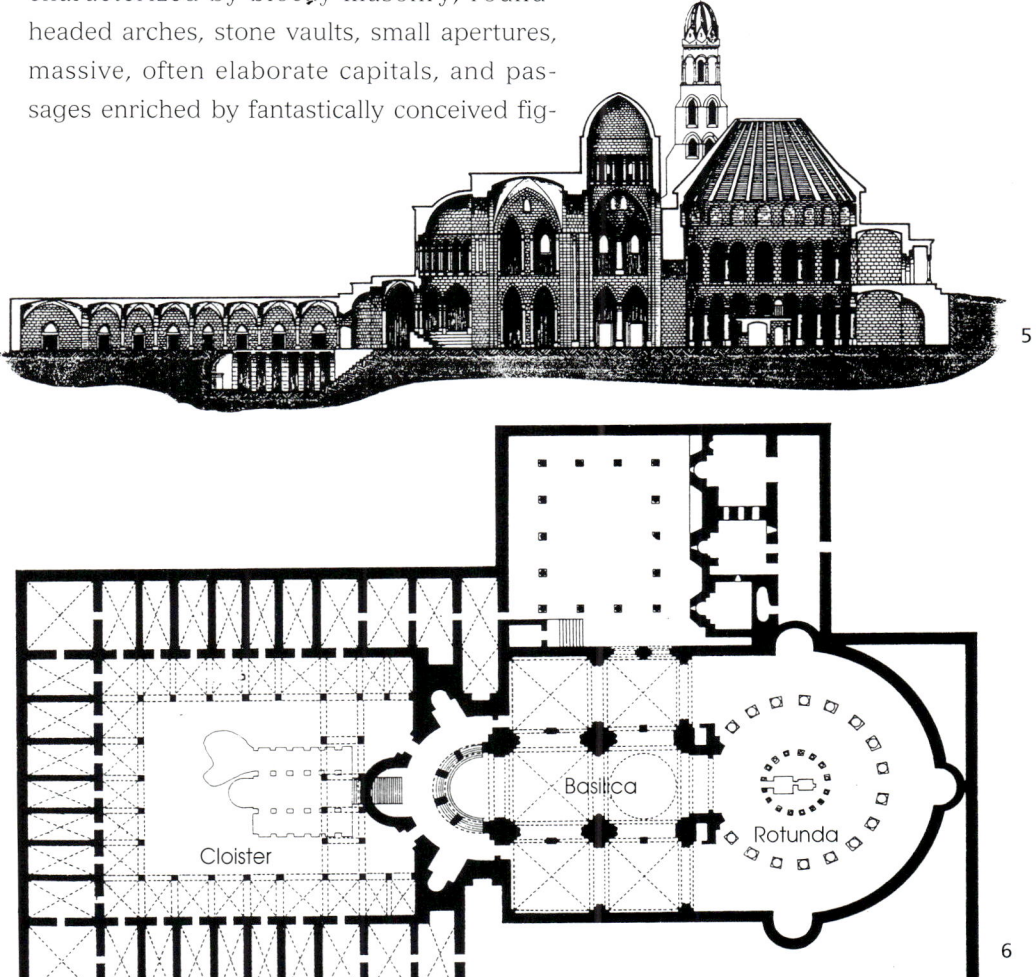

better security. Objective conditions in Palestine—a scarcity of timber—meant that church roofs were built of stone, as they had begun to be in Europe for reasons of fire prevention.

Indeed, a distinguishing feature of Crusader architecture was its integration of the entire array of Romanesque elements—masonry vaults, arches, pillars, and cupolas, ornamented capitals, lintel carvings—with the stone-cutting and other construction techniques characteristic of northern Syria and Palestine. Harbingers of the Gothic style, which would shortly succeed Romanesque in Europe, are evident in several Crusader churches, notably the ogive or pointed arches in both the Holy Sepulcher and St. Anne's. However, European influence abruptly terminated with the Crusaders' defeat in the Battle of Hittin in 1187. And when the second Crusader kingdom fell, in 1244, Jerusalem was lost to Christendom for nearly seven centuries.

In its present form the Church of the Holy Sepulcher, the most important monument in Christendom, dates almost entirely from the Crusader period. It was consecrated in 1149, the jubilee year of the Crusader conquest of the Holy Land. The original church had been built by the Emperor Constantine eight centuries earlier. The Crusader structure, erected on Byzantine foundations, contains a concentration of monuments directly connected with the crucifixion of Christ. The complex combines a circular memorial structure with a basilica for daily worship.

1, 2, 4. Romanesque grandeur: The southern façade and main entrance to the Church of the Holy Sepulcher fuses local stylistic influences with monumental construction imported by the Crusaders from Europe.

3. The Sepulcher itself, rebuilt in the early 19th century in the center of the rotunda of the church. The Crusader church incorporates the earlier Byzantine structure and houses the last five Stations of the Cross.

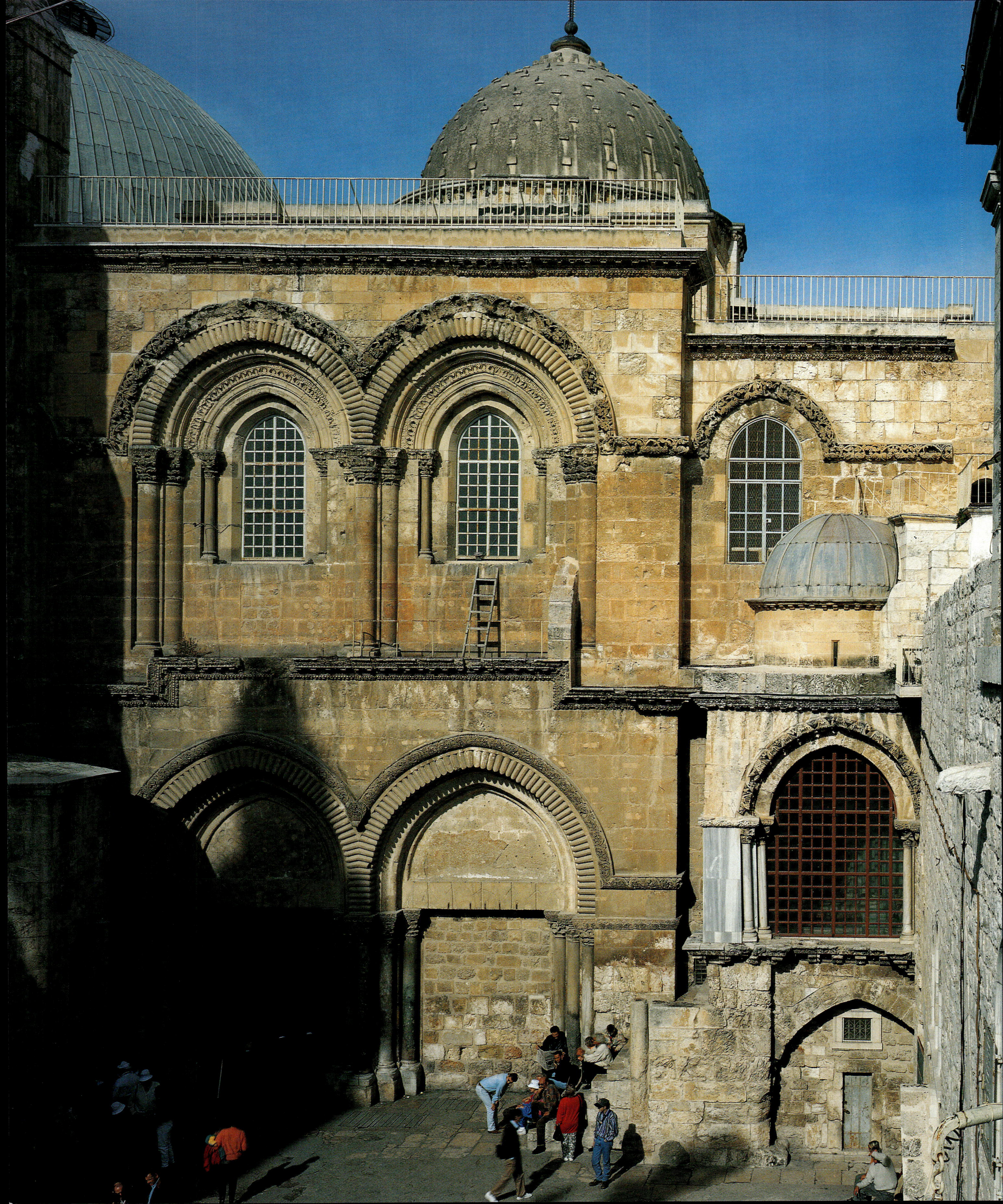

In keeping with its unique status, the Church of the Holy Sepulcher is architecturally unique as well. It is a vast structure incorporating monasteries, chapels, and residential areas, but the basilica and rotunda are of special importance. The monumental rotunda, towering above the tomb itself, is of Byzantine origin. The large basilica, a Crusader creation, has a nave, four aisles, and a transept, and it is domed at the juncture of the nave and transept. On its eastern side the basilica concludes in an ambulatorium and three radiating chapels, the arrangement typical of churches built in the Western Romanesque style but the only one of its kind in Jerusalem.

The main, southern façade of the Holy Sepulcher Chruch displays the full grandeur of the Romanesque, reflecting its importance as a selves drawn to the surroundings of the Church of the Holy Sepulcher. The sanctity of the Via Dolorosa ("Street of Sorrows"), the route taken by Christ from condemnation and crucifixion to burial, extending from Lions' Gate to the church (which houses the final five Stations of the Cross), was determined after the Crusader Period, and many churches and chapels were subsequently built along this important Old City axis.

The Church of the Monastery of St. Anne was built in c. 1140 to commemorate the home of St. Anne, mother of the Virgin Mary. It is an example of the most widespread type of Crusader church. Its basic basilican design—a rectangular structure in which colonnades divide the space into aisles and a nave terminating in an apse, or three apses in the case of St. Anne's—cathedral. Both the twin gates of the portal and the two large windows above are richly decorated. The form of the capitals on both sides of the double entrance and on the upper windows is extremely rare in the West, but widespread in Palestinian and Syrian churches erected between the 5th and 11th centuries. The actual sculpture was probably done by local Eastern Christian artisans, who inserted the geometric decorative elements familiar to them, forging a remarkable blend of Western and Eastern art and architecture.

Just as the Muslims clung to the area of the Haram al-Sharif, Christians found them-

1. East and West: Local building traditions combine with European influence—here, early Romanesque—on the entrance façade of the Church of St. Anne. Buttresses flanking the entrance reflect the building's interior division.
2. An arch with "cushions" ornaments a window on the façade of St. Anne's. The apertures in the marble window allow shafts of light to penetrate the hall of worship.
3. The interior of St. Anne's is divided into two colonnades by means of six piers that support the cross-vaulted ceiling.

combines early Romanesque with ancient local Christian traditions and Byzantine influences, such as the cupola above the intersection of the nave and transept. The Romanesque tradition, which imbues the church with a quiet elegance, produced in part by a restrained use of external decoration, is reflected as well in the cross vaults and the series of pointed arches borne by complex piers. The Neo-Romanesque Church of the Redeemer, erected more than seven centuries later by Lutherans, and discussed in the section on the Ottoman Period, has a similar structure. Suitably enough, the builders saw fit to integrate the portal of the ancient Hospitalers' Church of Maria Latina into the new Lutheran building.

The fortress architecture erected by the Crusaders was clearly influenced by European defense architecture. In Jerusalem they repaired the city walls, but invested their main effort in reinforcing the Citadel (Tower of David) and constructing a fosse around it. These security means were necessary because, adjacent to the Citadel, the Crusaders built a palace for their king, to which he moved from his former quarters in the Al-

4. The Church of St. Anne is part of a monastery compound in which the Pool of Bethesda—where Jesus cured the blind and the lame (John 5:2-4)—was unearthed in archaeological excavations.
5, 6. The Tower of David complex, one of Jerusalem's best-known landmarks, is a microcosm of the city's long history. The eastern arcade (top of drawing) dates to the Crusader Period.

1. Sweep of history: The courtyard of the Tower of David, now the Museum of the History of Jerusalem, contains remnants of the Hasmonean city wall (foreground), a Herodian tower (extreme left), an early Muslim tower base, a Mamluk polygonal tower, and an Ottoman minaret.

2, 4. A complex of Crusader buildings, consisting of a church, a hospice, and a hospital, was discovered in the 1970s during the restoration of the Old City's Jewish Quarter. The pointed arches, built around 1128 by German Knights Hospitalers of the Order of St. John, are typical of Crusader architecture in the Holy Land.

Aqsa Mosque on the Haram al-Sharif. Vestiges of Crusader construction, including characteristic arches, are still clearly visible in the Citadel's interior eastern wall. The Europeans erected strongly fortified towers at the corners of the city wall. The remains of one of these, the Tower of Goliath at the northwest corner (also known as "Tancred's Tower," after the Crusader prince who laid siege here in 1099), show that it was fashioned of massive stones in secondary use, taken from the ruins of Psephinus' Tower from the Herodian Period.

Of all the other structures built by the Crusaders—residences, hostels, hospitals, and markets—only the last remain. Occasionally renovated, these have been in use for generations. Economic and commercial activity, which attracted both local and European merchants, came together in three Crusader-built market and bazaar structures. They were originally located in the heart of the city, by the

3. Shafts of sunlight, streaming through apertures for light and air in vaulted Crusader structures in the narrow alleys of the market, create a striking play of light and shadow.

intersection of the ancient bisecting thoroughfares. The market streets, linked by internal passages, consisted of rows of shops. The roof covering the whole was made of a succession of cross vaults and pointed arches, about 20 feet (6 meters) above street level and 10 feet (3 meters) wide. Openings for ventilation and illumination were left on the top and sides of the roof, and the shafts of sunlight that stream in through them produce a picturesque effect.

Crusader architecture, which fused Western Romanesque with traditional Syrian building, was the basis for the distinctive style of construction in the lengthy period of Muslim rule that followed. It featured the integration of fragments removed from Crusader structures. Because of their decorative wealth and easy availability, Crusader columns, "cushioned" arches, and ornamented capitals became objects of demand in Ayyubid, Mamluk, and Ottoman times—yet another example of how West blended with East in Jerusalem.

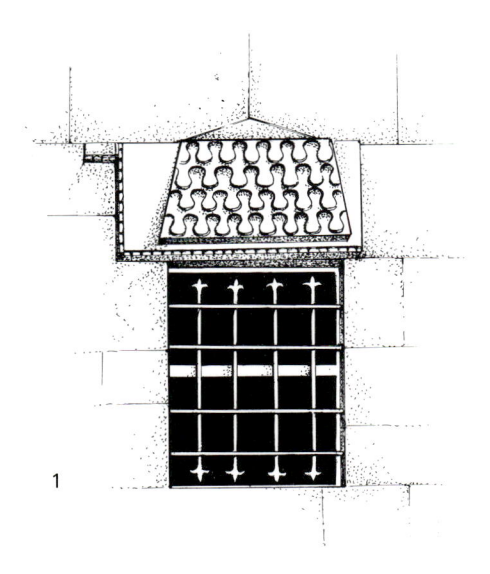

1-5. This Muslim theological center of study, or *madrasa* (the "Dome of Learning," 1207), is the only one from the Ayyubid period that has survived intact. At the center of the structure is a magnificent entrance ornamented with entwined marble columns from the Crusader Period in secondary use.

2. The principal Ayyubid structures are on the Haram al-Sharif:
A. The main façade of Al-Aqsa Mosque.
B. The Dome of Learning.

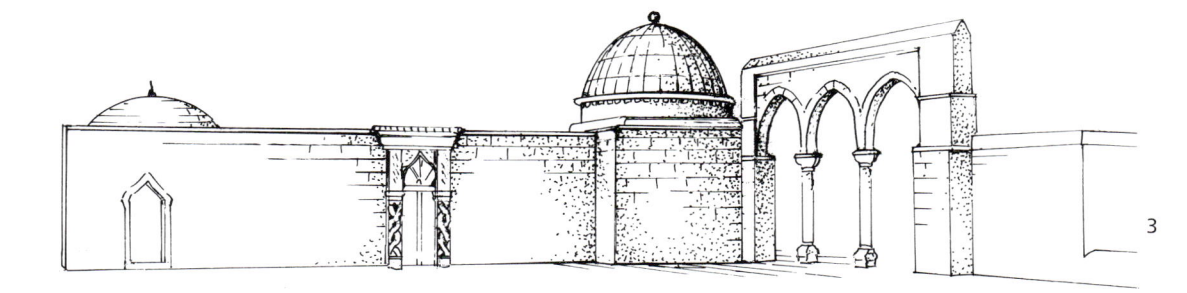

THE AYYUBID PERIOD: 1187-1250
Secondary Use of Architecture

Although of short duration, this was a period of varied construction in Jerusalem: religious, military, public-administrative. Most important, the Ayyubids, a Muslim dynasty founded by Saladin, produced an architectural masterpiece in the façade of Al-Aqsa Mosque, the holiest place of prayer in Islam outside Mecca and Medina. Al-Aqsa, which dates from the Umayyad Period, underwent radical alterations over the years, and in its present form the building lacks a defined and uniform architectural style. The bulk of the current structure was erected in 1035, under the Fatimid Dynasty, but the central section of the portal is Ayyubid (1217/18), as the inscription above the façade's central arch states.

The Ayyubids' contribution lies in the complex arches that form the present-day façade and create the structure's portico. The new exterior is a striking example of post-Crusader Muslim construction in Jerusalem, reflected in stylistic features drawn from Crusader architecture, as well as in an extensive secondary use of decorative and structural elements salvaged from Crusader buildings. The "zigzag" decoration on one of the arches, an innovative element in Muslim architecture, became a hallmark of Ayyubid and later construction. Supporting the arches on the façade are columns crowned with capitals—distinctly Crusader forms in secondary use.

The Ayyubids also contributed to the city's physical image through the *madrasa* (Islamic religious seminary), an institution that began to take root in this period, though only one intact Ayyubid madrasa remains today (on the Haram al-Sharif). Mostly, the Ayyubids "recycled" Crusader churches, converting them into madrasas. Thus, an Arabic inscription on the entrance lintel of St. Anne's Church attests to its Ayyubid phase. Overall, however, their primary architectural contribution lay in the original use they made of elements from earlier eras, particularly those of the Crusader Period, which can be seen as well in the Gate of the Chain leading to the Haram al-Sharif.

THE MAMLUK PERIOD: 1260-1517
Religious Splendor

Jerusalem under the Mamluks had limited political, strategic, or administrative importance; nevertheless, it had great religious importance, best seen in the distinctive mark left on the city by the Mamluks. These overlords were a military caste of former slaves who converted to Islam. Asian in origin, they subsequently ruled Egypt, Syria, and Palestine for nearly three centuries. The Mamluks endeavored, with some success, to make Jerusalem an international Muslim religious center. Tens of thousands of Muslim pilgrims flocked to the city, in a kind of antithesis to the Crusader Period, and they all needed places of worship and study, lodgings, and shops to purchase food and other commodities. The Mamluks responded by launching one of the most sustained and impressive campaigns of construction in the city's history, putting up splendid madrasas, mosques and minarets, hostels, bath houses, Sufi monasteries, markets, and mausolea. A major locus of pilgrimage, and hence of religious building, was the Haram al-Sharif (the Temple Mount) and its environs.

In Mamluk Jerusalem the Muslim theological center of learning known as the *madrasa* became the distinctive Muslim edifice, which figured prominently in the Mamluk drive to enhance the city's religious prestige. Thus,

6. Masterpiece of Mamluk architecture: Entrance to the Al-Ashrafiyya *madrasa* (theological center) on the Haram al-Sharif.
7. Entrance to the Mamluk Tankiziyya madrasa.
8. Mamluk construction (13th-16th centuries) is concentrated primarily along the northern and western flanks of the Haram al-Sharif, and in the adjacent streets facing west.

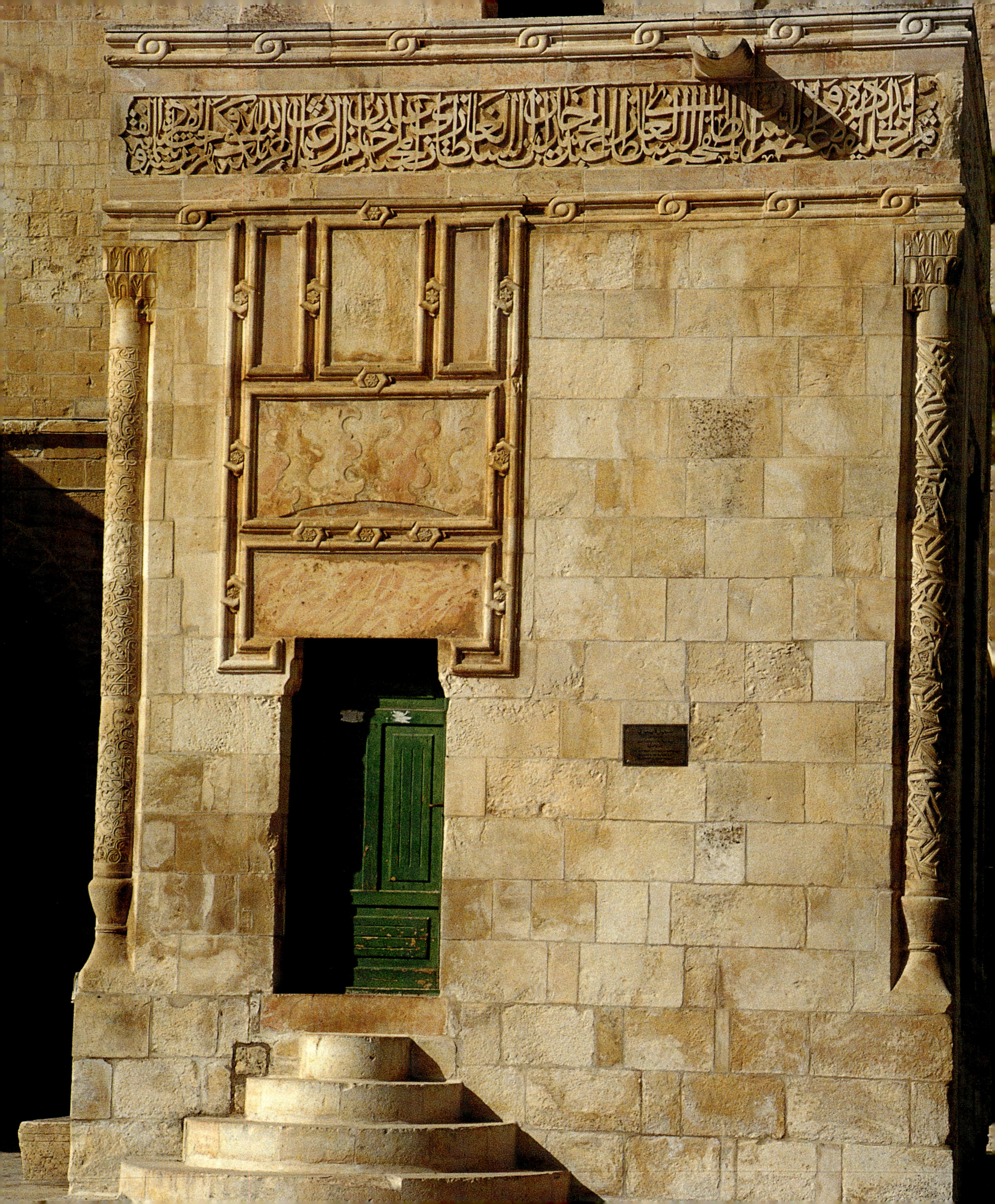

large madrasas came into being, mainly north and west of the Haram al-Sharif. The two most important are the Tankiziyya (1328-29), next to the Gate of the Chain leading to the Temple Mount, and Al-Ashrafiyya (1483), on the Haram al-Sharif itself. The design of the medieval madrasa followed a centralized plan, with four domed rooms (known as *iwans*) built around a central hall and open to this space. Like the mosque, the madrasa commonly has a prayer niche (*mihrab*) in the southern wall (*qibla*) facing Mecca.

Because Muslims believe that the events connected with the final Day of Judgment, including resurrection of the dead, will begin at the Haram al-Sharif, that area was much in demand for burial. The *turba* ("mausoleum") of Barka Khan, on the Street of the Chain, was the first of seven similar structures on that street, and eight more were erected adjacent to the western and northern sides of the Haram. The bodies of several important emirs (princes) who had died elsewhere were disinterred and brought to Jerusalem for reburial. Generally, the mausoleum is a one-room, dome-vaulted structure with an ornamented mihrab in the southern wall. Over time, additional stories would be added to many of the mausolea, necessitating the replacement of the original vault with cross vaults. The tomb itself is in the basement, where the burial chamber contains a horizontal monument of stone or marble, its corners decorated with bulbous marble knobs.

The dominant element of the Muslim skyline is the minaret, the tower usually above a mosque from which the muezzin calls the faithful to prayer five times a day. The Mamluks built or renovated four minarets around the Temple Mount to serve worshippers at Al-Aqsa Mosque. They erected two more in the Christian Quarter and a third near the site of the Hurvah Synagogue in the Jewish Quarter. All three stood in non-Muslim sections, probably intentionally, to stress the Islamic presence in the city. These minarets are still a dominant feature in Jerusalem's skyline.

1. Stone inscription inviting the "righteous servants of Allah" to quench their thirst with sweet water. Detail of the Qayt Bay *sabil* (drinking fountain) on the Haram al-Sharif.

2-4. Rich geometrical designs carved in stone on the façade of the *turba* (mausoleum) of Turkan Khatoun, a Mamluk woman, on the Street of the Chain.

5. "Jogglers" in red and white hues adorn stone benches at the entrance to the Al-Ashrafiyya madrasa.

1, 4. Square Mamluk minaret with a copper dome and a porch for the muezzin (who calls the faithful to prayer), which is supported by a series of graduated "stalactites" in the form of a projecting band of stone (*muqarnas*). Fakhriyya Minaret, southwest corner of the Haram al-Sharif.

2. Different types of *alam*, a decorative metal structure bearing the form of the Muslim crescent characteristic of mosques.

2, 3. Mamluk minaret at the Gate of the Chain topped with an alam.

5. The Mamluk Ghawanima Minaret, one of four square minarets around the Haram al-Sharif. Some of the decorative elements on the arches and on the columns of the upper windows are Crusader elements in secondary use.

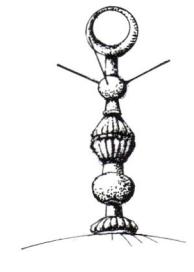

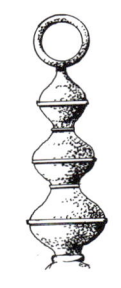

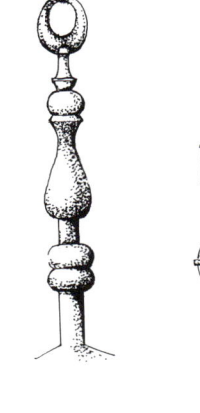

A minaret has a base, a tower, a porch for the muezzin, and a lantern above the porch and dome, ornamented with the Muslim crescent. Most minarets rise to an average height of 65 to 100 feet (20 to 30 meters, including the structure on which it stands) with a width of approximately 13 to 16 feet (4-5 meters). This ratio of 6:1 or 7:1 between height and width gives the minaret its slender, elegant appearance. All but one of the Mamluk minarets reflect the square Syrian plan, as opposed to the round type favored by the Ottomans and afterward. Besides the architectural function of rising above the skyline, minarets are important for their ornamentation, especially in the transition from base to tower. Mamluk minarets are divided into several "floors" by means of a *muqarnas*, a band made of projecting and stylized stone. The minaret at the Mosque of Omar, the highest in the Old City and among the handsomest, has four such floors.

To accommodate the thousands of pilgrims who swelled the city's population every year, hostels—separate for men and for women—were constructed near the Temple Mount. The two main hostel forms were the *khan*, built under the auspices of the authorities, and the *khanaqah*, for Sufi mystics. The khans for pilgrims, which also served merchants, government officials, and others, were two-story structures built around an open inner courtyard. A row of attached rooms ran along the building, linked (usually) by a covered arcade. The use to which these buildings were put subsequently changed, but the Khan al-Sultan on the Street of the Chain remains a good example of such a hostel, as does the khan above the Cotton Merchants Market. The Mamluks employed the revenue from that

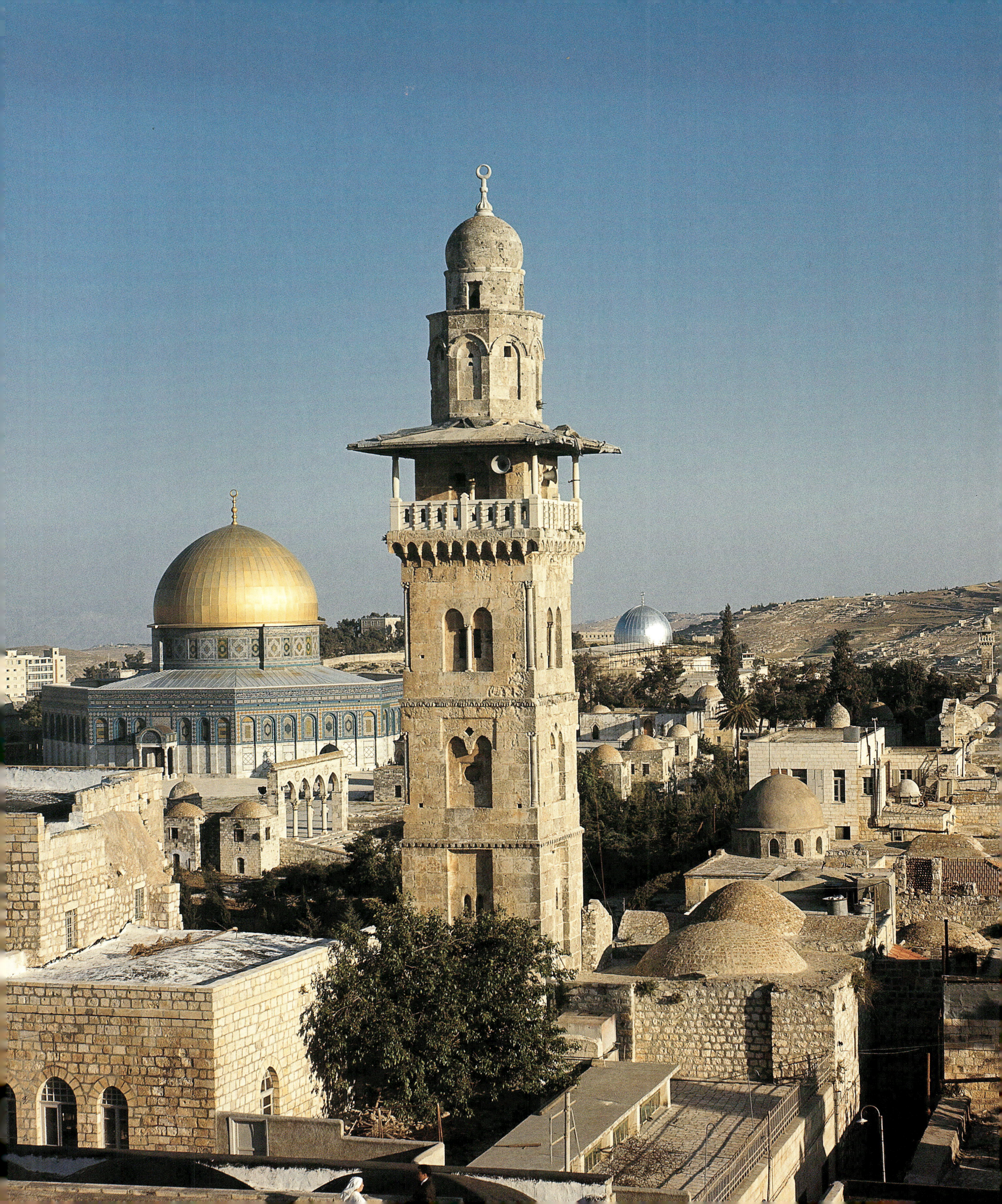

1, 2. The Cotton Merchants Market. A typical Mamluk structure decorated with graduated "stalactite" designs (*muqarnas*) and interlocking red and white and black and white stones (*ablaq*). On either side of the gate are stone benches, and a U-shaped staircase leads to the Haram al-Sharif.

combination of the commercial and the residential to pay for the upkeep of religious institutions.

Efforts to resuscitate the Cotton Merchants Market—made first by the British Mandate authorities in the 1920s and then by the Administration of Awqaf (Muslim Religious Endowments) in 1974—failed, largely because the market lies away from the main tourist route. The Khan al-Sultan, built probably by the Crusaders, underwent refurbishment in 1386 by the Mamluk Sultan Barquq and again some five hundred years later, this time by the Administration of Awqaf.

Two large public bath houses, or *hammam*, were built by the Emir Tankiz (1312-40) for both local residents and pilgrims. Modeled on Roman baths, the hammam contained a water-supply system, heating facilities, and runoff conduits. The visitor passed through successive, increasingly hot rooms. Built into the domes above some of the rooms were hollow clay pipes. Sealed with glass disks, these acted as windows through which shafts of sunlight penetrated, piercing the clouds of steam to create a unique atmosphere. The hammams, though still standing, have fallen into disuse.

Architecturally, the most important market structure in the Old City is the 14th-century Cotton Merchants Market. It is a covered, continuous, two-story structure, 315 feet (95 meters) long, containing fifty shops below and living quarters on the upper floor. The ceiling consists of a series of cross vaults, with an illumination opening at the center of every second vault. Within the structure are a khan and two bath houses (today used for storage and lodgings).

Although often different inside, Mamluk buildings display, to the outside world, common architectural features and decorations—that is, a distinct and defined vocabulary of construction. Most Mamluk buildings are attached to one another, or to earlier structures, and clustered near the Temple Mount as well as along its access streets. A continuous façade is thus created, with each building projecting a physical presence that is two-dimensional (since only the main entrance is visible from the street). But every structure is set apart architecturally by a repertoire of stylized elements. In the Mamluks' linear form of construction, the façade, and especially the main entrance, assumed unusual importance. The entrance was a structure in its own right, formed as a high niche within a rectangular frame. The richly ornamented niche endowed

50

the entrance with a kind of elegant grandeur.

Since inner courtyards provided ample ventilation and illumination, ground-floor windows facing the street were usually small and set high, enhancing the occupants' sense of privacy. Mausolea, however, had large windows at street level so that passersby could look in and listen to readings from the Koran. Ground-floor windows were usually protected by heavy rounded iron grilles. The upper stories of some Mamluk buildings have projecting, enclosed balconies (a widespread form of bay window or oriel known locally either by the Turkish term *kösk* or the German *Erker*).

Mamluk architecture also exhibits extensive use of *ablaq*—interchanging and/or interlocking colored stones, usually red and yellow (less frequently black and white)—on the main façade. Striking examples are the Al-Ashrafiyya madrasa and the splendid *sabil* ("fountain") on the Haram al-Sharif built by Sultan Qayt Bay, who ruled from Cairo (1468-96). That fountain also furnishes one of the finest examples of the Mamluks' use of highly ornate stone-engraved calligraphy. In this case, a broad stone strip surrounding the entire structure documents its construction, interspersing verses from the Koran. The use of interlocking geometric motifs or arabesques, especially in stone and wood, is another outstanding decorative element in Mamluk (and other Muslim) architecture, which the Qayt Bay fountain shows to good advantage. In some instances the geometric motifs are inlaid with colored glazed ceramic.

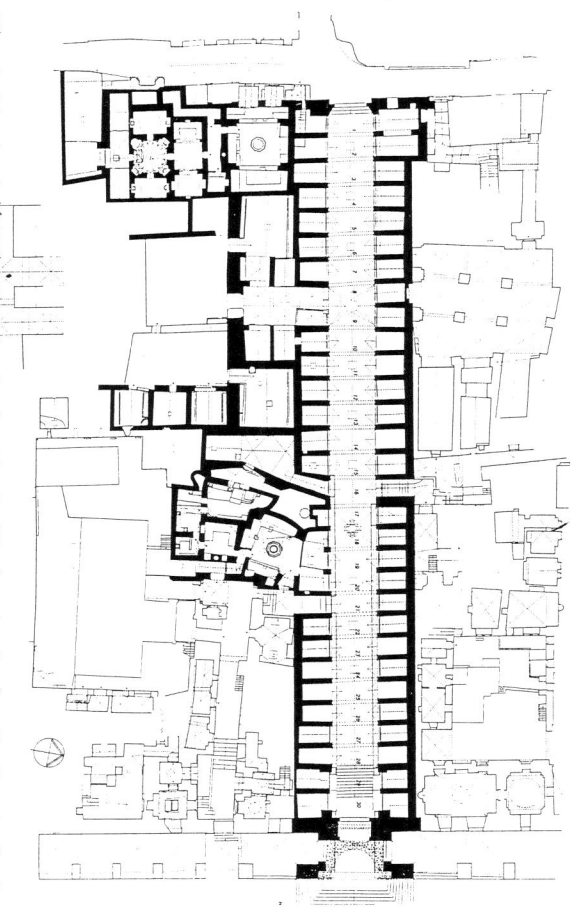

3, 4. The Cotton Merchants Market. The covered two-story structure contains some fifty shops. In the restoration work done in 1974, the inside of the cross-vaulting was left exposed to display the complex construction technology.

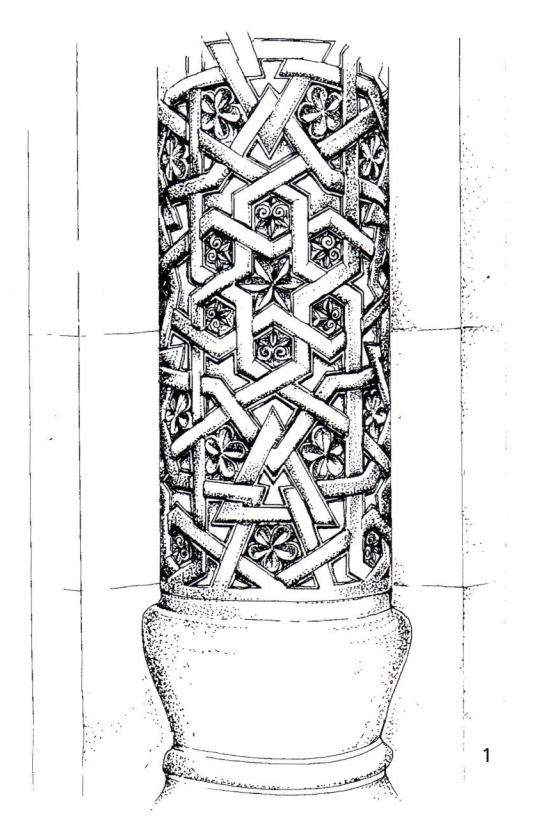

Mamluk architecture was enhanced by intriguing combinations of arches, vaults, and domes, the result of complex engineering techniques that produced sophisticated geometric spaces of unusual form and proportion. Construction was relatively speedy. The large and magnificent Al-Ashrafiyya madrasa took eighteen months to build, the Tankiziyya two years. Most of the work was done by local artisans and workers, although evidence suggests that itinerant craftsmen from Egypt and Syria also participated.

Despite the effects of time, climate, and war, about three-quarters of the Mamluk buildings in Jerusalem survive, for the most part in reasonably good condition. However, since the 18th century hardly any Mamluk building in the city has served its original purpose. Gradually, most of them would be occupied by destitute families, who sometimes put up makeshift structures in the courtyard that marred the building's form. Stones became loose, cracks appeared, and plaster crumbled; original doors and wooden shutters had to be replaced. Yet, the overall urban texture of Mamluk structures was only slightly affected, thanks to their having remained in continuous use. Even the additions were usually made of light, easily disposable materials.

1-3. The *sabil* (drinking fountain) built by Sultan Qayt Bay on the Haram al-Sharif is one of the most impressive 15th-century structures in Jerusalem. It blends red and yellow stones (*ablaq*), "stalactite" (*muqarnas*) designs, ornate calligraphy carved in the stone, and a dome ornamented with interlinked geometric arabesques.

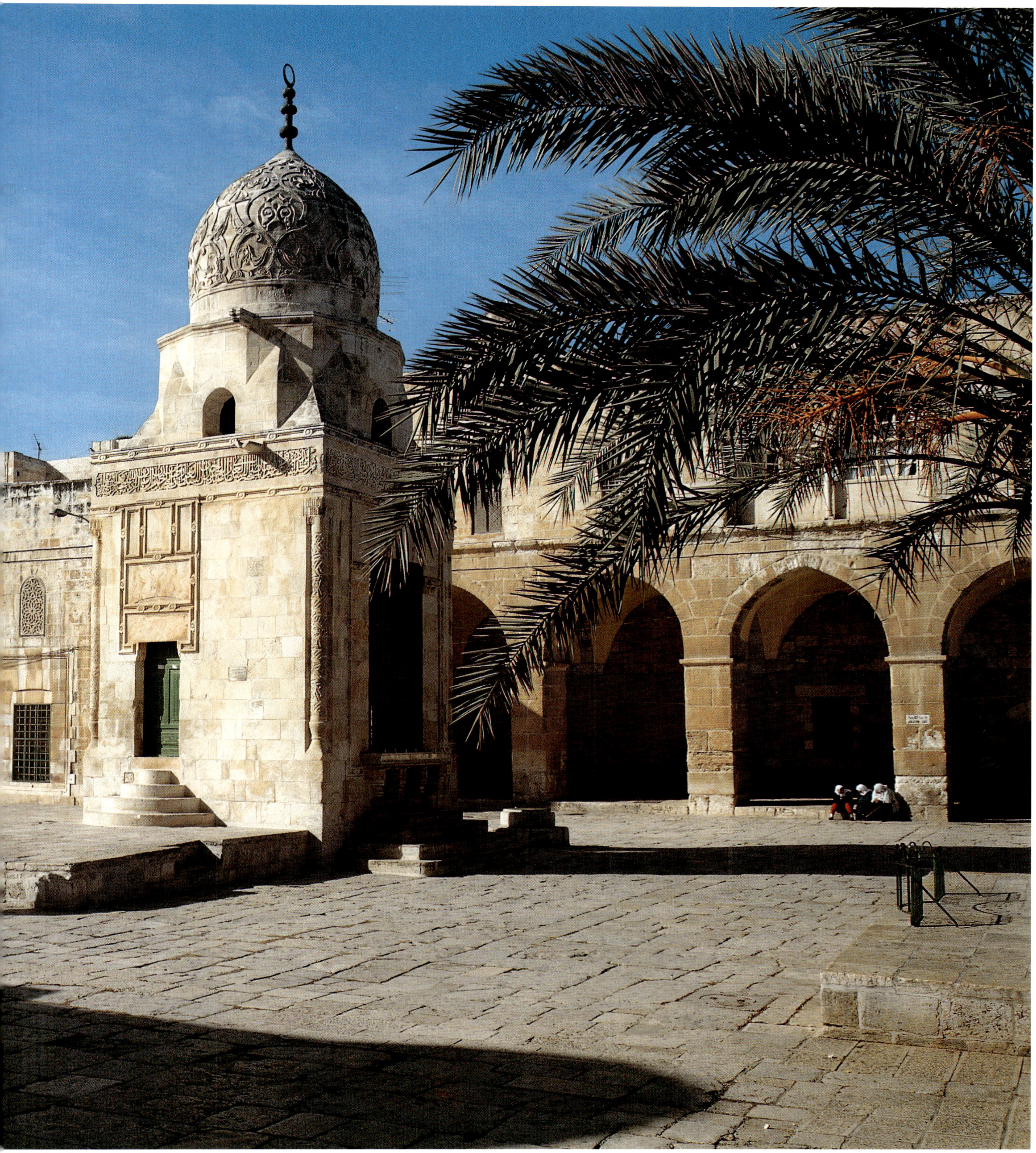

1, 2. A typical Mamluk wheel-shaped decoration formed by an inlay of interlocking red and yellow stones (*ablaq*) adorns the windows of the madrasa 'Uthmaniyya, located above the western covered arcade of the Haram al-Sharif.

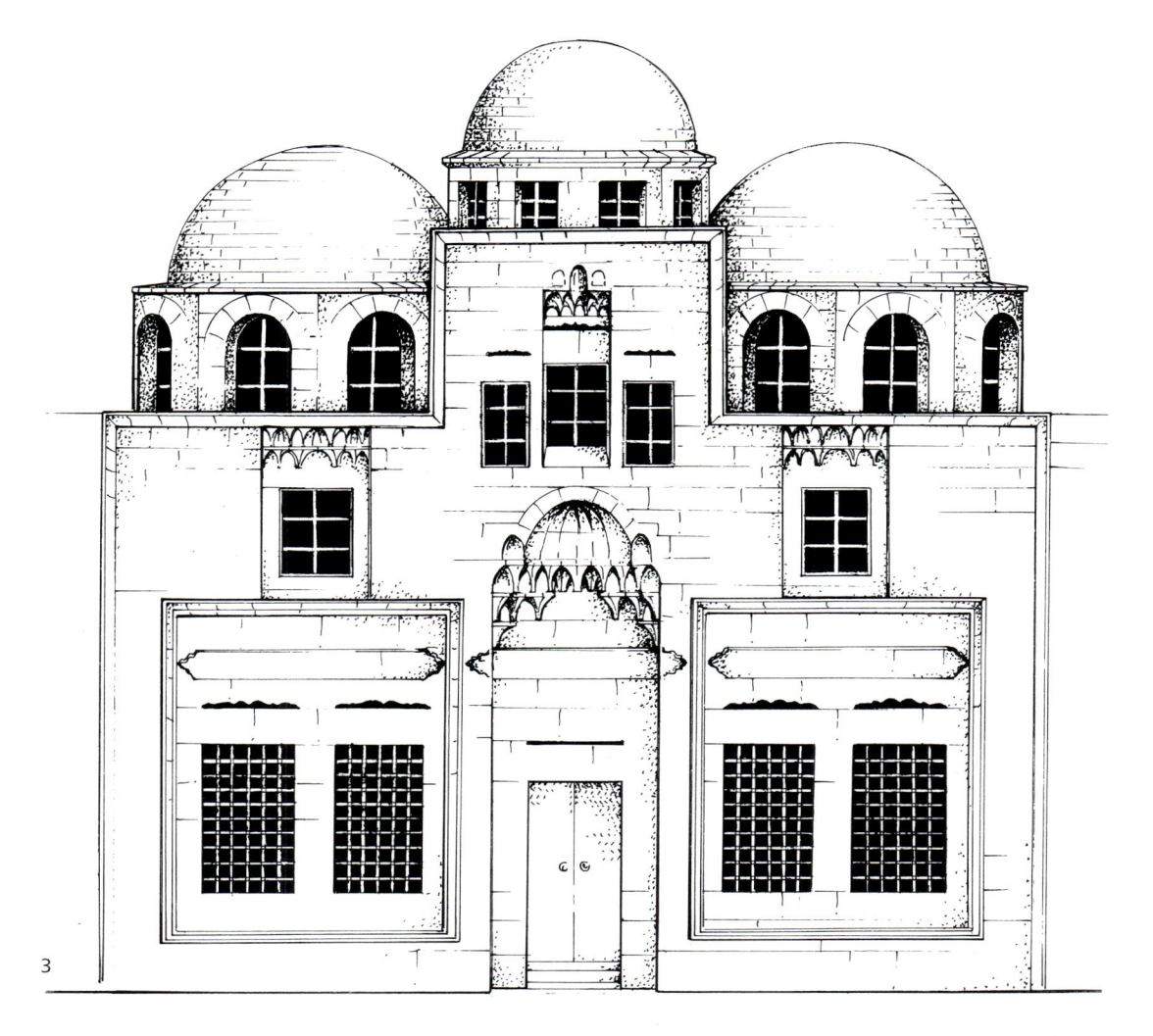

3, 5. Façade of Al-Kilaniyya *turba*, a typical Mamluk mausoleum with an imposing entrance and a niche topped with a dome. The iron-plated wood door is decorated with reliefs in the shape of barley seeds.

4, 6. The stylized façade of the Al-Is'ardiyya madrasa on the Haram al-Sharif. The prominent niche in the center emphasizes the location of the *mihrab* (prayer niche) in the building's mosque.

1 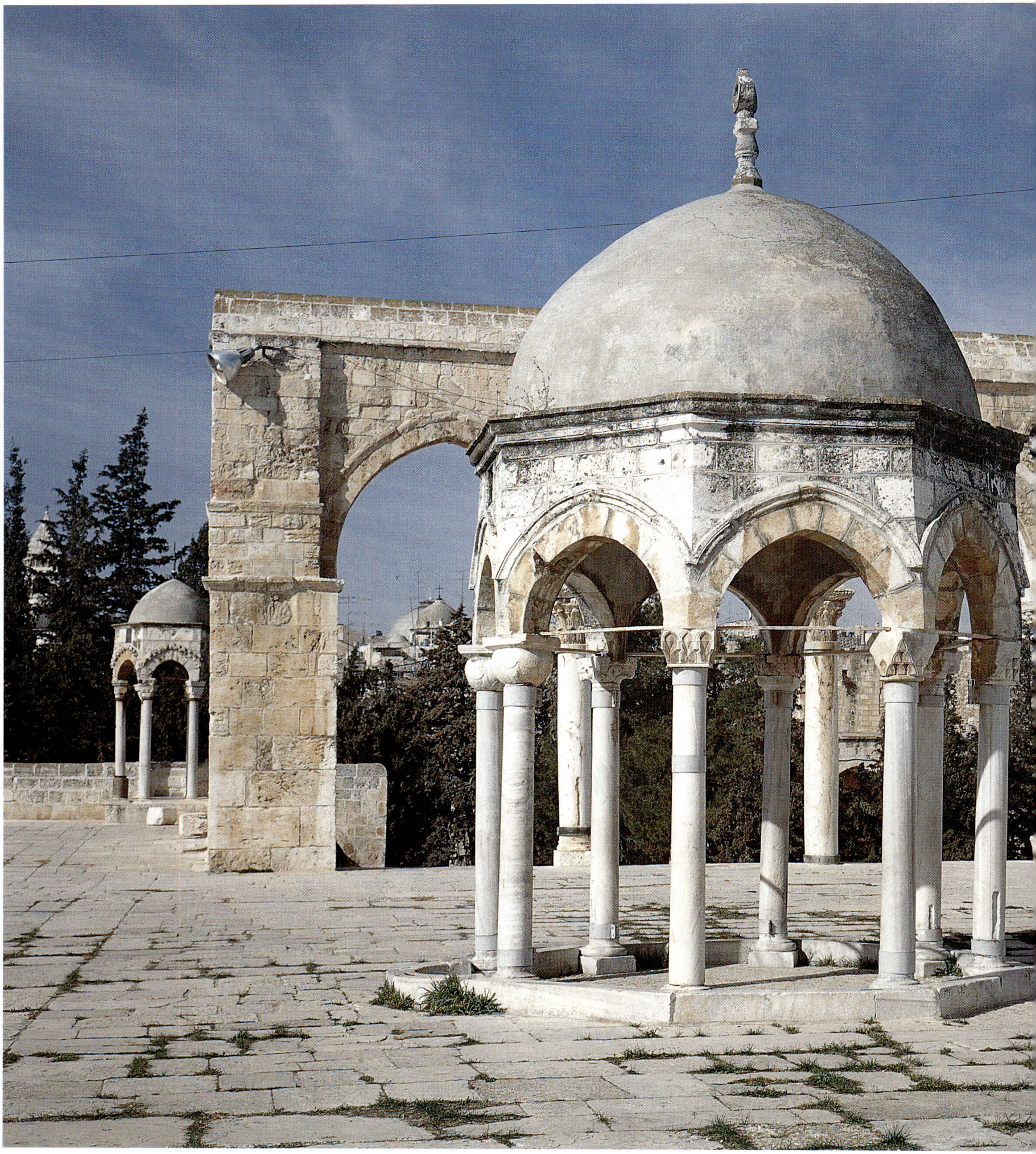

1. The Dome of the Spirit, one of similar memorial structures built on the Haram al-Sharif to commemorate historical personalities or events. In the background is the northwest colonnade gate (*qanatir*), with its typical wheel-shaped Mamluk decoration (2), combining black and white marble with stone dentils on the perimeter.
2. One of eight Mamluk colonnade gates around the upper level of the Haram al-Sharif that define the stairs leading from the lower platform.

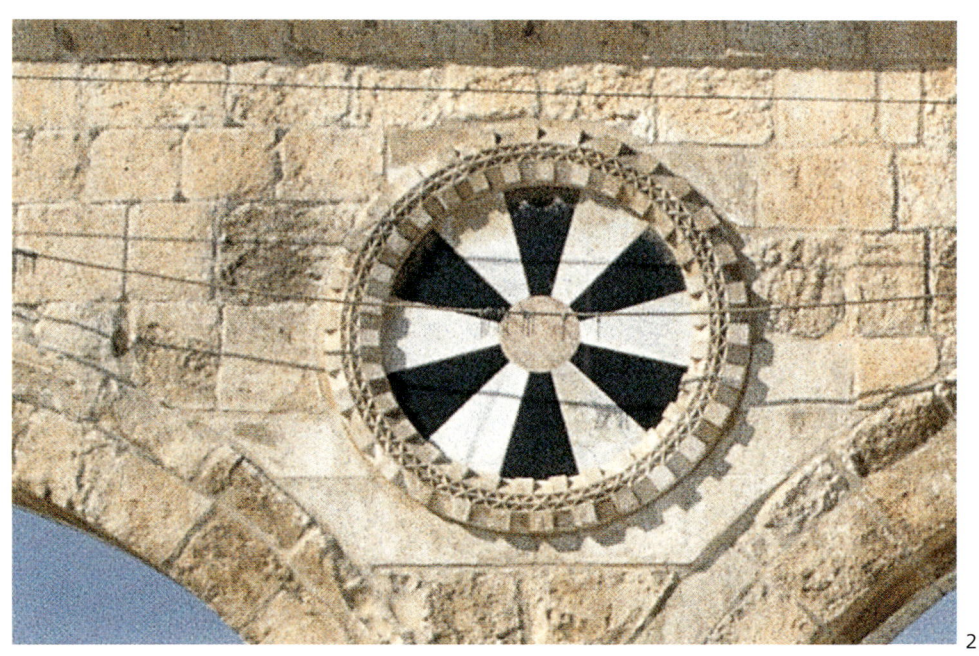

THE OTTOMAN PERIOD: 1517-1917
A Tapestry of Styles

From Constantinople, their capital, the Turkish sultans ruled Jerusalem for four centuries. A burst of building energy, much of it religiously motivated, marked the initial period of Ottoman rule, and it changed the face of the Old City. Thereafter, for about three-quarters of the Ottoman Period, Jerusalem, like the rest of the empire, had less magnificent buildings to offer. Still, the construction that did take place during the lengthy period of Ottoman hegemony produced a mélange of forms and styles, since the three monotheistic claimants to Jerusalem all undertook significant construction, each in its own image. First came the Ottoman Muslims and then, some three centuries later, the European Powers and Christian communities, as well as Jewish religious and public institutions. During the 19th century, ironically, the Muslim Quarter, which contained the great majority of the Old City's population, began to deteriorate into a sorry physical state, from which it has yet to emerge.

Palestine, and Jerusalem in particular, initially benefited from the Ottoman conquest. Economic development and administrative efficiency were the hallmarks of the reign of Suleiman the Magnificent, the dynamic Sultan of the Ottoman Empire in its golden age (1520-66). Suleiman, impressed by Jerusalem's religious and historical importance, gave the city a major facelift. He sent his architects to supervise the ambitious and spectacular enterprise of building the great wall that symbolizes the Old City to this day. Suleiman modernized the water-supply system and built six splendid public drinking fountains. He showed his religious devotion by renovating the exterior of the Dome of the Rock, a campaign that replaced the chipped and flaking original glass mosaics with glazed ceramic tiles richly decorated with colorful floral motifs—a resplendent new element, used in Ottoman architecture since the 15th century.

Commercial life flourished. Several of the suqs, or markets, were reorganized and renovated, while new ones were built, in part to further the Ottomans' imperial trade policy. For example, one purpose of the new spice market was to help the empire compete with the Portuguese, then opening new sea routes to the East, in the lucrative purchase and sale of spices.

Suleiman's Walls and Gates

Jerusalem has always been a fortified city. The present wall and gates were constructed some 450 years ago (1536-41) on the foundations of the medieval ramparts, which themselves stood on the ruins of still earlier walls, built on bedrock, from the Second Temple Period. Architecturally, the wall is a highly successful fusion of the functional and the aesthetic, the paragon of all 16th-century walls. At the same time, it inevitably determined Jerusalem's urban texture, framing a given area of land that could not be extended.

In addition to reasons of prestige and economics, Suleiman built the wall for protection against marauding Bedouin tribes and, more urgently, against a new crusade rumored to be in preparation by the Holy Roman Emperor Charles V (1519-56). Charles' defeat at Algiers, however, delivered Jerusalem from this threat, which enabled the Sultan to redirect his builders to more pressing assignments elsewhere. Thus, the interiors of about half the towers were left unfinished.

The wall's statistics are imposing enough, the total length (with angles, towers, gates, and the Citadel) running to 2.7 miles (4,325 meters). The height ranges from 17 feet to 50 feet (5 to 15 meters), and at some points it is nearly 10 feet (3 meters) thick at the base,

1, 2. The present-day wall surrounding the Old City was built by the Ottomans more than 450 years ago, from 1536 to 1541. More than any other structure, it symbolizes Jerusalem.
3. The western section of the Old City wall, leading to Jaffa Gate (right).

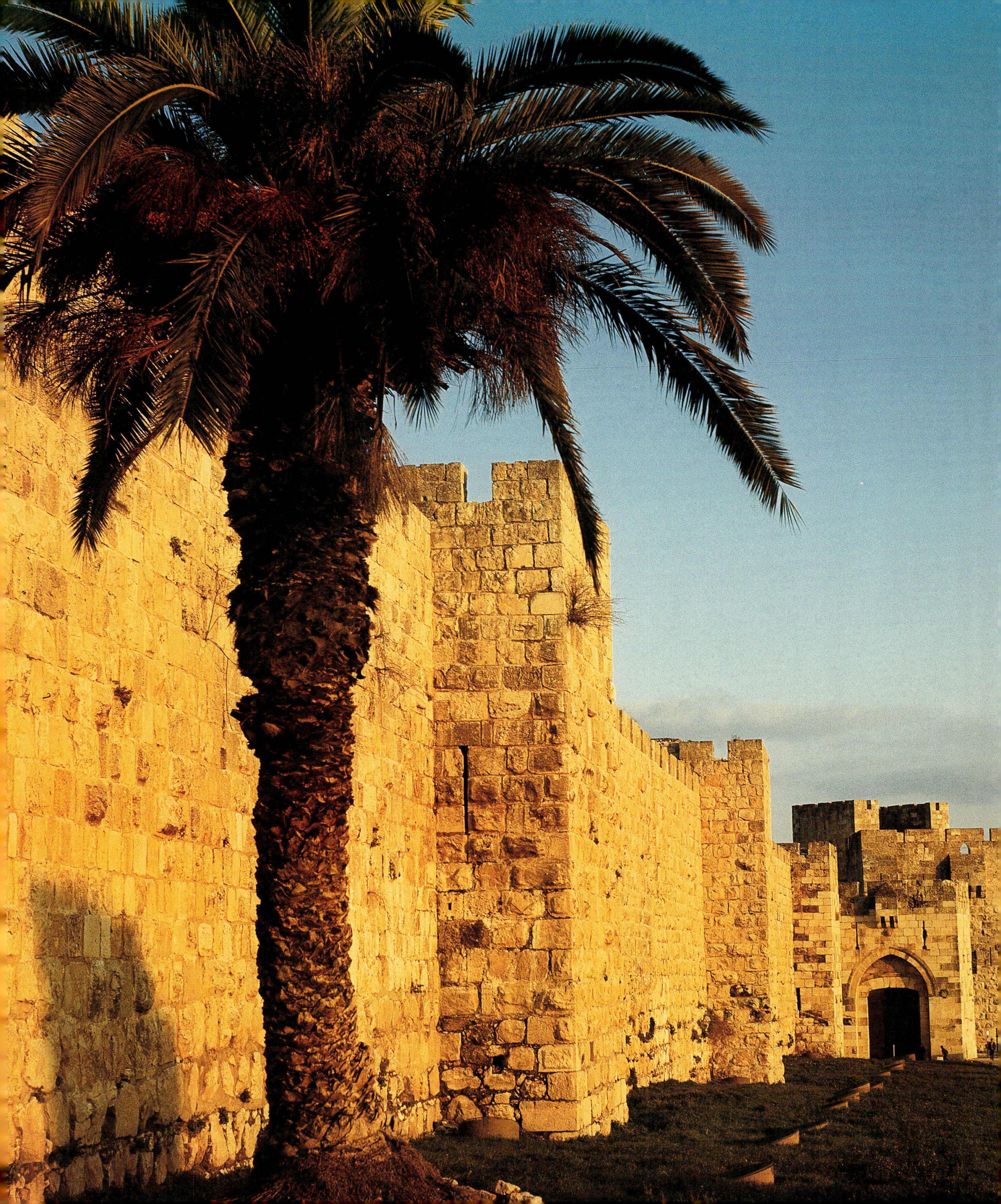

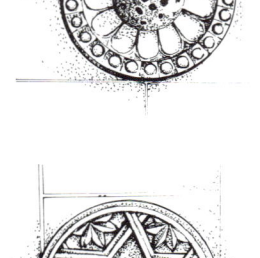

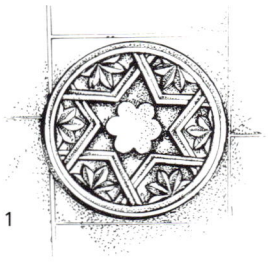

about half that at the line of the firing slits and half again at the uppermost level. The wall does not encompass the strategically located Mount Zion, and legend has it that the two graves just inside Jaffa Gate are those of architects who were executed at Suleiman's command for not including that area. A different version has the two being put to death to ensure that no one else could hire them to build another wall as magnificent as Jerusalem's.

The external rampart on the west side of the Citadel/Tower of David is part of the Old City wall. However, the Citadel itself is an independent structure with its own system of defenses and gates. Suleiman had the Citadel repaired in 1531, a few years before work began on the walls, probably to symbolize his presence and to serve as a barracks for the troops stationed in the city shortly after its conquest. The Ottomans deployed a relatively large garrison in Jerusalem, equipped with cannons emplaced in the Citadel.

Since the professional work force available in the Jerusalem area proved insufficient for the project, experts were summoned from Cairo, Aleppo, and elsewhere. The hugely expensive enterprise was financed from taxes collected in Palestine and as far afield as Damascus.

Massive gates constitute a major element in the wall's fortress architecture. Located at the center of each side of the wall, the four main gates—Jaffa Gate on the west, Lions' Gate on the east, Damascus Gate on the north, and Zion Gate on the south—give access to the two thoroughfares that bisect the city. To ease the flow of traffic, two smaller entrances, passable by both individuals and animals, were built: Herod's Gate in the north and Dung Gate in the south. A seventh entrance, west of Damascus Gate and known simply as New Gate, was breached in the wall in 1889, with the permission of Sultan Abdul Hamid II, at the request of the European powers and Christian institutions, to create a more convenient approach to the New City from the Christian Quarter.

Three of the gates—Jaffa, Lions', and Zion—had an L-shaped internal structure, the built-in 90-degree turn obviating a direct breach. (This element was later removed from Lions' Gate, to provide access for motor vehicles.) Each of these gates is crowned by a

1. Stone medallions with geometric and floral designs adorn the Old City ramparts.
2. Jaffa Gate (left) and the Tower of David are the most prominent architectural elements in the western façade of the Old City wall.

machicolation, an upper battlement with an opening, common in medieval fortified structures, through which missiles, hot liquids, or stones could be hurled onto attackers. Defense was further enhanced by heavy wooden, iron-plated double doors. Damascus Gate, the largest and grandest of the four, built as a double L, stands at the lowest geographical point in the Old City on the remains of a late-Roman gate that led to the Cardo. Two prominent, ornamented turrets flank the gate, and, in addition to machicolations, medallions, and firing slits, the entrance climaxes in slender turban-like "pinnacles," giving the effect of a lace crown.

The wall is punctuated at unequal intervals by thirty-five towers, located at corners and other vulnerable points. These differ in height, exterior design, and number of fighting positions. Seventeen machicolations were built in order to fulfill an obvious functional purpose—for which, incidentally, they were never used—but also to enhance the wall's aesthetic merit. There are 344 firing slits, or loopholes, and an additional 60 in the interior walls of the Citadel. The slits, meant for riflemen (the bow-and-arrow was already obsolete), average 5 feet (1.5 meters) in height and 5 inches (13 centimeters) in width. Some are decorated with stone medallions engraved with geometric or floral motifs.

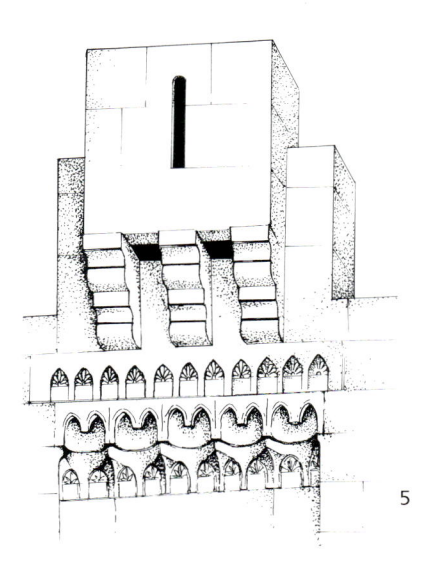

3, 5. Stylized decorations adorn the battlements (machicolations) protruding from the upper section of the ramparts and gates. In addition to their functional purpose—boiling oil could be poured on attackers through an opening at their base—they played an aesthetic role.

4. The façade of Lions' (St. Stephen's) Gate, on the eastern side of the Old City wall, is topped by crenellations and studded with stone carvings. On either side of the gate are panthers, the heraldic emblem of the Mamluk Sultan Baybars. They are here in secondary use.

1, 2. Some of the medallions adorning the Old City ramparts are actually the protruding extremities of small stone pillars that were inserted into the wall to reinforce the construction.

3. Damascus Gate, the most monumental and magnificent of the Old City gates, is adorned with battlements, carved medallions, and stylized lacelike pinnacles. An inscription declares that it was built by Suleiman the Magnificent in 1536-38. Damascus Gate stands on the ruins of an early gate from Roman times (seen as an arch on the left). The preservation and restoration of the Old City ramparts and gates is one of the major projects carried out since Jerusalem's reunification in 1967.

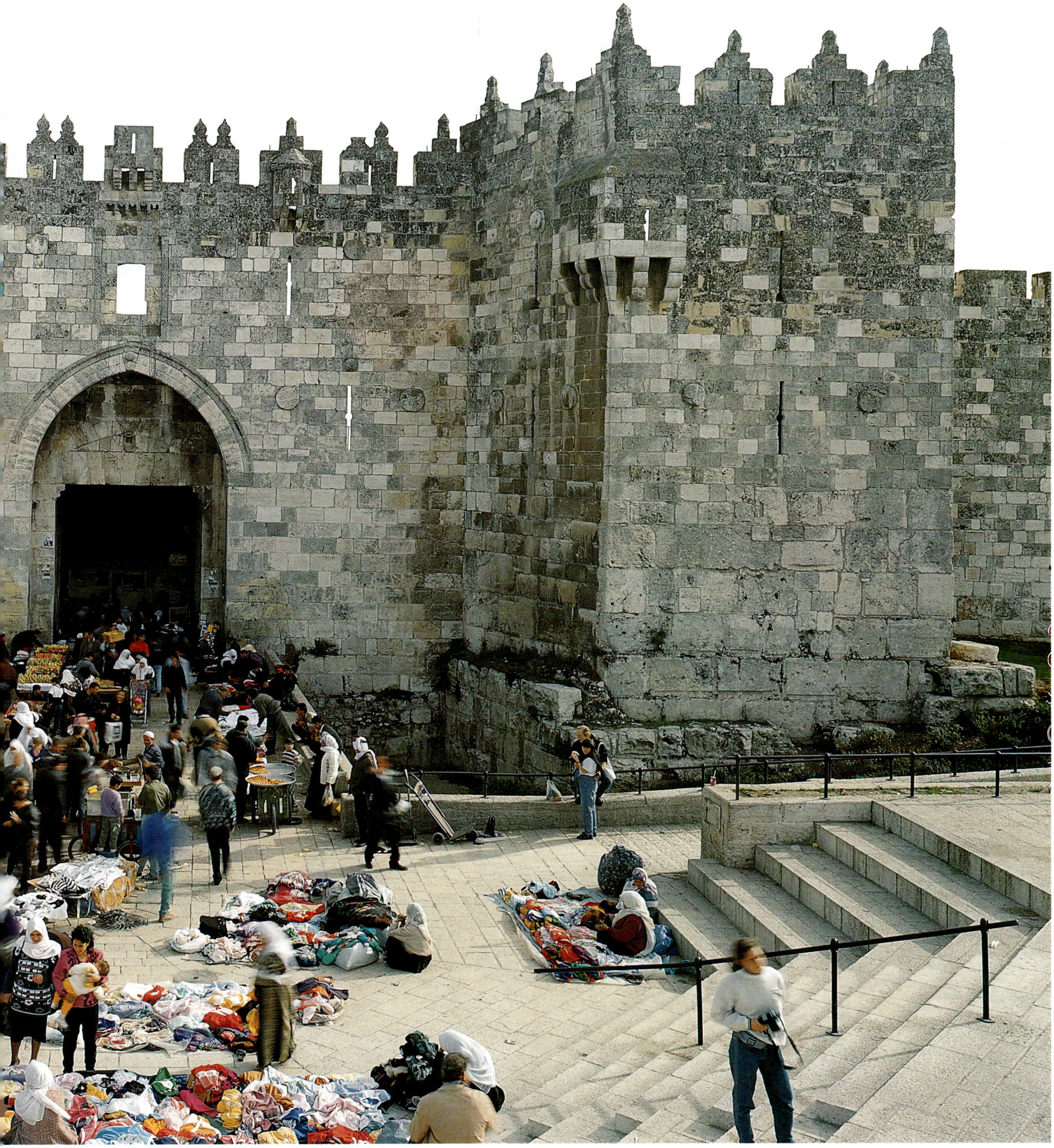

1, 2. The Sabil Suleiman is the finest and best preserved of the six fountains built by Suleiman the Magnificent.
2. A 19th-century engraving of the Sabil Suleiman.
3. Lions' Gate, the entry to the Old City from the east, leads on to the Via Dolorosa.
4. Bullet marks in the stones around Zion Gate bear witness to the fighting that raged here during Israel's War of Independence in 1948.

Inserted in the wall are sixteen incised stone plaques commemorating Suleiman and giving the construction date of that section along with verses of thanksgiving. Inscriptions above the gates provide a chronological record of the building process, which began in 1535 or 1536 on the city's northern, and strategically most vulnerable, side. The western, and final, section was completed in 1541. The base of the wall is a historical potpourri, made of stones from earlier periods and varying in style, cut, size, and color. These were taken from ruined and abandoned buildings in the city, including churches no longer in use. The stones in the upper courses, however, were cut especially for the wall and hence are more uniform in shape and size.

Within a single year, 1536-37, Suleiman erected six magnificent public drinking fountains, known as *sabils*: five within the Old City and a sixth just outside the wall, at the edge of Sultan's Pool. The finest and best preserved of these watering places stands next to the Gate of the Chain. Besides quenching the thirst of the population, the fountains also served the ritual-cleansing needs—of the face, hands, and feet—of the faithful who visited the Haram al-Sharif. One of the cleansing fountains was on the Temple Mount and four others on adjacent streets. Most of them disclose clear secondary use of pre-Ottoman architectural elements, producing a tapestry of mutual influences and thus an architectural form unique to Jerusalem.

After Suleiman, the Ottoman Empire plunged into a protracted period of economic, political, and social decline. Constantinople lost interest in Jerusalem, where construction, development, and maintenance came to a virtual halt. The population—particularly the Jewish community—dwindled, and Jerusalem gradually sank into that "mournful and dreary and lifeless" condition described by Mark Twain, who visited the city in 1867, just as a spurt of European and Jewish building was beginning.

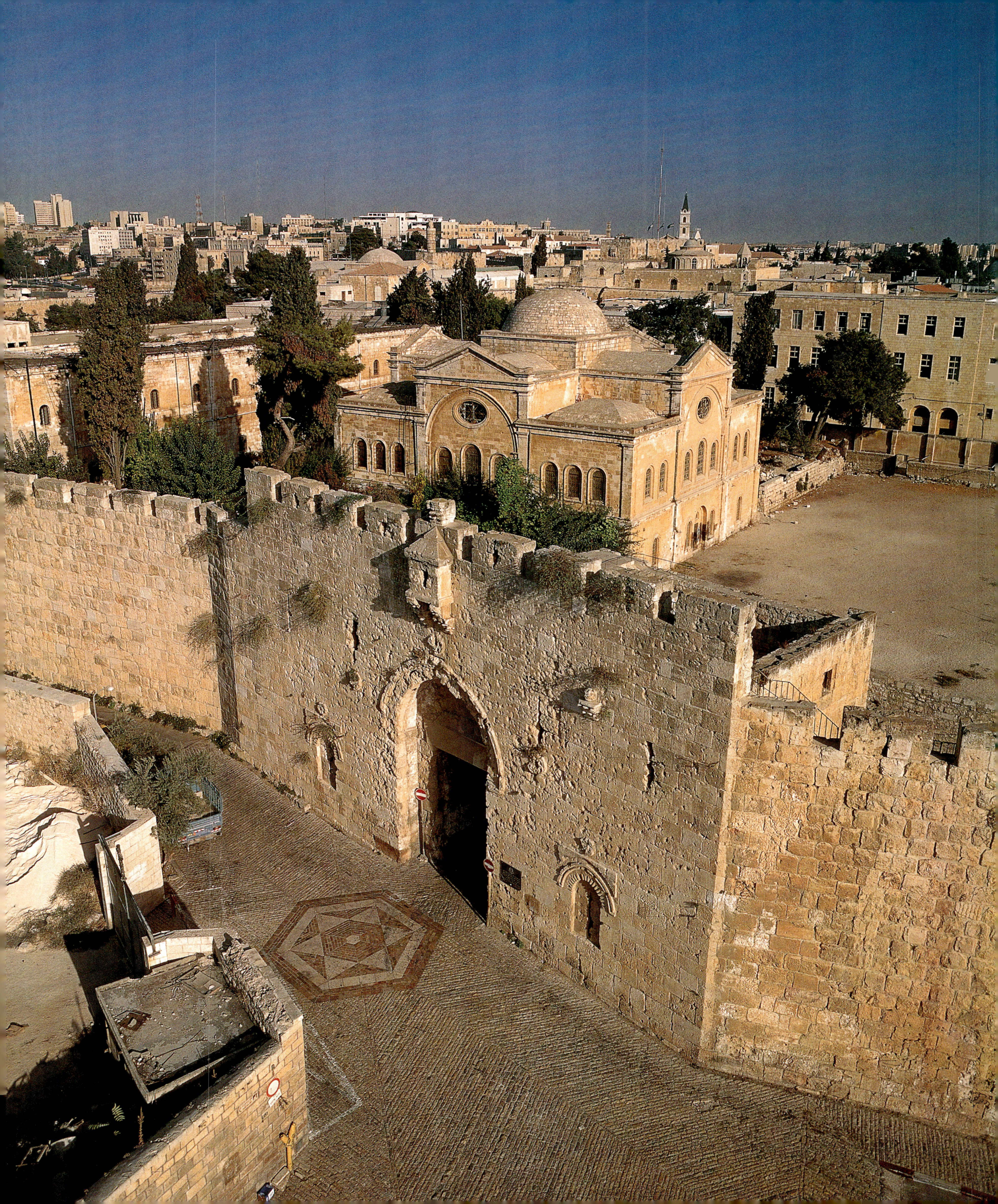

European Christian Building

In the 19th century, international and regional developments conspired to produce a burst of construction activity in Jerusalem, sponsored by the European Powers and Christian communities. Building was concentrated in three areas: around the Church of the Holy Sepulcher, at the eastern extremity of the Via Dolorosa, and in the Armenian Quarter and its environs. Religious motivation played a large part in the construction drive, but so did availability of land and its cost. Political connections and bribes to Ottoman officials often proved helpful. Missionary groups sought locations near their target populations, mainly in the vicinity of the Jewish Quarter. Besides reflecting the city's importance in Christian tradition, the new building campaign enabled the Christian sects to demonstrate their own presence and influence, particularly by means of religious activity, organized pilgrimages, and humanitarian works centered about the new structures.

As the number of clerics, monks, nuns, and others engaged in religious activity increased, large compounds—virtual minitowns—rose to accommodate them, in both their spiritual and their everyday material needs. The three major compounds are those of the Greek Orthodox, the Armenian Quarter, and the Franciscan Monastery of San Salvatore. The dearth of hotels in Jerusalem during most of the 19th century meant that the thousands of pilgrims who visited the city lodged in church hostels or in sections of monasteries set aside for that purpose. The Austrian Hospice (1869), on the Via Dolorosa, and the Franciscans' Casa Nova (1866) in the Christian Quarter were built exclusively for Christian pilgrims.

Nor was the indigenous population neglected. To upgrade the perceived substandard educational level of the local (i.e., Arab) population, and coincidentally augment their own influence, European Christian organizations erected

1. The Church of the Holy Sepulcher was a magnet for much European Christian building in the late 19th century and the early 20th.

2, 3. Some of the courtyard structures in the Armenian Quarter feature arcades with cross vaults. The Armenian Museum (2), originally a hostel for students at the Armenian Theological Seminary, built in the mid-19th century.

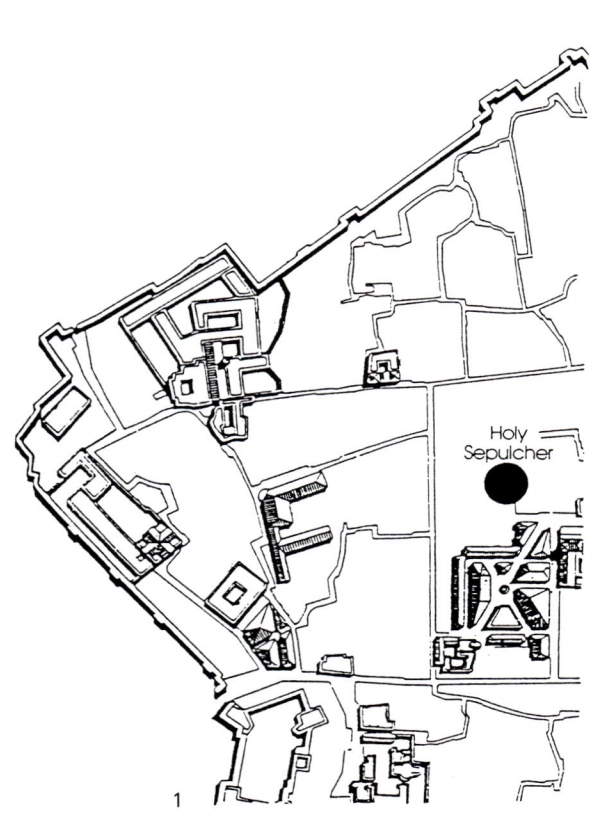

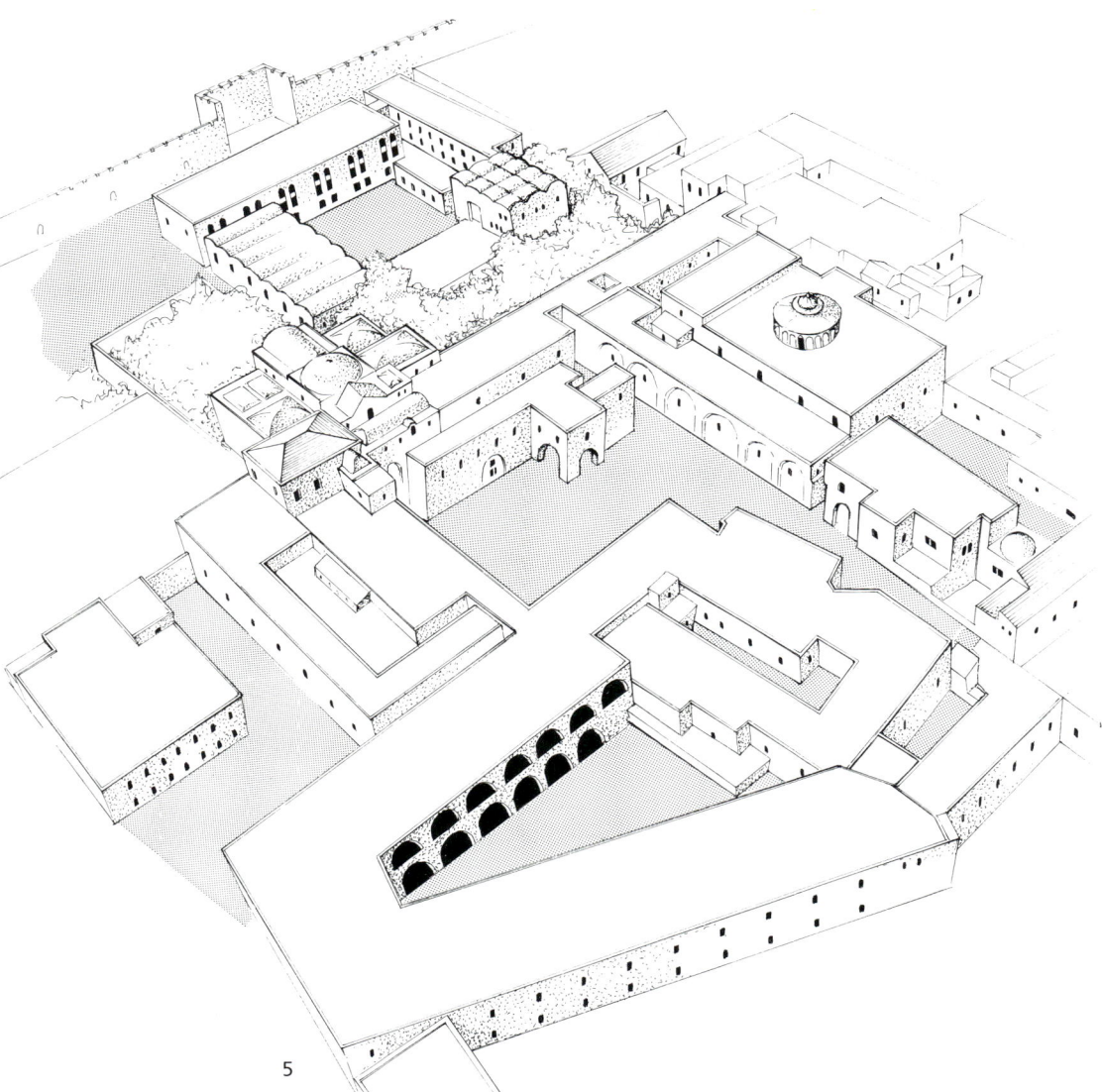

4, 5. Inner courtyards of religious, educational, and residential buildings characterize the architecture of the Armenian Quarter in the Old City.

6. A protruding grille allows those inside the residence to observe the narrow space of the alley below.

7. A series of traditional buttressing arches on St. Mark's Street in the Armenian Quarter.

1. This intricate and stylized iron grille on the main entrance to the Cathedral of St. James is typical of construction in the Armenian Quarter.

2. The stone plaques on the walls surrounding the entrance courtyard to St. James's Cathedral are known in Armenian as Khatchkars (*khatch* = cross, *kar* = stone). They were dedicated by Armenian pilgrims to Jerusalem.

3. The Neo-Byzantine style is well displayed in the former Armenian Theological Seminary (1857).

4. St. James's Cathedral, built in the 12th century on the foundations of a Byzantine church, is the most important Armenian place of worship in the Holy Land. Its massive dome rests on four great piers. View to the east, with the iconstatis and altar.

a series of schools in the Christian Quarter, with Catholics and the Greek Orthodox taking the lead. The Franciscans built a school for girls, the Collège de Terre Sainte, in 1841; in 1876 the French Catholics opened a school for boys, the Collège des Frères; and in 1891 the Franciscans built an orphanage. The Greek Orthodox effort included a girls school across from the Great Greek Monastery, inaugurated in 1862, and, later in the century, a combined elementary and high school nearby.

As in medieval times, some Christian communities undertook commercial construction to help finance their activity. Thus, for their two main projects, the Greek Orthodox built a shopping arcade inside Jaffa Gate (1884-89), as well as a hotel, called Grand New Hotel (today the New Imperial Hotel), and the Aftimos Market (1903) in the Muristan area, close to the Church of the Holy Sepulcher. Both projects have the same plan, with entrances from various directions and the center underscored with an architectural element.

Most of the residential buildings erected by the Greek Orthodox monasteries, and scattered mainly in the Christian Quarter of the Old City, were rented out. The symbol of the Greek Orthodox Patriarchate, the *Taphos* (meaning "tomb" and thus signifying the Holy Sepulcher) is engraved on the keystone above the community's many religious and commercial buildings.

Building by Christian communities was one of the principal means through which the European Powers sought to gain a religious and political foothold in Ottoman-Muslim Jerusalem, at a time when the Near East assumed growing international importance. The Turks, for their part, hampered such construction wherever they could. The trials and tribulations faced by the builders of Christ Church, the first Protestant house of worship in Palestine, exemplify the problems faced by Christian institutions. The foundations for the

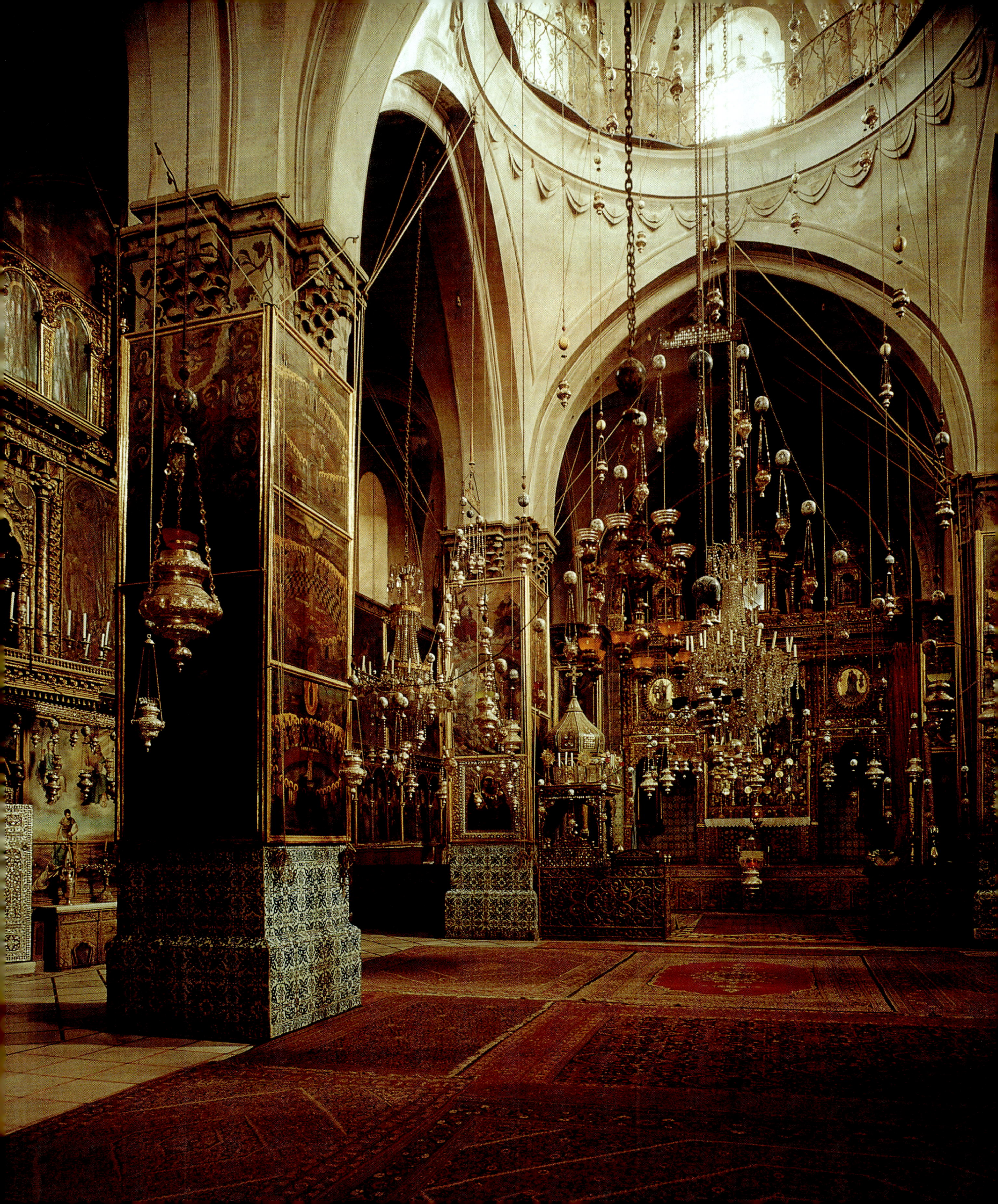

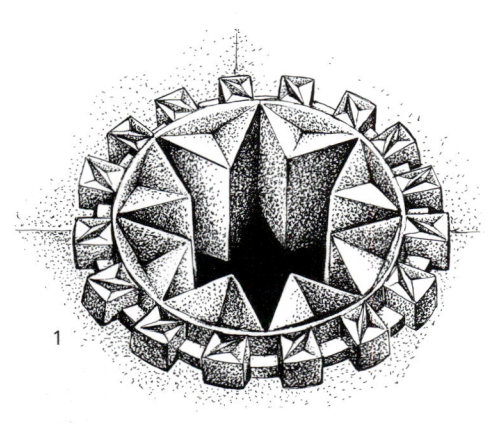

1. A ventilation opening in a Christian Quarter residence.
2. The bell towers of Greek Orthodox churches and monasteries are virtually of uniform traditional design. Church of St. John the Baptist in the Christian Quarter.
3. The urban texture of European Christian building in the Old City was often that of a mini-city serving religious and educational purposes, together with residences for monks and nuns. The great Greek Orthodox Monastery.
4. Projecting windows that face on to the street and provide much-needed extra living space for the small, cramped quarters.
5. The multilevel Franciscan Monastery of San Salvatore was built by stages, since the 17th century, as a mini-city.

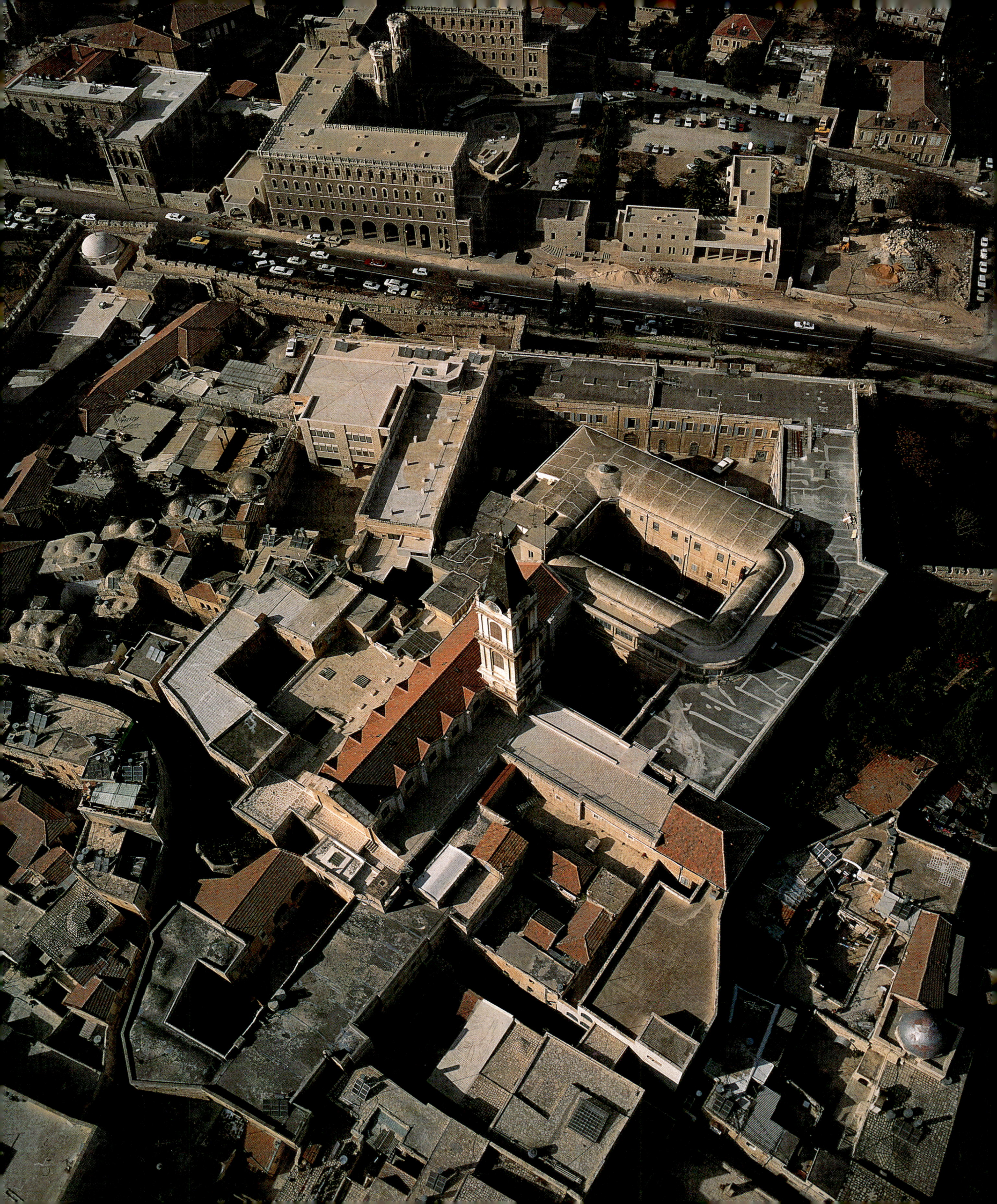

1-6. Aftimos Market built in 1903 by the Greek Orthodox Patriarchate next to the Church of the Holy Sepulcher. Its two diagonally intersecting streets contain some seventy shops and create the suq's distinctive X-shape. At the point where the two streets intersect stands a fountain (6) in the Neo-Baroque style—water streaming from the mouths of two gargoyles, one animal (5), and one human. The market was renovated in 1993.

Anglican structure were laid opposite the Citadel/Tower of David in 1841, but the Ottoman authorities ordered the construction halted in January 1843. The Rev. John Nicolayson—a missionary of the London Society for Promoting Christianity among the Jews, under whose auspices the church was erected, and a resident of the Old City—thereupon went to Constantinople to apprise the British ambassador of this development. The latter asked King Friedrich Wilhelm IV of Prussia to intercede with the Sultan, but to no avail. The original plan drawn up by the British architect J.W. Johns for a cathedral structure with four high corner towers had to be abandoned. It was not until September 1845, after pressure had been brought to bear by the British Foreign Office—in the wake of a petition signed by the Archbishop of Canterbury, the Bishop of London, 1,400 senior clerics, and nearly 15,000 of the faithful—that the Sultan issued a decree allowing construction to resume. Christ Church was finally consecrated in January 1849.

Thanks to the political significance placed by the European Powers on Christian building in Jerusalem, heads of state became the direct patrons of some of the period's most notable structures. Patronage involved both personal lobbying of high Turkish officials and financial donations. In 1869, while on a visit to Palestine after attending the inauguration of the Suez Canal, Prussia's Crown Prince received as a gift from Sultan Abdul Aziz the plot of land in the Muristan on which the Lutheran Church of the Redeemer would be built. Kaiser Wilhelm II, who eventually consecrated the church in 1898, not only raised funds for the structure but also helped plan its lofty tower. The Austrian Emperor Franz Josef made a sizable donation to the building of San Salvatore Church and to the upkeep of the Austrian Hospice when he visited Jerusalem

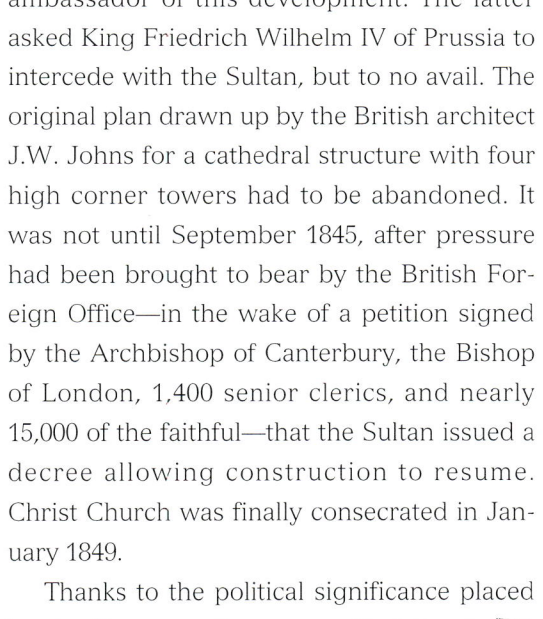

1-4. The Anglican Christ Church compound is built around an inner courtyard. The cruciform church itself (consecrated 1849) is in the English Neo-Gothic style. The fine stone construction was executed by masons brought especially from Malta.

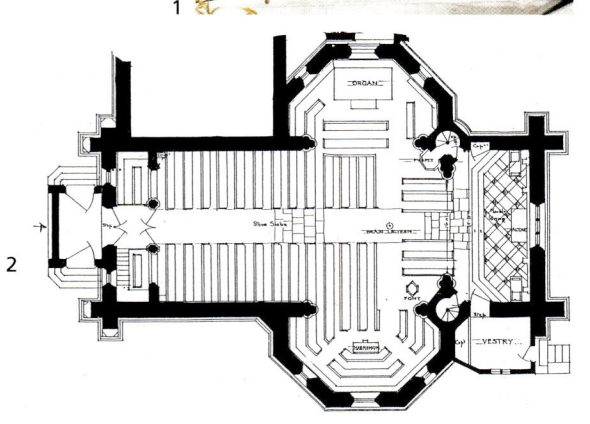

5-8. The German Lutheran Church of the Redeemer, Neo-Romanesque in style, was consecrated in 1898 by its initiator, Kaiser Wilhelm II. At the entrance portal (6), the German eagle appears on the upper left, the cross of the German Order of the Knights of St. John on the right.
The lamb in the center symbolizes Christ the Redeemer.

5. Original drawing of the Lutheran Church of the Redeemer by the building's architect, Friedrich Adler.

8. Church of the Redeemer. The complex was built on the foundations of the 12th-century Crusader Church of Maria Latina. The cloister (7) retains some Crusader parts.

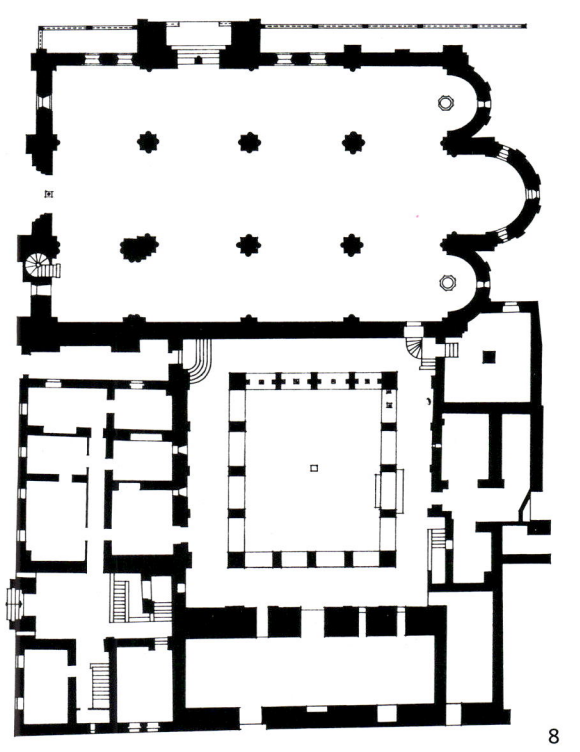

stone walls and sealed with heavy gates and doors. They are mostly institutional compounds, usually built in stages and consisting of numerous structures connected by courtyards. All were designed for maximum spatial exploitation and minimal loss of ventilation and illumination. Another widespread form was a cluster of buildings grouped about a small inner courtyard. The Greek Orthodox monasteries in the Christian Quarter belong to this type, as do the Ethiopian Patriarchate structures and the Syrian-Assyrian monastery and church. In religious buildings an atrium and cloister often defined the courtyard, which might be square, rectangular, or triangular, its shape dictated by the structure of the surrounding edifice and the plot of land available.

There are also monolithic structures without courtyards, such as the Alexander Nevsky Church (Russian Orthodox) next to the Church of the Holy Sepulcher, the two Greek Orthodox monasteries on the Via Dolorosa, and the Austrian Hospice. This category also includes European buildings not intended for religious purposes, a number of which are hotels located just inside Jaffa Gate.

Many of the religious institutional buildings have the structure of a single rectangular unit, or attached rectangular units. There are two basic forms: a long central corridor with rooms on either side, and a corridor running along one side with rooms along the other. The "long corridor" is utilized primarily in institutional architecture, which is formal and cold and reflects the purpose the building was designed to serve.

Adjacent to many Christian institutions is a church or chapel, linked by a passage to the main building. In some cases the church is an integral part of the building, but its presence is deliberately understated, as in the Austrian Hospice. Other institutions have separate places of worship, among these the Church of the Redeemer and San Salvatore, with the significance of each underscored by means of a high bell tower and a richly ornamented façade. Generally, the location and importance of a church are symbolized by an elevated dome or tall tower. The glittering silver dome of the Church of St. John the Baptist on

in 1869. Duke Maximillian of Bavaria underwrote construction of the Franciscan Chapel of the Flagellation on the Via Dolorosa.

In the Greek Orthodox community, the patrons of religious and commercial construction were usually the patriarchs themselves. Similarly, John of Smyrna, head of the Armenian Patriarchate from 1850 to 1860, was responsible for three major edifices in the Armenian Quarter: the Patriarchate building (1853), the former theological seminary (1853), now the museum, and the new seminary (1857).

In keeping with the spirit of Old City construction, the majority of Christian structures erected in this period are surrounded by high

1. Neo-Gothic façade of the Latin Patriarchate Church, consecrated in 1872. Its structure is that of a basilica.
2. Walls and narrow alleys conceal the headquarters of the Latin (Roman Catholic) Patriarchate, revealed in this reconstruction drawing.

3-5. The Russian Orthodox Alexander Nevsky Church, near the Church of the Holy Sepulcher, was consecrated in 1890. It has an ornate Neo-Baroque style with courses of pink and white stones. Atop the building is a broken pediment bearing the symbol of the "Imperial Russian Orthodox Palestine Society."

Christian Quarter Street is not visible from the main entrance but stands out prominently from the Muristan. The narrow perspective created by the lanes of the Old City obstructs our "reading" of many buildings, making it virtually impossible to view from the Via Dolorosa the impressive dome atop the Sisters of Zion Convent. Again, the casual stroller in the Old City will simply not see the church of the Maronite Convent and other churches situated within the compounds of Greek Orthodox monasteries.

A distinctive feature of Christian structures in the Old City is the bell tower. Greek Orthodox bell towers, located on the roofs of the community's churches and monasteries, are traditional and almost uniform in design, which takes the form of a broad, low (up to 10 feet, or 3 meters) gate with one or two registers, inside which hang the bells. Interesting bell towers belonging to other communities include the one designed by the architect Conrad Schick for the former residence of Bishop Alexander in the Christ Church compound and the square Crusader tower at the Church of the Holy Sepulcher. In some

1. The Franciscan Church of the Condemnation was restored in 1903-04 by architect Bro. Vendelin Gierlich according to the Byzantine church that had stood on the site. The structure has five domes borne on drums punctuated with windows. View to the west, with the dark dome of the Ecce Homo Church at the Convent of the Sisters of Zion (Catholic) in the background.

2. The metal dome of the Ecce Homo Church on the Via Dolorosa dominates the foreground. The convent was built from 1856 to 1868 on the site where, according to Christian tradition, Pontius Pilate mockingly presented Jesus to the people, saying *Ecce homo* ("Behold the man," John 19:5). The multilevel convent structure designed by Daumet has archaeological remnants from the Roman Period on display at the lowest level. View to the southwest toward the Haram al-Sharif (Temple Mount).

monasteries the bells are set in a special, prominently situated niche, a striking example of which can be found at the Ethiopian monastery Deir al-Sultan, located on the roof of the Church of the Holy Sepulcher. The two most prominent bell towers belong to the Church of the Redeemer (149 feet, or 48 meters) and the San Salvatore Church (98 feet, or 30 meters).

The differences between Catholic, Orthodox, and Protestant church architecture in the Old City (and in the New City too) are apparent mainly in structure and internal design. Protestant places of worship are generally less grandiose, as in Christ Church (Anglican) or the Church of the Redeemer (Evangelical Lutheran), where the interior space is simple and spare by comparison with San Salvatore Church (Franciscan) or the Cathedral of St. James (Armenian). Catholic and Orthodox churches tend to be "heavy," as well as dense with ornamentation—frescoes, stained-glass windows, stylized iron grilles—and replete with expensive materials such as marble, alabaster, and wood.

Nineteenth-century public architecture in Europe (as well as in the United States) is characterized by a revival of the past. In Jerusalem these eclectic influences are pro-

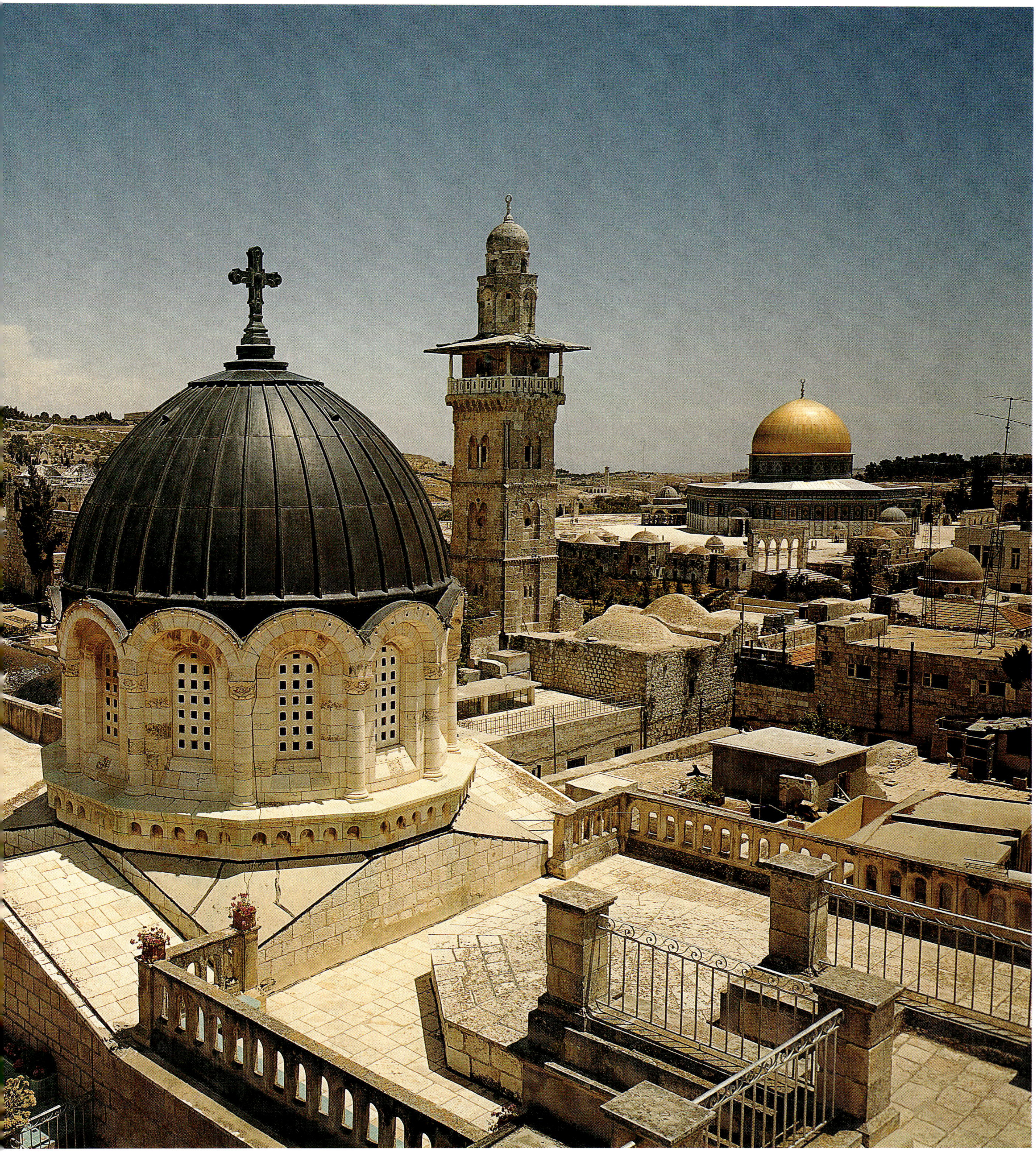

2

nounced both inside the walls and in the New City. Only a handful of buildings are stylistically "pure." The vast majority are a mélange of forms, making it virtually impossible to identify a particular building with a particular style. Still, six styles dominate 19th-century European architecture in the Old City: Neo-Classical, Neo-Byzantine, Neo-Romanesque, Neo-Gothic, Neo-Renaissance, and Neo-Baroque.

Nineteenth-century builders in the Old City had to cope with more than the corrupt Ottoman bureaucracy. One problem they faced—still encountered by builders—was how to cope with the archaeological finds that almost invariably turn up whenever a shovel is plunged into the earth of Jerusalem. In some cases, as in the construction of the Austrian Hospice, archaeological remains were simply covered over or destroyed by the workers. However, some 19th-century planners altered their original design to incorporate the old into the new. As mentioned in the case of the Crusader Church of Maria Latina, architect Friedrich Adler integrated its cloister into the Church of the Redeemer after unearthing the ruins while excavating the site prior to construction.

Very often, though, before builders could delve into the soil, they had to clear away huge mounds of debris—testimony to generations of neglect. Stability required that foundations be laid on bedrock, even if this added to the time, and the cost, of construction. An illustration prepared by J.W. Johns, the architect of Christ Church, for a fund-raising pamphlet, shows underground foundations 43 feet (13 meters) high. Every large building encountered this kind of challenge. In the case of the Austrian Hospice, five hundred professional workers and three thousand day laborers toiled for seven months on the groundwork alone, and in 1857, when the building was supposed to be dedicated, only the foundations had been laid. Meanwhile, the cost had already exceeded the original estimate by a factor of four.

Transporting materials entailed equally prohibitive expenses. Construction stones that could not be extracted from the building site itself were brought from quarries in the Jerusalem area and paid for "per camel load." The cost of bringing water to the site was calculated "per skin," and the removal of debris "per ass load." Timber, almost all of it imported, had to be conveyed from the port of Jaffa in units of 300 kilograms (660 pounds) known as *cantahrs*. The furniture and roof beams for Christ Church were manufactured in London and then shipped on a specially chartered new steamship together with two experts to install them. The long-term effect of European building was the contribution made by master craftsmen from abroad to the revival of local building skills. In his book of 1844, J.W. Johns writes that nearly all the workers, with the exception of stone masons brought from Malta, were local people, the majority of them Catholics. Destitute Jews, however, refused to do actual construction work for Christians, although Johns employed them in metal work and other crafts. Impoverished pilgrims, pri-

1. Neo-Classical symmetry characterizes European Christian building of the late 19th century and the early 20th in the Old City. Franciscan orphanage on St. Francis Street in the Christian Quarter.

marily from Russia and Poland, also found employment, eager as they were to work for any pay.

Owing to the combination of political, technical, and budgetary difficulties, the various structures of the Christ Church compound took some sixty years to complete. This was a familiar pattern in the Old City, buildings going up in stages, often with long intervals between each phase. The most extreme case was probably San Salvatore Church, where construction began in 1560 and continued over the next three centuries. Architecturally, though, this sporadic process afforded an aesthetic benefit, inasmuch as the absence of a uniform design, stemming from a mixture of styles and technologies, produced clusters of buildings that nonetheless combine to yield an integrated, colorful harmony. Certainly 19th-century European Christian construction brought new standards of quality and precision to Jerusalem, where European planning and construction methods were hardly known before the mid-19th century.

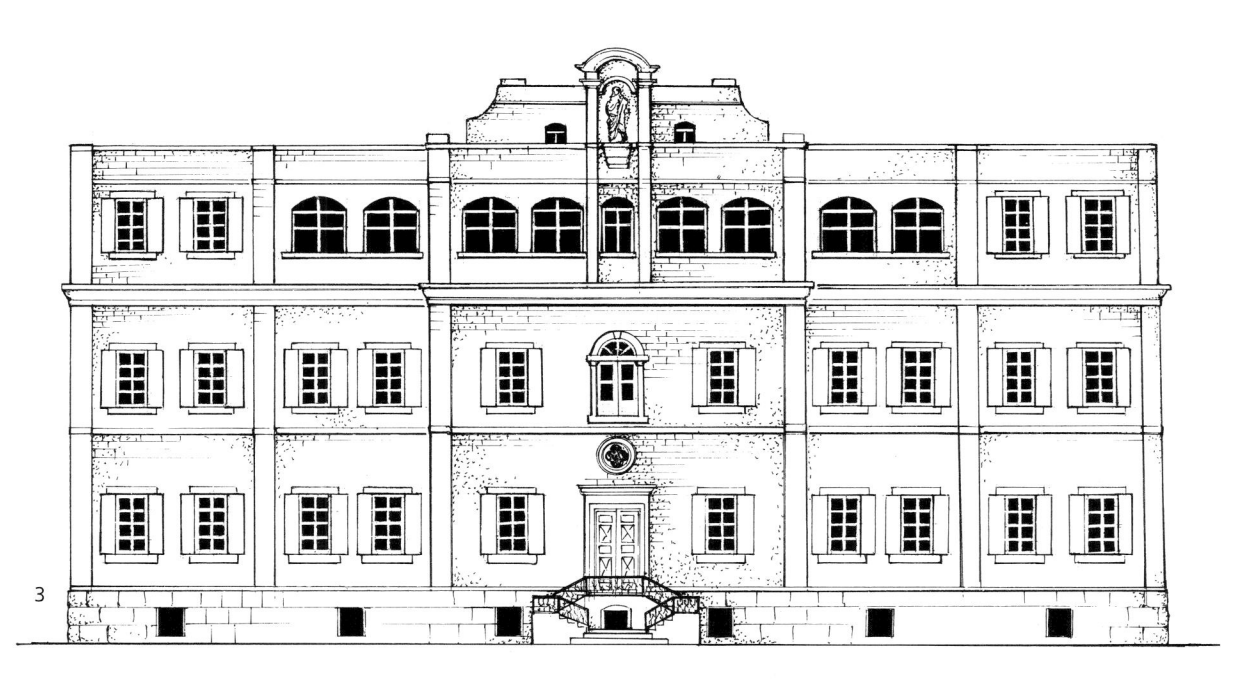

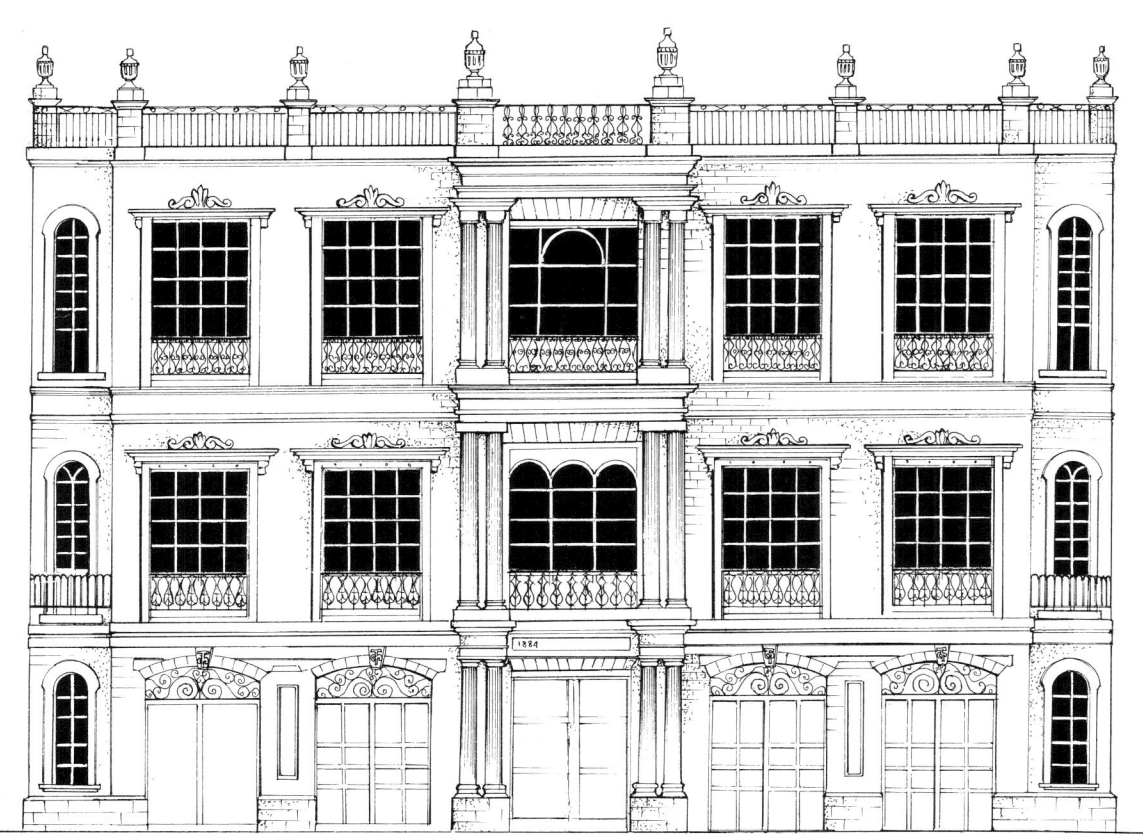

2, 3. The Franciscan Collège des Frères, adjacent to New Gate, was founded in 1882. Most of the buildings of the period had a "heavy" rectangular shape in the Neo-Renaissance style. They also featured an accentuated main entrance and staircase, as well as uniformly spaced windows on the façades.

4. The present-day New Imperial Hotel, just inside Jaffa Gate, was built from 1884 to 1889 by the Greek Orthodox Patriarchate as an investment for leasing. The symmetrical Neo-Classical façade is decorated by pairs of pillars on every story and on either side of the main entrance, and by a stylized roof balustrade with stone urns. On the ground floor is a row of shops.

The Muslim Quarter

The Muslim Quarter has changed little over the centuries. Today, in an area of 75 acres with some 26,000 inhabitants—twice as many as all the other neighborhoods combined—the Muslim Quarter is the Old City's largest and most densely populated section. Its multitude of traditional *hosh* ("inner courtyard") units, mostly built in late Ottoman times on the remnants of earlier structures, cover about a quarter of the Old City's total area. As a consequence of Ottoman neglect, much of the quarter deteriorated and became a slum, unrelieved by urban development or significant new construction. In the late 19th century, when Christian institutions had the support of the European Powers and the Jewish community received donations from abroad, the Ottomans remained indifferent to the needs of their fellow Muslims. Yet, this state of prolonged stagnation lends the area an architectural authenticity that permits the contemporary observer to become acquainted with traditional residential forms (modified, of course, by the devastations of time).

The old houses in the Muslim Quarter reflect the gradual evolution of Arab residential construction, from the rural village home, some elements of which continue from Biblical times, to concrete urban structures. The use of building materials is similar not only to that found in Arab villages outside the walls but also to Jewish Quarter houses in Ottoman times. The structures face inward, with family or clan units grouped about an inner courtyard. The rooms are square, and attached without connecting corridors or inner stairwells, and those belonging to the same residential unit are linked by internal openings. Most structures were originally built with a domed roof, advantageous in a hot climate because some part of it remains in shadow for some of the day. The thick outer walls assured stability and permitted high rooms that could bear the weight of heavy stone domes; in addition, they acted as superb insulation and allowed deep niches to be excavated for the storage of bedding and other household items.

Instead of professional architects, rare at the time, a master builder oversaw the entire project, from plans to the installation of the crowning dome. Family members and neighbors did the work, and a rich folklore attests to the great importance that Arabs in general, and villagers in particular, attach to the building of their houses. Construction usually proceeded sporadically, over time, with lengthy intervals between stages dependent on the availability of funds. To exploit every inch of space, one- or two-story overpasses, each supported by a broad arch, frequently span the narrow streets.

Efforts to ward off the evil eye, apparent on the façades of many homes in the Muslim Quarter, take the form of amulets or lintels and windowpanes painted turquoise. Traditional Islamic wall paintings and inscriptions, executed next to the main entrance, assure a colorful greeting for members of the household returning from the *hajj*, the pilgrimage to Mecca. In the past these were invariably homemade, but today they are increasingly replaced by commercially painted plaques with wooden frames. Indeed, in the late 1980s and the early 1990s, after the start of the *intifada* (the Palestinian uprising in the Israeli-held territories), nationalist graffiti, usually in the colors of the Palestinian flag—red, green, black, and white—became favored "wall paintings."

The inner courtyards continue to serve functional and social needs, even though they are usually crammed with makeshift structures fashioned of concrete blocks, plaster, tin,

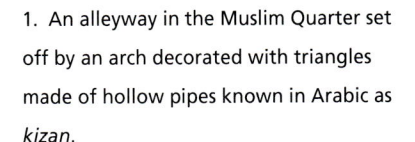

1. An alleyway in the Muslim Quarter set off by an arch decorated with triangles made of hollow pipes known in Arabic as *kizan*.

2. The traditional residential fabric in most of the Muslim Quarter consists of structures with inner courtyards abutting one another, square buildings, arched windows, and stone domes.

and plastic. Owing to a shortage of space and the Muslim family's distinctive way of life, much housework is done outside, in the courtyard. Later on, after the day's work, the courtyard becomes the center of social activity and leisure.

Most houses in the Muslim Quarter now have running water, but their courtyards still retain the old wells. These are replenished by rainwater running off the roof through clay and/or tin pipes, or from open canals on the ground. The water, used for cleaning as well as for nourishing potted plants and herbs, is drawn up by a hand pump or, less commonly, by old-fashioned rope and bucket.

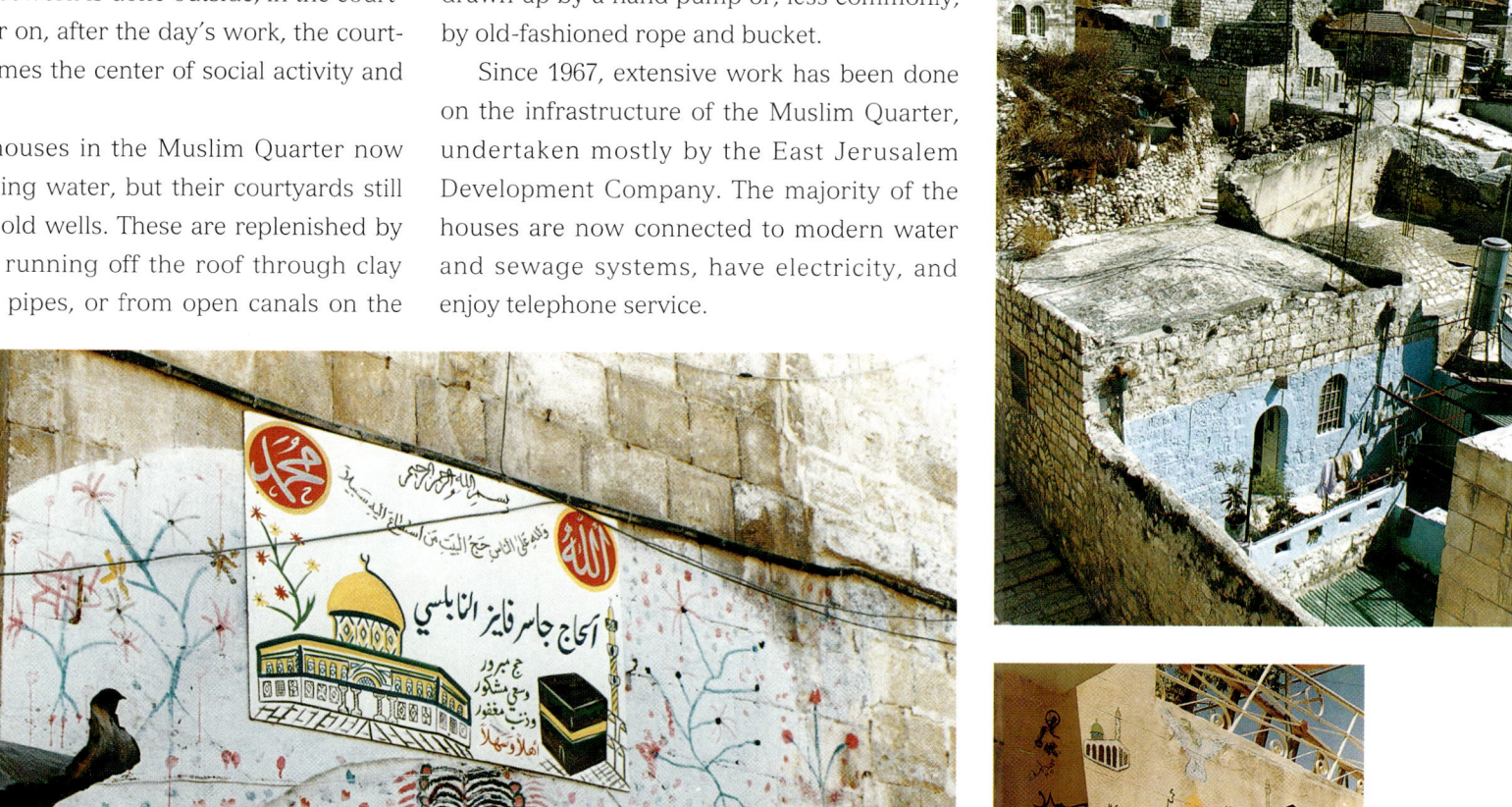

Since 1967, extensive work has been done on the infrastructure of the Muslim Quarter, undertaken mostly by the East Jerusalem Development Company. The majority of the houses are now connected to modern water and sewage systems, have electricity, and enjoy telephone service.

3, 5. Paintings around the entrance to the house honor the return of members of the household from the pilgrimage (*hajj*) to Mecca. Motifs depicted usually include the Ka'ba (central shrine of Islam) in Mecca and the Dome of the Rock.
4. Courtyard of a traditional residence in the Old City's Muslim Quarter. In the East the color turquoise is considered to offer protection against the evil eye.

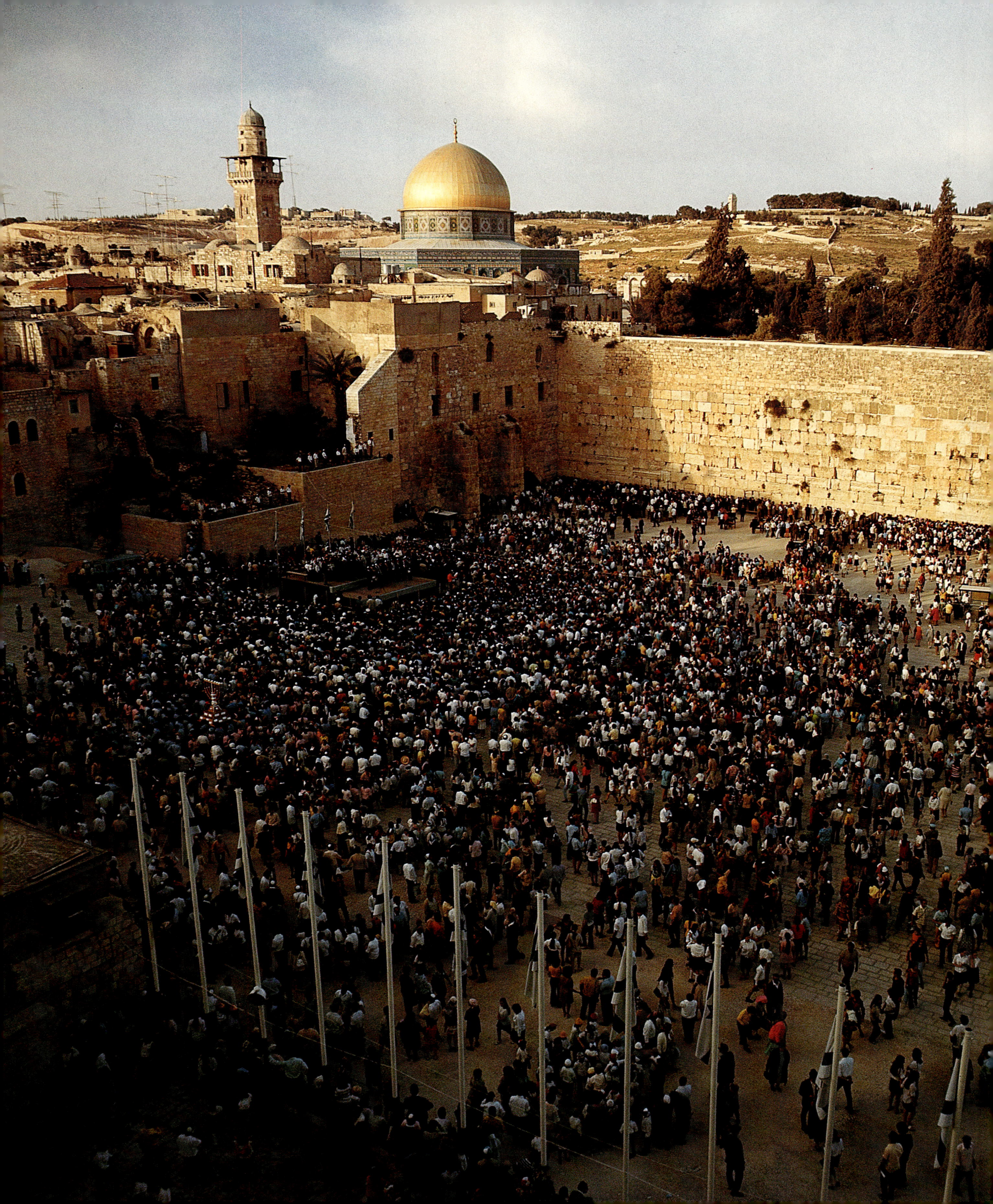

THE OLD CITY IN MODERN TIMES
Preservation and Reconstruction

Jews have lived in the area of today's Jewish Quarter, in the southwest corner of the Old City, since First Temple times in the 8th century BC. The Quarter within its present boundaries dates from the Mamluk Period. During most of the Quarter's existence, Jerusalem was ruled by Ottoman Muslims, whose attitude toward the Jews was uneven. One of the more benign eras began in the 1860s. By the late 1870s the Old City's 15,000 Jews, divided about equally between Sephardim and Ashkenazim, constituted half the total population of Jerusalem. These years saw the emergence of the Ashkenazi "Old Yishuv" community, which devoted itself to prayer and Torah study. For its material sustenance, this group depended on donations, known as *halukka* ("division") funds, from Jewish individuals and communities abroad. The name was apt, since the division of the funds sparked disputes and altercations between yeshivas and communal organizations (*kolels*) based on cities and countries of origin.

As a whole, the Jewish community, being desperately poor, resided in rented quarters. The majority of buildings in the Jewish Quarter were owned by Arabs, because until 1856 the Turks did not permit foreign nationals to purchase land. Ottoman restrictions and the Jewish community's economic straits virtually ruled out "private" Jewish residential building.

The bulk of Jewish public building took place in the second half of the 19th century, concurrent with European Christian construction. Although no distinctly "Jewish" architectural style emerged during the Ottoman Period, certain distinguishing features are discernible in Jewish construction, deriving from the community's singular religious-social composition, economic difficulties, and restrictions imposed by the Turkish authorities.

Just as Christians congregated around the Church of the Holy Sepulcher, the Jewish community kept as close as possible to the Western Wall below the Temple Mount. Unlike Christians, however, Jews could draw on neither a rich architectural heritage nor on the wealth of the European Powers. The two most prominent Jewish structures, spiritually and physically, built in the Jewish Quarter in the 19th century were Ashkenazi synagogues: Hurvah (dedicated 1864) and Tiferet Yisrael (1876). Their domes, each at a height of nearly 80 feet (24 meters, or 8 stories in present-day building), towered above the Old City and

1. Since the destruction of the Second Temple the western supporting wall of the Temple Mount has been an object of reverential yearning by the Jewish people. Prayers and assemblies have been held here since the city's reunification in 1967.

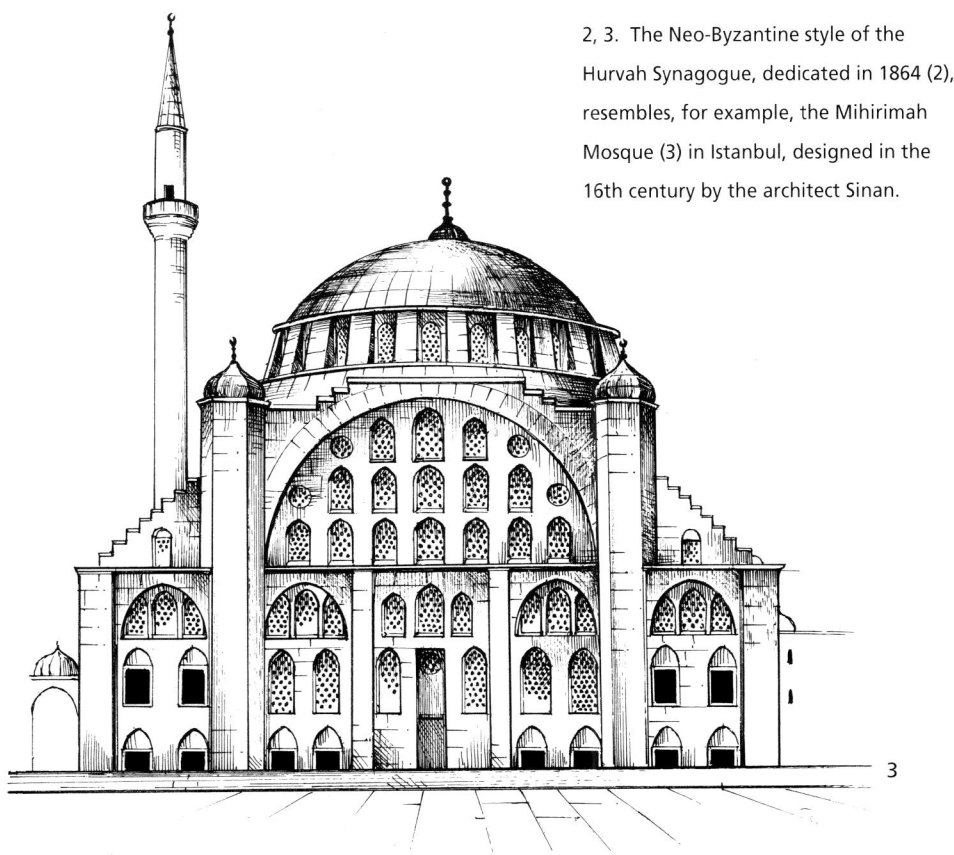

2, 3. The Neo-Byzantine style of the Hurvah Synagogue, dedicated in 1864 (2), resembles, for example, the Mihirimah Mosque (3) in Istanbul, designed in the 16th century by the architect Sinan.

1. Interior of the imposing Hurvah Synagogue, dedicaterd in 1864 and destroyed in Israel's 1948 War of Independence. The model was made in the early 20th century.

2. Remnants of Tiferet Yisrael Synagogue, destroyed in the 1948 War and deliberately left in its gutted state for commemoration.

3. The central square of the Jewish Quarter with the arch commemorating the Hurvah Synagogue, which stood on this site until it was leveled in 1948, in the center.

competed visually with Muslim minarets and Christian towers. Both buildings, like most of the other synagogues, yeshivas, and public structures erected by the Jewish community in this period, were systematically demolished by the Jordanians after 1948.

Synagogue architecture of the Ottoman Period can be seen today in the four Sephardi houses of worship located at the center of the Jewish Quarter. The oldest of the four is Eliyahu Hanavi ("Elijah the Prophet") Synagogue, dating from 1586. In 1835 it was rebuilt in Neo-Byzantine style as a box structure (460 square feet, or 42.25 square meters) with barrel vaults supporting a round drum topped by a semicircular dome. Johannan Ben Zakai Synagogue, the largest (1,742 square feet, or 160 square meters) and most splendid of the group, dates from the 17th century, when it had a timber ceiling. In 1839, renovation replaced the old ceiling with four cross vaults. A rosette-shaped medallion was placed in the center of each vault, so that the point of intersection would not suggest a Christian cross.

The narrow, elongated Middle Synagogue, as it is called (but also known as Kehilat Tsion or "Community of Zion"), was built in the 19th century in a space originally used as a courtyard and passage between the other houses of worship. The fourth synagogue (1764), known as Istanbuli because it was built by Jews who hailed from the capital of the Ottoman Empire, is similar in construction to Eliyahu Hanavi. Above its original entrance an ornate inscription gives the renovation date: 1835.

Two of the Sephardi synagogues, Istanbuli and Eliyahu Hanavi, shared a common architectural style with the more resplendent Ashkenazi Hurvah and Tiferet Yisrael houses of worship—as well as with Porat Yosef Synagogue, built from 1914 to 1923 as part of a yeshiva complex, which the Jordanians also leveled. All five were constructed in the Neo-Byzantine style characteristic of such Greek Orthodox architecture in and near the Christian Quarter as John the Baptist Church. They have a square box structure topped by a large, elevated dome resting upon a drum whose circle of windows permits light to enter the area of worship below. The common source of all Neo-Byzantine architecture is the 6th-century Hagia Sophia in Istanbul, which influenced architecture throughout the East.

Synagogue architecture is relatively modest in character, its representational splendor expressed primarily in the stone ornaments decorating the portals, in windows, and in various interior elements. Most Old City synagogue decorations utilize geometric shapes prevalent in both Byzantine and Muslim architecture. Undomed religious and public structures built during this period in the Jewish Quarter were accented externally by means of stylized windows and doors. Etz

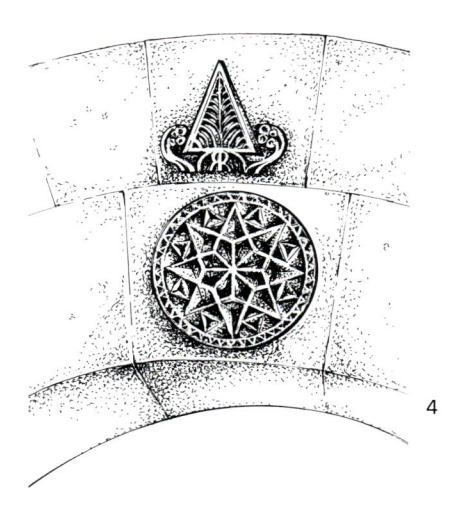

4. Geometric designs adorn the interiors of the Sephardic synagogues.

5. The Middle Synagogue, one of the four Sephardi synagogues in the Old City complex with rosette-shaped medallions at the intersection of the cross vaults so as not to evoke a Christian cross.

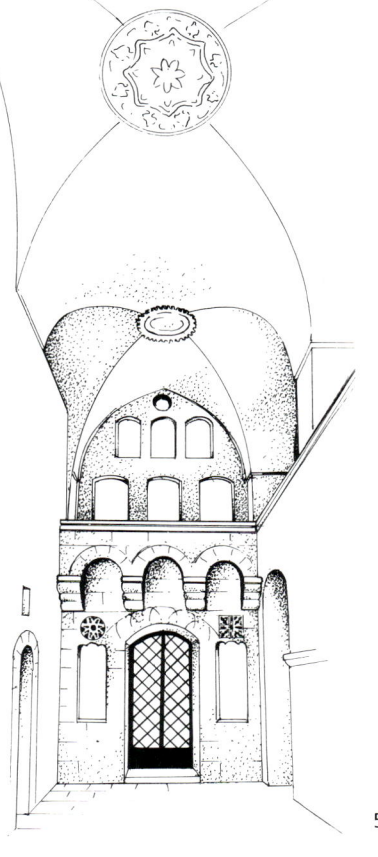

Hayyim Yeshiva, for example, was erected in 1841 as a series of simple two-story rectangular structures, their physical presence enhanced with ornamented upper windows. By hiring Turkish rather than Christian architects—both to maintain good relations with the Ottoman authorities and to avoid emulation of monumental Christian structures then being built in the Old City—the Jewish community was effectively drawing on Byzantine material culture.

1, 2. The Johannan Ben Zakai Synagogue is the largest and most important of the four Sephardi synagogues restored after 1967. The Neo-Gothic "windows" serve, in fact, as the synagogue's Torah ark. The four adjoining synagogues are situated below street level because when they were first constructed, Ottoman law forbade any building to be higher than a mosque.

3. Since there are no outward-facing windows, the synagogues receive their light through skylights in the stone domes, which are raised on an octagonal drum.

The 19th-century visitor to the Jewish Quarter (or the Muslim Quarter) could easily go astray in a maze of dark alleys and cul-de-sacs. Here, urban texture was determined largely by courtyard neighborhoods. In the Ottoman Period there was no such thing as a master plan or an organized, legal planning system. The Jewish Quarter's dense courtyard housing consisted of clusters of simple one- or two-story structures erected about an inner courtyard. For reasons already mentioned, Jews, few of whom were Ottoman nationals, generally rented quarters in buildings owned by Arabs. Courtyard neighborhoods were typically named after the *kolel* whose members resided there, after the local synagogue, or after the courtyard's owner.

In the pre-1948 Jewish Quarter some courtyards had "mixed" Sephardi and Ashkenazi populations, creating a kind of "melting pot." During the day the courtyard gate remained open, but at night it was bolted shut to keep out thieves. Rooftop sleeping was popular on hot nights. Whitewash covered walls and fences, while potted plants and medicinal herbs stood in every available space. Less pleasant was the presence of communal latrines, positioned inside the courtyard gate. Tiny kitchens often drove housewives into the courtyard to do their cooking.

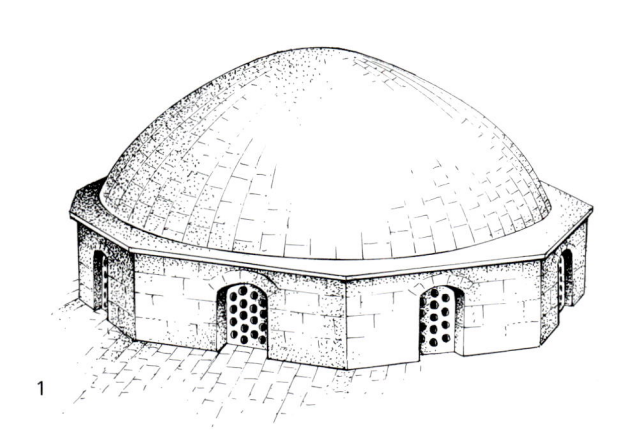

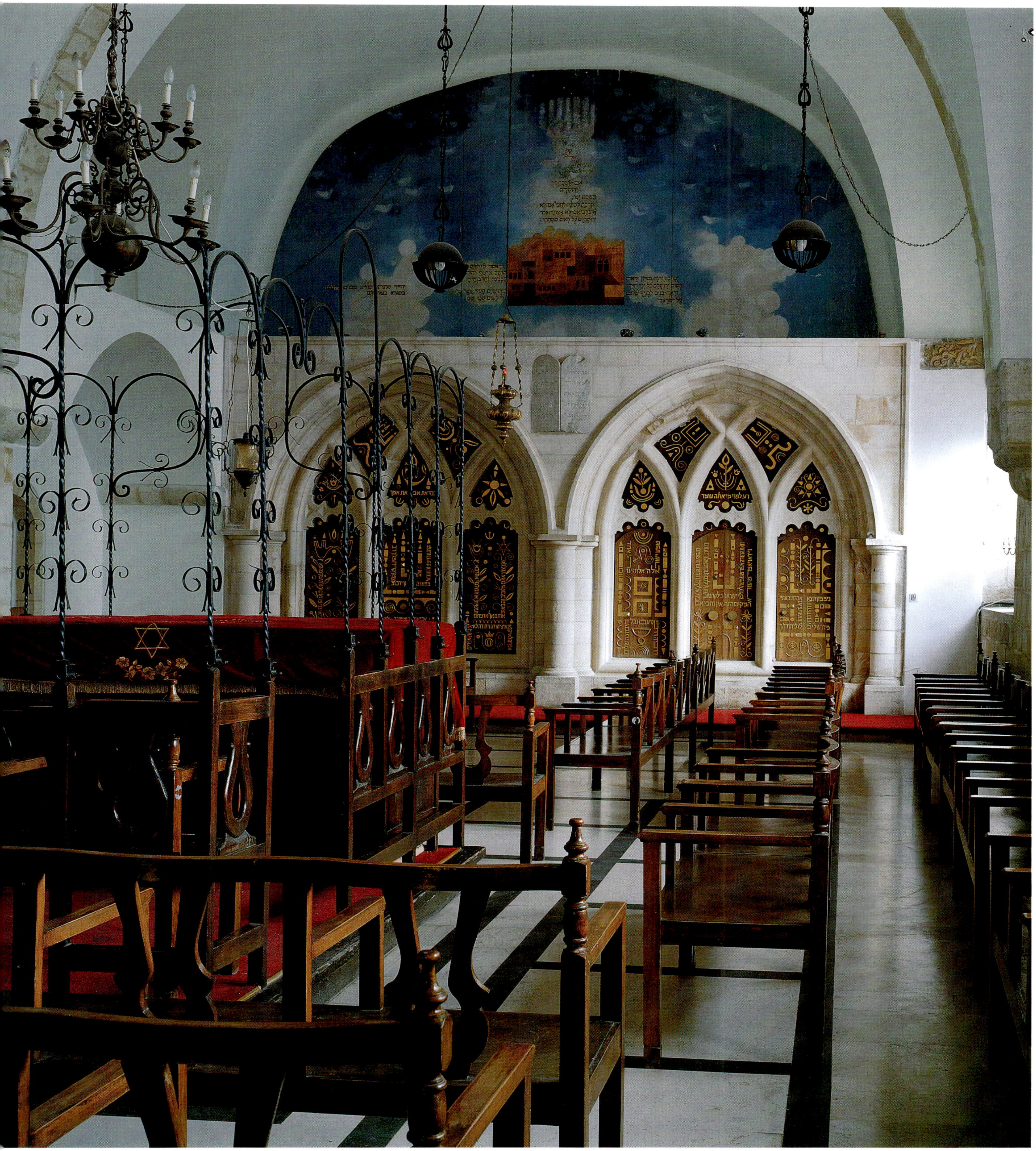
3

1, 2. The most elegant of the buildings erected in the Jewish Quarter as part of the organized housing construction in the 19th century is Rothschild House (1871), financed by Baron Wilhelm von Rothschild from Frankfurt. His family's emblem is engraved on the upper part of the front façade. The apartments were constructed in a linear row along a covered corridor set off by a large stone arcade, and the number of each flat was engraved in Hebrew letters in its headstone.

No original pre-1948 courtyard complexes remain in the Jewish Quarter, although something of their community flavor may be gleaned from the first but still-standing Jewish neighborhoods built outside the Old City. Today, the basic physical structure of courtyard-neighborhood architecture can best be seen in the Muslim Quarter, although makeshift building caused by population growth has wrought large-scale changes.

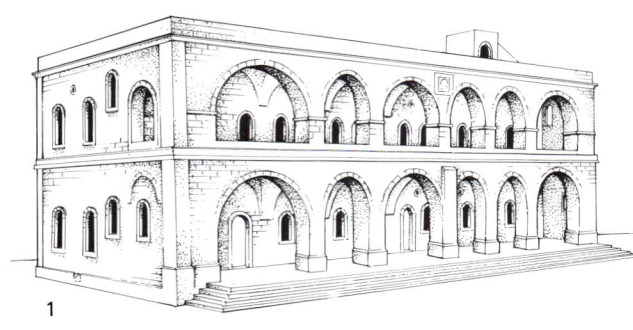

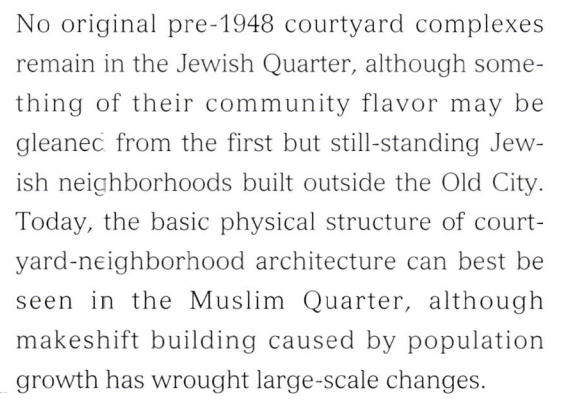

In 1856, following the end of the Crimean War (caused in part by a dispute over control of the Christian sacred places in the Holy Land), the Turks, who emerged from the struggle weakened vis-à-vis the European Powers, eased restrictions on both Jewish and Christian land purchase and building. In 1857 Kolel "Hod" (comprising Jews from Holland and Germany—*Deutschland*—hence the acronym) acquired a three-acre plot of land for housing in the southwest corner of the Jewish Quarter. Planning and construction were carried out under the auspices of the Austrian Consulate and financed by donations in 1862, having been financed by philanthropists who wished to perpetuate their names or those of their dear ones. The complex consisted of clusters of buildings erected on two adjoining flanks of what was then called the *Deutsche Platz* ("German Square"). The bulk of the construction, which ultimately produced about a hundred apartments and two small synagogues, took place from 1861 to 1891. The most spacious of the structures was Rothschild House (today containing the offices of the Company for the Reconstruction and Development of the Jewish Quarter), completed in 1871 and financed by Frankfurt's Baron Wilhelm von Rothschild, whose family crest is emblazoned on the building. More than any other structure, Rothschild House symbolizes the improved living conditions enjoyed by part of the Jewish population. Six families occupied the two-story edifice on five-year leases. The apartments were constructed in a linear row along a covered corridor set off by a large stone arcade. A broad staircase on either side of the building connected the upper and lower arcades. Construction of Batei Mahseh, the first housing complex for the poor of the Old City built by an organized Jewish group, got underway in the same year (1860) that Mishkenot Sha'ananim, the first Jewish neighborhood outside the Old City walls, was completed. Batei Mahseh would remain *sui generis*, for henceforth the housing problems of Jerusalem's Jewish population would be addressed in the emerging New City.

collected in Europe by the Batei Mahseh Society, founded in 1859. The organization's full name also served as a statement of its mission: "Society for Shelter Houses for the Poor and for Receiving Guests on Mount Zion in the Holy City of Jerusalem May it Be Speedily Rebuilt in Our Day, Amen." Chosen by lottery, the tenants paid little or no rent, and their leases ran for three years, although in practice tenancy extended for much longer periods.

A first group of eight flats, each with two rooms and a kitchen, was ready for occupancy

The Jewish Quarter, like the rest of the Old City, suffered during the fifty-year period that began with the British Mandate (1918-48) and continued through the era of the divided city (1948-67), which—apart from short-lived efforts at renovation and preservation—witnessed neither a substantive contribution to the texture of the Old City nor the emergence of a distinctive architectural style. Besides sheer neglect, much of the Jewish Quarter underwent malicious destruction by the Jordanians, who controlled the Old City from 1948 until Jerusalem's reunification nineteen years later.

The main effort during the Mandate lay in preserving and restoring historical structures. In 1918 the city's British Military Governor,

1. Restoration of the Jewish Quarter in the Old City after 1967 followed a middle ground between total excavation in search of archaeological finds, and the idea of building new houses on pillars so that digs could be carried out beneath. The open section of the Byzantine Cardo was preserved without construction above.

2. The Byzantine Cardo's covered section was restored so that a modern residence—architecturally in keeping with the Jewish Quarter's traditional character—could be built above.

Ronald Storrs, founded the Pro-Jerusalem Society, whose members included both British officials and public figures from the Arab and Jewish communities. The society, which set itself the goal of physically preserving the Holy City, remained active until 1922. Its chief projects were the repair and renewal of the ancient walls and gates, the installation of a promenade along the rampart, and the renovation of the Citadel/Tower of David. The society also brought about the demolition of a public fountain and a clock tower built early in the 20th century by the Ottomans in front of, and atop, the Jaffa Gate, and helped restore the Dome of the Rock and the Cotton Merchants Market. In addition, it encouraged such popular arts as pottery and ceramic tiles, resulting in the use of colorful tiles for street signs throughout the city.

The widespread employment of Armenian glazed tiles outside the walls was spurred by the restoration work on the Dome of the Rock. For this, Ernest Richmond, the British architect in charge of the Mandate government's Antiquities Department, had brought a group of Armenian artists from Turkey. Three of them later established their own workshops in the city, gaining renown for their glazed tiles and other colorful ceramics.

Inactivity marked the period of Jordanian command over the Old City, in the aftermath of the 1948-49 war. Devastated by Jordan's Arab Legion, the Jewish Quarter lay desolate, and the rest fared little better. Some restoration was undertaken in the Haram al-Sharif/Temple Mount area, and a few additions were made to existing residential buildings, primarily in the Christian and Muslim quarters.

After Jerusalem became one again following the Six-Day War in 1967, there developed a striking architectural style in which a contemporary look managed to blend old and new. This can be seen in the massive restoration and reconstruction carried out in the Jewish Quarter from 1967 to 1987. The distinctive and homogeneous manner that evolved here reflects the aspiration of architects to rework the traditional world of forms by utilizing modern concepts of design, construction, and technology. What came forth was a new architectural vocabulary, rooted in old traditions. It yielded a clear, highly defined style. Encompassing about 20 percent of the walled city, the post-1967 style constitutes a significant layer in the age-old sequence of periodic construction witnessed by the Old City.

The renovation included repaving streets and public squares with flagstones, installing street lamps, and refacing as well as reinforcing structures in the Jewish, Christian, and Muslim quarters and around the gates in the wall. Here, too, an attempt was made to create a new architectural language grounded in the past.

The twenty-year restoration of the Jewish Quarter is a landmark in Jerusalem's development. Moreover, the intriguing manner that emerged there went on to influence the Neo-Oriental style so prominent in the post-1967 satellite neighborhoods in the New City.

In 1968 the Israeli government set up the Company for the Reconstruction and Development of the Jewish Quarter. Its goals were to restore the area's former glory and to assure the historical continuity of Jewish settlement, thereby symbolizing Israel's determination to prevent any possible future partition. Rigorous planning involved a special team assigned to prepare a comprehensive program for 650 families to reside in the Jewish Quarter's 30 acres. The plan would designate areas for residential, commercial, and public buildings, set a height limit, and bar construction close to the

3. Intriguing blend of new and old: Visitors to the restored Cardo's covered section can shop while viewing Crusader pointed arches and cross vaults. Covered shafts allow viewing finds from earlier periods. On the street above are newly built residences. Design by architects Peter Bugod and Esther Niv-Krendel.

wall on both sides. It also recommended optimal access routes, new streets designed to strengthen the quarter's link with the Western Wall, and the preservation and restoration of structures with archaeological, historical, and religious import.

The planners had to contend with ancient myths and symbols, while solving practical problems entailed in the revival of a residential neighborhood, the better to save the Jewish Quarter from becoming a lifeless museum display. The wide range of different approaches ultimately produced a mélange that translated into a distinctive architectural style. Buildings designed in a romantic manner, nostalgically evoking traditional Oriental-Middle Eastern elements, such as arch, vault, and dome, stand alongside structures utilizing synthetic materials and modern construction.

Another aspect of the old-new fusion concerned the wealth of archaeological finds in the Jewish Quarter. Indeed, the entire sector, located in the Upper City of the Second Temple Period, was declared a historic site. There were some who called for the excavation of the entire area, even if that meant destroying buildings designated for preservation. Others wanted all new structures to be built on pillars, so that digs could be carried out beneath them. In practice, a middle way was found, one that would allow no construction before a dig could be undertaken at the site by an archaeological team. Finds of secondary importance would be dismantled or recovered after being documented, while major finds were to be left for the edification of visitors or integrated into buildings. Plans often had to be altered, as in the case of the Cardo.

In the winning plan submitted for a 1971 international competition, the Aronson, Bugod, Niv-Krendel firm of architects proposed to design the Jewish Quarter's central commercial area by reconstructing the ancient Cardo, which had run through that section of the Old City. The main street of Roman and Byzantine Jerusalem, which bisected the city from north to south, the Cardo is clearly visible on the famous 6th-century mosaic map found in 1884 at Madaba in Trans-Jordan. In 1976, during construction on the new commercial center, a team led by archaeologist Nachman Avigad unearthed part of the monumental arcaded Cardo (74 feet, or 22.5 meters, wide) beneath the Street of the Jews, just where the Madaba Map shows it to have been. Restored to complement the three Crusader-built covered markets on the north, the Cardo is once more open for business. But whereas the markets still cater to the everyday needs of the Old City's inhabitants, the Cardo appeals to tourists, even though Jewish Quarter residents live in apartments right above the ancient street.

Another case involved the "broad wall," a remnant from the First Temple era, which had to be preserved, despite its width of 23 feet (7 meters). Accordingly, architect David Best altered his plans for the apartment buildings slated for construction on the site and created a two-level square to accommodate the wall and permit it to be viewed. Similarly, the discovery of a complex of residences from the Second Temple Period at the site designated for Yeshivat Hakotel ("Western Wall Yeshiva") obliged architect Eliezer Frankel to revise his original plan and location for the building's foundation pillars. This yielded a large underground space beneath the yeshiva, which now houses the Wohl Archaeological Museum devoted to finds from opulent Herodian mansions.

Although displaying diverse architectural approaches, the new residential buildings in the Jewish Quarter—mostly clusters of three- or four-story structures grouped around an inner courtyard—generally preserve the neighborhood's original character. Some of the different solutions reveal themselves in the façades of the buildings on the 19th-century Deutsche Platz, where two structures—Rothschild House and Batei Mahseh—have been refurbished in keeping with their original design. Still, the new apartment buildings that surround the repaved Deutsche Platz evince a powerful plasticity. In the first block, designed by Eliezer Frankel, this is stressed by means of ornamented bay windows, whereas in the eastern block, Sa'adia Mandel produced a more moderate plasticity, effected in arched concrete apertures. Meanwhile in the northern block, Mandel muted the plasticity quite notably, calling into play spatial proportions characteristic of Old City building but not its traditional forms.

A significant element in the reconstruction of the Jewish Quarter, both as a residential neighborhood and as a magnet for tourists, was the rebuilding of its synagogues and religious seminaries. The four old Sephardi synagogues had been turned into storage rooms by the Jordanians. Impressively restored as a single complex, according to a design by Dan Tanai, this cluster of synagogues was reopened to the public in 1972. It demon-

1. The largest of the few open spaces in the densely built Jewish Quarter is Charles Clore Square, adjacent to the ruins of the Hurvah Synagogue (arch on the left). Powerful plasticity and exploitation of light-and-shadow effects mark the design of the adjacent residences.

strates, perhaps more than any other structure, that the special physical character of the Jewish Quarter derived not from planning but from continuity throughout generations. Built sporadically, patchwork style, over a lengthy period, the synagogue complex is a rich and surprising amalgam of forms that fuse into a harmonious whole.

Among the new buildings in the Jewish Quarter, the two most prominent are also religious institutions—Yeshivat Hakotel and Porat Yosef Yeshiva—which represent post-1967 Jewish monumental construction in the Old City. Architect Moshe Safdie rebuilt the latter on the site of its forerunner adjacent to the Western Wall Plaza. Constructed by means of advanced technologies, Porat Yosef evinces a present-day look, blending "traditional" with "modern." In both texture and color, the stone walls echo the dominant building material of Jerusalem. The synagogue is a substantial structure of six stories, with seating for 450 worshippers. The edifice is covered by a large, semitransparent dome that permits light to enter by day, while at night it glows with interior illumination.

Yeshivat Hakotel, dedicated in 1980, presents an extreme example of traditional forms reused in a modern context. Not only are two of its façades ornamented with oriels, recesses, protrusions, and minitowers; it is also crowned by a series of finely dressed masonry domes that rise clear and free of the Jewish Quarter's skyline. However, owing to the narrow streets surrounding Yeshivat Hakotel, the viewer cannot grasp its full scale and architectural power. Indeed, despite their large number, the physical presence of Jewish religious structures in the Old City is negligible if measured against that of Christian and Muslim edifices. Over the centuries the masters of Jerusalem forbade or restricted Jewish construction, and the Jordanians razed the three monumental buildings that did exist. The spatial gap created by their destruction has been partially filled by the rebuilt Porat Yosef and by Yeshivat Hakotel.

As for their monumental predecessors, the Hurvah Synagogue is commemorated by a large arch, signifying the four arches that once supported the building's dome, while remnants of Tiferet Yisrael were cast in rough plaster, thereby emphasizing the devastation wrought by the Jordanians. Helping to set off the Hurvah is one of the few open spaces in the Jewish Quarter.

The urban texture of the Jewish Quarter thus comprises a series of physical elements that interlock to form a distinctive architectural mosaic. Those elements include the neighborhood's basic skeleton—streets, lanes, public areas, and inner courtyards—fleshed out by features that constitute an innovative and original interpretation of the old, well-known architectural vocabulary of the Oriental/romantic world of forms. The new grammar integrates functional engineering solutions with aesthetic needs. The architecture of restoration endeavors to make richly diversified use of traditional features in order to create a modern, sculptural architecture, while also exploiting the play of light and shadow that is a hallmark of Jerusalem.

Residential buildings rise in an irregular, seemingly arbitrary, and unplanned manner, creating a "broken," asymmetrical effect, the better to evoke the Jewish Quarter's historically

2. A touch of mystery and adventure is created by the eastern street grid of the Old City, where narrow passages branch off in unexpected directions, lanes have different widths, and dead ends are common.

1, 2. Architectural mélange: Restoration of the Old City's Jewish Quarter was guided by a romantic approach that sought to merge traditional Oriental elements like arch, vault, and dome with such modern construction technologies as industrialized concrete and domes made of synthetic materials. Residences (2) designed by architect Moshe Safdie opposite the Western Wall Plaza.

3. Around Batei Mahseh Square in the southern Jewish Quarter, restored 19th-century traditional dwellings (such as Rothschild House, at top) are integrated with new houses built after 1967 in a traditional-modern style. Many roofs were planned for leisure, some serving as terraces for the apartment above.

colorful and haphazard urban structure. Some of the new buildings recapitulate the old, intimate courtyards, linked to the street by covered passageways. The widespread use of terraced building, in which the roof of one story serves as the courtyard or balcony of the story above, permits light and air to penetrate even ground-floor dwellings. Much effort has gone into planning the roofs, which are visible from various points in and beyond the district. The majority are faced with natural stone, and some have modern versions of the Muslim Quarter's pierced balustrades. Although old structures were renovated or rebuilt with stone-clad domes, new buildings usually have flat roofs. Some of the terraces on Moshe Safdie's housing complex, built against the slope descending to the Western Wall Plaza, have white domes made of a hard plastic material (like the monumental dome of Safdie's Porat Yosef Yeshiva). The continuous roof above the Cardo combines traditional barrel vaults with modern technology in the form of exposed concrete.

An element of deep architectural resonance is the oriel, which, as seen, proliferated during the Mamluk Perdiod and now survives in various forms throughout the Old City. In the Muslim Quarter the walls of the traditional *kösk* (Turkish and Arabic for a bay window or enclosed balcony) are made of delicate wooden latticework, enabling Muslim women to look into the street below without themselves being seen. This feature emerged more or less everywhere in the restored architecture of the Jewish Quarter (also in the Neo-Oriental buildings of post-1967 extramural Jewish neighborhoods). The majority of the façades in the Jewish Quarter boast one or more oriels. The modern version is a projecting stone or plaster structure supported by a concrete console that evokes not only the corbeled windows of the Muslim house but also the machicolations—the battlemented parapets—that Suleiman the Magnificent had built into the Old City wall in the 16th century. Aesthetically, the oriel is a form that stands in relief against the wall of a house and thus casts a deep shadow, enhancing the façade and imbuing the overall structure with formal plasticity. Functionally, it may be the broad-

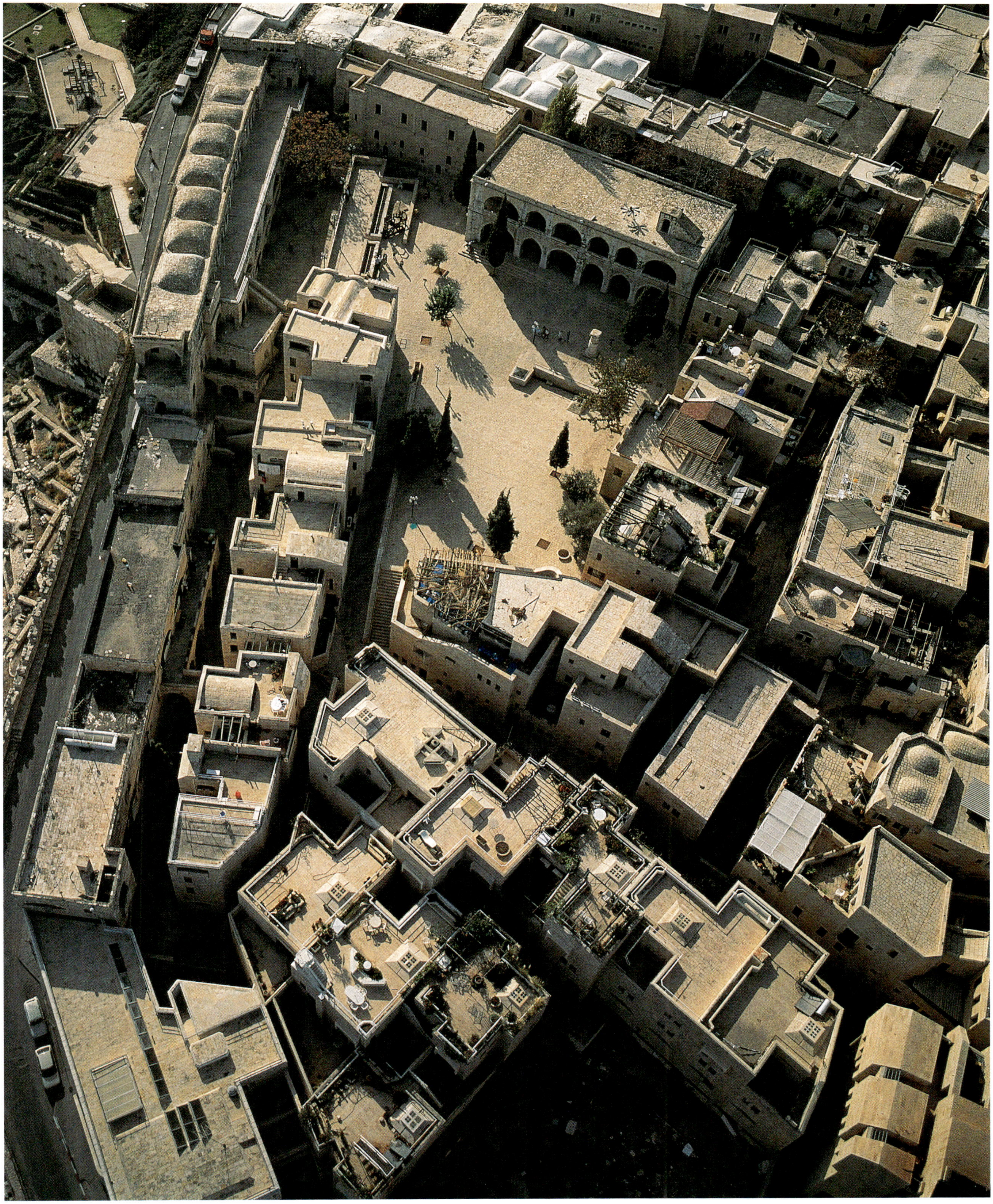

3

1. Entrance to Batei Mahseh Square, where organized housing was built, at the end of the 19th century, for the poor of the Jewish Quarter. Low-rent, or free, flats were distributed by lottery.

windowed extension of a room, or it may be a lavatory and thus sealed except for high, narrow windows.

Other traditional Old City elements adapted for use in the revitalized Jewish Quarter are "bridge" rooms—overpasses—that help alleviate spatial shortage while facilitating passage from one side of the street to the other. Equally present are stone buttresses that, like the overpasses, "float" above the street, creating a counter-pressure to help stabilize exterior walls. Then come the arches, the single most widespread architectural component in Jerusalem. In the Jewish Quarter, however, they are made of precast concrete rather than traditional stone, which satisfies nostalgia more than the needs of engineering. In addition, there are the over-present exterior stairs, which, although modern, recall the traditional courtyard houses that create a separate entrance for each dwelling, thereby eliminating the interior stairwell of the typical Israeli condominium.

The ongoing project of repairing and preserving the Old City walls and gates began in June 1967, immediately after the reunification of Jerusalem. Following long neglect, compounded by war damage, the initial task was to remove debris and shattered buildings along the wall's western section, between Jaffa Gate and New Gate. For the first time in generations, the rampart stood revealed in all its height and glory. Restoration of the wall and gates became part of a comprehensive program, devised by Mayor Teddy Kollek and Jacob (Jan) Yannai, then director of the National Parks Authority, to create a national park around the walls of the Old City. The program's basic principles—exposing the wall, repairing the gates, building a promenade on the battlements, installing illumination below them, and providing access roads for both pedestrians and goods—have been realized gradually, under the leadership of the Jerusalem Municipality and the Ministry of Tourism, in collaboration with the East Jerusalem Development Company assisted by the Jerusalem Foundation.

The promenade on the battlements, restored with great sensitivity thanks to architect Nahum Meltzer, is 2 miles (3.4 kilometers) long. It encompasses the entire Old City with the exception—for political and security reasons—of the section between Lions' Gate and Dung Gate, bordering the Temple Mount. The most extensive restoration was done at Damascus Gate, which showed the effects of severe neglect even though the structure is architecturally and functionally the most important of the portals. Architects Peter Bugod and Eunice Figueiredo treated the approach to the gate as if it were a theater, complete with a spreading "fan" of steps and ramps for unloading merchandise. Space for taxicabs was arranged nearby, and a drinking fountain, in the form of an Ottoman *sabil*, built opposite the gate. The market area inside the gate underwent total redesign. Its picturesque masonry domes, recalling the traditional cupola of the *hammam* ("bath house"), crown a row of one-story shops, their façades renovated and the street area repaved. While working on the infrastructure, engineers discovered the Roman gate of Aelia Capitolina, the city established by the Emperor Hadrian in place of Jerusalem in the 2nd century AD, and made it accessible to the public.

Extensive restoration was also undertaken on Dung Gate. Here, the wide concrete lintel installed by the Jordanians, when broadening the gate for vehicular traffic, was removed and the structure redesigned with traditional stone elements. Other gates required less work, primarily cleaning and repaving. A special station for Christian pilgrims, designed, together with a sculpture garden, by architect Arie Rahamimoff, was built inside Lions' Gate, which leads on to the Via Dolorosa. In 1992, major infrastructure work began at the interior plaza of Jaffa Gate, in accordance with a plan drawn up by architect Moshe Safdie.

In 1978 the Administration of Awqaf undertook a survey of Mamluk buildings outside the Haram al-Sharif. It found a third of them being used as residences, a third as offices and public institutions (such as schools), and a third for other purposes. In the 1980s, the structures were for the most part merely given "first aid," which meant cleaning façades and reinforcing those buildings in particularly poor condition. Restoration began along the main commercial and tourist routes, adjacent to the Jewish Quarter. A major pro-

2. Modern architecture without traditional Oriental motifs but with narrow windows suggesting firing slits inserted deep in thick stone walls. Nebenzahl House, one of the first residences built in the Jewish Quarter after 1967, was designed by British architects Ahrens, Burton, and Korralek.

3. Traditional bridge rooms that "hover" over narrow alleyways—a picturesque architectural feature of the Old City—have been converted to modern use in the restored Jewish Quarter.

ject involved the Al-Ashrafiyya *madrasa*, its pristine glory recovered in the course of a five-year campaign (1986-91).

The Awqaf's Archaeological Department is training a new generation of artisans capable of working in stone, plaster, and iron. As a matter of policy, traditional techniques are utilized, rather than such modern methods as sandblasting or chemical-spraying to clean exterior surfaces. Most of the work is done by hand, with steel brushes. Flawed stones are usually replaced with *malaki* ("royal") stones, which are rare and expensive but strong and conducive to carving. In every building a section of the original is left in order to underscore the transformation that has been wrought.

A different type of transformation was caused by the *intifada*, the Palestinian uprising that erupted at the end of 1987. Walls of many Mamluk buildings are continuously covered with political slogans and graffiti, which the Israeli army blots out with more thick layers of paint. However, the real problem lies elsewhere. Thus, restoration is aimed in part at easing conditions for the impoverished occupants of many historic buildings, where the Administration of Awqaf and its professional staff are hard put to make architectural preservation the highest priority. Families without running water and decent sanitary facilities are not always receptive to arguments for the urgent need to spend money on renovating centuries-old ornamentation.

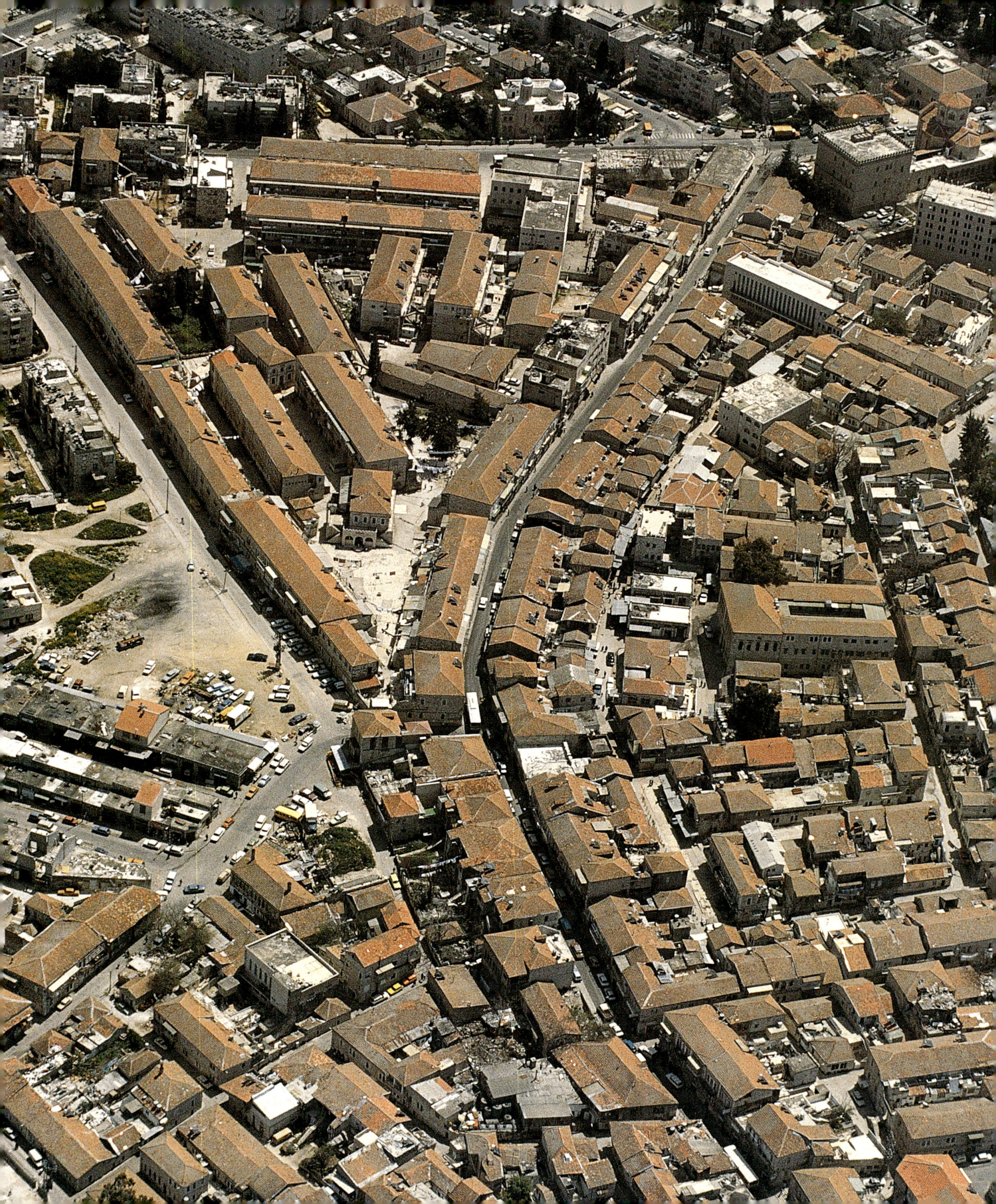

Jewish, Arab, and European Christian Building in the New City
Architecture with Ethnic Identity

The distinctiveness of the Old City's urban texture is particularly striking in comparison with the urban pattern outside the ancient ramparts. The differences stem from different objective conditions—a wall-enclosed area of some 460 acres contrasted with a large, unbounded area of 27,500 acres (9,500 before the reunification of 1967), an area that has grown and developed gradually only since the middle of the 19th century. The Old City is dense and cramped in its pattern, with narrow alleys and few genuine streets or open areas, whereas the New City is composed of proper roads, broad avenues, parks, and free spaces between the neighborhoods. The sealed, inward-looking urban structure produces short, squeezed perspectives; meanwhile, the urban pattern outside offers long, distant views, making it possible to "read" or apprehend the physical presence and the merits of large buildings or whole neighborhoods.

Thanks to its compressed environment, the Old City is urbanistically and architecturally more homogeneous than the New City. Only a limited range of building types proved feasible in the Old City, but New City builders work in a freer, more creative manner. The result is a community with a heterogeneous texture, a world composed of physical patterns that diverge in both form and character. This range results from differences—in cultural-religious makeup, in material demands, and in economic ability—among the many and diverse ethnic, national, and religious groups that have established the new neighborhoods outside the walls.

JEWISH BUILDING: 1860-1914
Communal Courtyard Architecture

Until the mid-19th century, walled-in Jerusalem was surrounded by barren hills and a few unpaved tracks and trails. By the 1860s, Jews, weary of the insufferably cramped conditions in their quarter, began buying land beyond the walls, especially where it could be had cheaply.

The first neighborhood to rise in what would become the New City was Mishkenot Sha'ananim (1860), built adjacent to its distinctive windmill at the initiative of British philanthropist Sir Moses Montefiore. By 1914, some seventy Jewish neighborhoods had been established, all quite similar in population makeup, intimate community life, and adminis-

1. Dense urban texture marks the late-19th-century traditional Jewish neighborhoods such as Me'ah She'arim (right) and Batei Ungarn (upper left). Houses were to be erected around open inner courtyards, but over time those spaces also filled with dwellings.

2. This decoration, representing the palm of the hand and known as a *hamsa*, is thought to bring good luck and ward off the evil eye. It is commonly found in houses of Jews from the Oriental communities and in Arab dwellings.

3. The main residential neighborhoods built outside the Old City walls between 1860 and 1918.

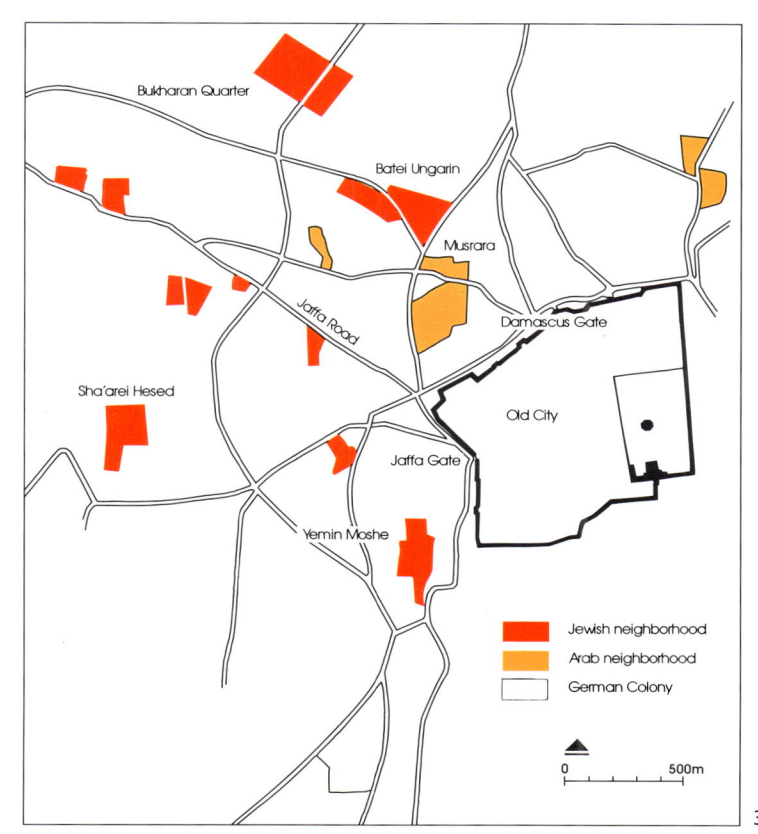

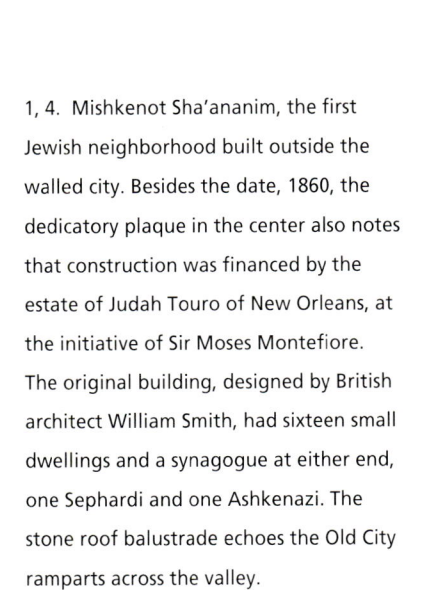

1, 4. Mishkenot Sha'ananim, the first Jewish neighborhood built outside the walled city. Besides the date, 1860, the dedicatory plaque in the center also notes that construction was financed by the estate of Judah Touro of New Orleans, at the initiative of Sir Moses Montefiore. The original building, designed by British architect William Smith, had sixteen small dwellings and a synagogue at either end, one Sephardi and one Ashkenazi. The stone roof balustrade echoes the Old City ramparts across the valley.

2, 3. Elevation and plan of Batei Ungarn neighborhood. The third floor was a later addition to the modest, cramped row flats, consisting of an entrance hall, kitchen, and main room.

trative organization. Eventually, these Jewish quarters, which produced New Jerusalem's initial neighborhood structure, merged to form a continuous block of settlement, extending like a half-crescent around the Old City to the north and west. The large built-up Jewish areas stood in marked contrast to Arab building, which was both scattered and private, as well as to the institutional and religious edifices of the Christian communities.

Jewish homogeneity expressed itself in the virtually uniform patterns of planning and construction. Settlers from Eastern Europe often appeared intent upon transplanting the ambience of their native town to Palestine. The size of the new neighborhoods ranged from the one-building Beit David to such large compounds as Me'ah She'arim, which contained three hundred and sixty apartments at the turn of the century. Each neighborhood generally had an ordinance that governed planning, construction quality, tenant relations, the use of public facilities, and so forth. The principal forms of organization were:

—The religious charitable trust with buildings donated by private philanthropists for the needy. These neighborhoods were generally run by appointed trustees.

—"Kolel" neighborhoods populated by residents from a particular country or city in Europe and administered by a committee. Here, the apartments were built with funding from the country of origin and remained *kolel* property, but tenants paid a nominal rent. Under kolel regulations, religious precepts dictated all social activity. The community, emulating its former way of life in Eastern Europe, kept to itself apart from the surrounding world.

—Ethnic community neighborhoods such as Mahaneh Yisrael, founded by immigrants from North Africa, or the Bukharan Quarter. Other neighborhoods, among them Yemin Moshe, had separate sections for Sephardi and Ashkenazi Jews.

In addition, there were corporate housing quarters and neighborhoods built at private initiative by commercial firms that purchased the land, erected houses, and then sold them.

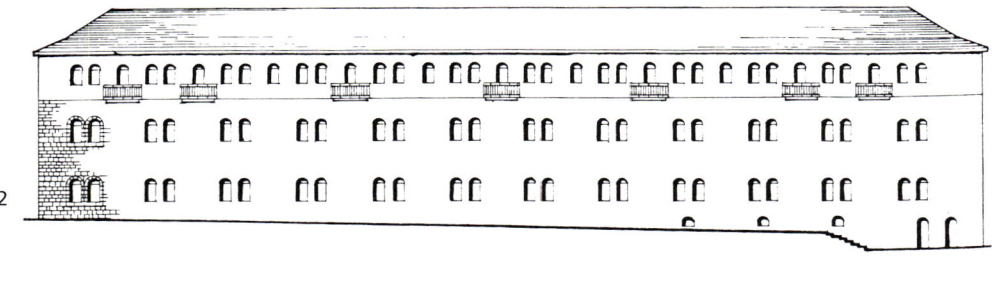

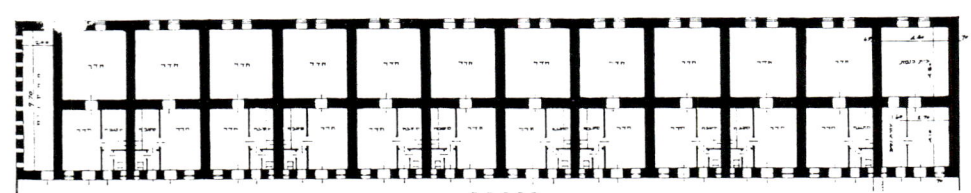

The typical residential unit built between 1860 and 1914 was a rectangular, one-family flat measuring about 645 square feet (60 square meters). About half its total area was given over to a large living room with a 15-foot-high (4.5-meter) ceiling and, at the far end, twin arched windows protected by wrought-iron grilles. The stone walls, up to a meter thick, had excavated niches that served as wall closets. Today it is almost impossible to make out the original designs, owing to changes and extensions made over the years.

The single-family row house, resting upon a narrow rectangular plot, consisted of a basic dwelling unit with a front courtyard enclosed by a stone wall. While courtyards generally faced inward, toward the public square, the adjoined rear walls of the houses faced the street, creating a continuous protective barrier around the neighborhood. The kitchen, generally of light construction, stood in the courtyard, adjacent to the front door, and the small latrine structure near the courtyard entrance. The roofs of private houses built in the 1870s and 1880s usually featured Oriental-style domes. However, by the 1890s, improved technology permitted ceilings to be borne upon metal rails and surmounted by tiled roofs. As the New City grew, residents relieved the housing shortage by erecting

5. Religious identity: Doors of 19th-century Jewish houses in Jerusalem were often decorated with the Star of David and the word "Zion" in Hebrew.

6. Architectural contrast between the continuous flat façade and the jumble of unplanned additions: Mishkenot Yisrael neighborhood, built in the 1890s.

1. Dedicatory plaque above the gateway to Ohel Moshe commemorates the neighborhood's founder, Sir Moses (Moshe) Montefiore, and the year, 1883.
2. In the late 19th century, entrances to Jewish neighborhoods, such as this one to Mazkeret Moshe, were locked at night with iron gates.

extensions in the courtyard, or adding a second story, with the result that single-family dwellings evolved into two- or even three-family homes.

A second type of residential structure, typical of the kolel, took the form of one- or two-story communal row housing, with rows running as long as 230 feet (70 meters). Kitchens were located in the entrance hall and communal latrines at the end of each building in a tower-shaped structure. Upper-floor dwellings were reached by an external staircase connected to a gallery extending the length of the building and serving for social activity on hot summer days. Some buildings had a basement that might function as a water cistern or *mikveh* ("ritual bath"), house a neighborhood bakery, or, more conventionally, serve for storage.

The mikveh and bakery—along with a combined synagogue and study hall—were public buildings that usually went up during the first stage of a neighborhood's construction. A rather simple, one- or two-story box-like structure with a tiled roof, the synagogue took pride of place at the center of the main courtyard, declaring its importance through the ornateness of its façade.

Neighborhood bylaws were derived from religious law. Thus, because on the Sabbath a Jew is proscribed from walking more than 3,673 feet (1,120 meters) beyond his town limits, the first new Jewish quarters were built close to the Old City. But as the New City spread, the same law automatically permitted additional neighborhoods to be located farther and farther away.

Just as in the Muslim community, the specialized professions of town planner, architect, and engineer did not exist when Jerusalem's first extramural Jewish neighborhoods came into being. Typically, craftsmen acquired on-the-job experience and only in time became experts at planning and constructing particular building types. The neighborhoods were, for the most part, erected by Arab contractors employing skilled Arab laborers from Bethlehem and Beit Jalla south of Jerusalem.

Soon a building-materials industry developed in the Jerusalem area. As early as the 1880s, the Schneller German-Arab Vocational

3. The first "railway carriage" houses in Palestine were erected in Jerusalem's Batei Ungarn neighborhood (1891). The long, two-story structures formed a defensive block around a large triangular courtyard.

1. Many houses in the traditional Jewish neighborhoods, such as this one in Zichron Moshe, were deformed over the years by additions made of different materials.

2. Buttresses in Batei Ungarn neighborhood provide structural support for adjacent buildings and set off the passageway "sculpturally."

School was manufacturing bricks and roof tiles, followed in 1880 by a roof-tile factory set up by Jews at Motza west of the city. Still, much had to be imported.

A reasonably clear idea of what a Jewish neighborhood of the time was like can be gained from three typical quarters: Me'ah She'arim (1874), Batei Ungarn (1891), and Batei Neitin (1903). Me'ah She'arim, whose name comes from the harvest blessing conferred on Isaac (Genesis 26:12), had a distinctive layout, characterized by organized construction supported by charitable "distributions" (*halukka*) from abroad. The other two, by contrast, had communal public housing of the kolel type. Even so, all the neighborhoods observed the crucial principle whereby the common good must take precedence over individual desire when it came to open spaces, cisterns, markets, and houses of worship.

The original plan of Me'ah She'arim, conceived by the renowned German-born architect and builder Conrad Schick, had to cope with adverse objective conditions. Foreigners wishing to purchase land faced an array of Ottoman administrative obstacles. In the case of Me'ah She'arim, the ground on which the neighborhood would stand (8 acres) had to be acquired in three stages, leaving its shape to be determined by the availability of land. The overall plan was based on the peripheral layout of narrow, contiguous row houses grouped about a sizable inner, open courtyard containing cisterns and the usual types of public building. Subsequently, a small market arose in the central courtyard, compromising its original character. The disorderly, asymmetrical arrangement of public structures, in relation to one another as well as to the open area, may have been caused by objective limitations or by the obligatory process of building in stages.

In marked contrast to Me'ah She'arim, Batei Ungarn ("Hungarian Houses") and Batei Neitin ("Neitin Houses," so named for the Chicago philanthropist who "endowed" the neighborhood) have remained virtually unchanged in their layout. This features a continuous peripheral arrangement of long buildings, surrounding a large triangular inner compound. Passageways between or under the buildings lead into the central area, which discloses groups of buildings in parallel rows separated by long rectangular courtyards. Dark, narrow gateways gave access to each quarter between groups of row houses. Me'ah She'arim originally had four gates, with two more added later, while the Batei Ungarn-Batei Neitin compound had nine. In 1915, the iron gates at the entry points, locked at night against marauders, were removed by order of the Turkish authorities.

The architectural identity of these neighborhoods—Me'ah She'arim in particular—lay in the sum of their parts rather than in individual elements. Narrow alleys, a mélange of structural additions, sloping tile roofs at skewed angles, tunnel-like passageways between buildings, winding stairways, open or closed balconies, and notices of all kinds plastered everywhere—these create the neighborhoods' unique texture and identity. Reflecting economic destitution, political and security concerns, and a disregard for material satisfaction, the architecture was of a "social" order that expressed close community and family ties, religious and ideological solidarity, and a tendency toward detachment and introversion.

Additional construction, largely makeshift and entirely against the bylaws, was inevitable, but it ended by deforming most of the neighborhoods. Demographic pressure proved relentless as the population of the new Jewish neighborhoods increased from 2,000 in 1881 to nearly 29,000 in 1914. This growth also created the need for a large number of public buildings—synagogues, yeshivas, and charitable organizations among them—some of which stand out against the modest and rather somber backdrop of the residential structures. Still, the fact that Jewish community buildings were situated in densely packed residential areas reduced their visual impact, especially in comparison with the magnificent Christian edifices then being erected in Old Jerusalem.

The Bukharan Quarter is unique among the pre-1914 Jewish neighborhoods built outside the Old City, inasmuch as it was fully planned from the outset and contained buildings of genuine architectural interest. The founders sought a "European" look, very likely in order to recall the towns they came from in Central Asia, then part of Westernized Russia. The quarter's orderly, grid-pattern layout, wide streets, and large, spacious houses contrasted with the crammed architecture of oth-

3-5. External stairways in late-19th-century Jewish neighborhoods are impressive architectural elements, their sculpturesque quality relieving the monotony of long façades. Functionally, they allow access to the balcony running the length of the building.

er contemporary Jewish neighborhoods. At the turn of the century, the Bukharan Quarter was considered Jerusalem's finest neighborhood, and by 1914 its community numbered about 1,500—a sevenfold growth in twenty-five years. However, the ravages of time have severely eroded the district's once noble character, yet without obliterating its progressive European planning.

Although most of the façades in the Bukharan Quarter appear symmetrical at first glance, they actually are not, a fact evident in the uneven divisions between the wings of the houses as well as in the unequal distances between windows. This may result from faulty design, but more probably it emerged as an expression of the East's fatalistic outlook, which holds that perfection, which symmetry denotes, is a divine attribute and thus not a suitable goal for mere mortals.

Most structures in the Bukharan Quarter were built around an inner courtyard, much like the homes in Bukhara, where the residents belong to patriarchal "tribal" families. The buildings had long dimensions and one or more wings, each of them housing consanguineous or socially close families. Many of the Bukharan courtyards were not fully closed, owing to incomplete buildings. The splendid façades boasted arched windows protected by decorative grilles. A narrow entrance with an iron latticework gate led into the courtyard paved with flagstones and planted, in some instances, with fruit-bearing trees. Verandas were often glorified by an impressive wood ceiling, similar to those found at the homes of wealthy Arabs. Some affluent Jews from Samarkand and Tashkent managed to erect mansions in European styles. Many regarded their Jerusalem houses as "summer homes," staying there with their families on visits to the Holy City. These extravagant villas, even when evocative of Bukhara, were apparently designed by Italian architects working more or less in the Neo-Renaissance style then all the rage in Italy. This meant stone pomp and grandeur, including façades punctuated by windows decorated with embellished stonework.

A mélange of architectural styles, the Bukharan Quarter exhibits not only German, Italian, and Russian influences but also elements derived from Muslim building, both local and elsewhere in Central Asia. The cosmopolitan effect is especially striking in the mansions, with their wood-carved Turkish ceilings, Neo-Renaissance or Neo-Gothic windows, tiled European roofs, Italian marble, Neo-Moorish arches, and naturalistic wall paintings of European landscapes. Needless to say, Jewish motifs, particularly the Star of David, found their place, appearing, sometimes with the word "Zion" and a surrounding rosette, in a wide variety of forms. It constituted a visual expression of the Bukharans' "Return to Zion."

1. The double-height roof on Davidoff House (1906), one of the magnificent dwellings in the Bukharan Quarter, had a purely aesthetic function. Such crowning features of architectural design are commonly found in Italy's Tuscany region as well as in wood synagogues of 18th- and 19th-century Poland.

2. "The Palace" (the Yehudayoff-Hefetz house) in the Bukharan Quarter is in Neo-Classical style, featuring pilasters with Corinthian capitals, cornices, rosettes, and stone urns on the roof balustrade.

The Zichron Moshe neighborhood, built mainly from 1906 to 1909, represents an important stage in the development of New Jerusalem, given that it emerged as the first neighborhood of "modern," culturally enlightened Jews. In physical character and social makeup, it somewhat anticipated Rehavia, the "garden neighborhood" built some twenty years later. Innovative principles were incorporated in the Zichron Moshe plan and reflected the experience gained in the building of earlier neighborhoods. Zichron Moshe was not a continuous, unified quarter; rather, it was divided into two halves, with the houses in the eastern section standing on plots twice the size of the others.

To enhance the quality of life, residents agreed to build houses in pairs, "so that each house will have open space on three sides," as the neighborhood ordinance called for, and a path 10 feet (3 meters) wide between each pair. Building requirements in older quarters, governing the interface between private and public domains, were meant to ensure a well-ordered community life, but the Zichron Moshe regulations went well beyond the necessary minimum. Each pair of houses was considered a single planning unit, one in which the two parts had to be architecturally harmonious. Well-dressed stone was mandatory for façades, as were projecting cornerstones and lintels above doors and windows.

Zichron Moshe heralded the end of a severe crisis in Jerusalem's building industry. The housing project had been initiated by the Moses and Judith Montefiore Foundation, established in 1874 to improve the lot of the local Jewish community. The foundation also supported the construction of other middle-class neighborhoods, all of them, like Zichron Moshe, named for Moses (Moshe) Montefiore: Mazkeret Moshe (1882), Ohel Moshe (1883), Yemin Moshe (1891), and Kiryat Moshe (1924). Zichron Moshe could count many of New Jerusalem's intelligentsia and leading public figures among its 550 residents. Sephardim made up about a quarter of the population, and small groups of Russian and Georgian Jews also lived there.

Until World War I, public buildings in the new neighborhoods served the immediate

3. Colored glass in stylized windows characterizes many elegant houses built in the Bukharan Quarter in the late 19th century and the early 20th.

4. An ambience of "majestic" Neo-Classical grandeur is evoked by the monumental stairway and raised entrance to "The Palace" in the Bukharan Quarter, which now serves as an Orthodox girls' school.

1. Local splendor with Neo-Renaissance windows, their protruding stone gables supported by pilasters. The Star of David decorations on the windows symbolize the Bukharans' "Return to Zion." Davidoff House in the Bukharan Quarter.
2, 4. Stylized rosettes were a common decorative element on the iron doors of entrances to Jewish, Muslim, and Christian houses in the late 19th century.

population, inasmuch as central synagogues, for instance, were virtually nonexistent. For health, education, and welfare services, various organizations erected buildings dedicated to those purposes. Initially, the most important Jewish (and some non-Jewish) public institutions outside the Old City were constructed along or near Jaffa Road and Prophets Street—today's downtown. Many of them had been operating in the Old City, until prompted to move by the same considerations that drove residents of the Jewish Quarter to the new neighborhoods outside the walls. Severe overcrowding and poor sanitation led two Old City hospitals—Bikur Holim and Rothschild—to relocate where they could function as modern medical facilities. Similarly, educational and welfare institutions, such as the Laemel School and the Ashkenazi Old Age Home, moved out of cramped quarters in the Old City to new extramural premises. Most of the buildings rose on large plots allowing for future expansion, and many, now hemmed in by dense, relatively high-rise construction, offered magnificent views of the Old City and beyond.

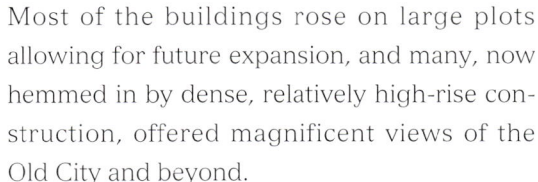

The original character of those first Jewish neighborhoods in the New City has suffered a prolonged process of erosion. Few buildings still exist in their original form. The accumulation of additions, planned and makeshift, and the city's exponential growth after 1967 have created a situation quite different from that envisaged by the founders. British planners who drew up master plans for Jerusalem had earmarked many of the old neighborhoods, including Nahalat Shiva, for demolition. Legal problems, economic realities, and altered perceptions about the importance of preservation have enabled the New City's first neighborhoods to survive (and some to thrive), but many display rampant deterioration and chaotic attempts at renovation.

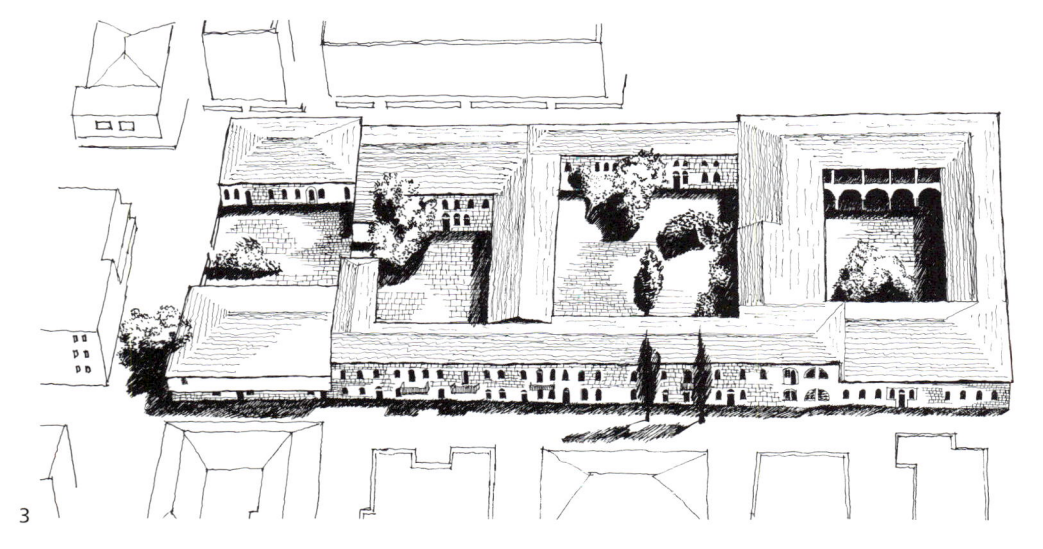

In most of the New City neighborhoods, which occupy prime downtown land, space for new construction has long been unavailable—but large-scale building has taken place nearby. Sha'arei Hessed (1908), which once overlooked the beautiful Valley of the Cross, now lies in the shadow of a high-rise residential project. The sixteen-story towers, just 100 feet (30 meters) distant, radically altered the character of the rustic old neighborhood. However, a preservation plan has made it possible for significant extensions to be built and makeshift additions to be demolished, without vitiating the neighborhood's original texture. As a result, Sha'arei Hessed, like other old neighborhoods such as Zichron Moshe, has been undergoing gentrification. Always a religious neighborhood, it is home to a new population consisting largely of ultra-Orthodox families from Western countries who can meet the high price of land and renovation, the price stemming from the neighborhood's location near the city center and adjacent to the prestigious Rehavia neighborhood.

A strikingly successful example of commercial revitalization is Nahalat Shiva, a neighborhood in the heart of downtown Jerusalem. One of the oldest quarters of the New City, Nahalat Shiva was created in 1869 by members of seven long-established Jerusalem families. Security, more than anything else, would seem to have determined its location, on the main Jaffa-Jerusalem road and close to the Russian Compound, the latter built several years earlier. In the early 1950s, a plan to raze the quarter and put up modern buildings gained approval, which, in 1959, allowed eleven structures to be replaced by a bland office block named after Yoel Moshe Salomon, one of the seven founders of Nahalat Shiva. However, following a series of policy reversals, the neighborhood received a complete facelift and turned into Jerusalem's "Soho." The main street became a pedestrian mall (dedicated in 1989), and today many components of the original architecture are again visible, while pubs, restaurants, and boutiques make Nahalat Shiva one of Jerusalem's most popular leisure-time areas.

ARAB BUILDING: 1860-1918
Rural and Urban Residential Architecture

Like the Jewish community, Jerusalem's urban Arabs did not begin building outside the Old City walls until the mid-19th century. There were, however, scattered Arab villages around Jerusalem, among them the village of Silwan, southeast of the Temple Mount. Now virtually a semi-urban neighborhood, Silwan has roots dating back almost three thousand years. Today, Arab villages form a ring all about Jerusalem, some of which exemplify the local vernacular architecture. Silwan and Lifta, especially, are typical of Arab rural building in the Jerusalem area, or indeed throughout Israel, but such construction is most evident in the Judean Hills, the Hebron area, and Galilee.

Built over a Crusader site on the slopes of a picturesque valley, Lifta is now a deserted settlement on the city's western approaches, but it remains a fascinating architectural preserve. Some of the houses, even though empty since the 1948 war, have survived the ravages of time, mainly because access to the site is difficult. The abandoned dwellings serve as mute testimony to a traditional vernacular architecture now on the verge of disappearing. As for Silwan, which began in Biblical times as a "city of the dead" and then developed into a village during the Byzantine era, it displays distinctive rural architecture of a type evolved over hundreds of years.

Various elements determined the location of Arab villages, such as the all-important one of proximity to a source of water. Both Silwan and Lifta have their own springs, but in order to ensure a steady water supply in drought years, the villagers dug numerous wells in low-seepage rock strata. Security also played a prime role. Hilltops gave defenders a tactical advantage over invaders and constituted lookouts to prevent theft of agricultural produce. The rural population lived mainly off agriculture, although the hilly terrain meant that most plots were split, while some lay at a fair distance from the village. Almost no building took place in valleys because land there was the most fertile. Moreover, slopes and hilltops provided stone for construction as well as a solid-rock foundation.

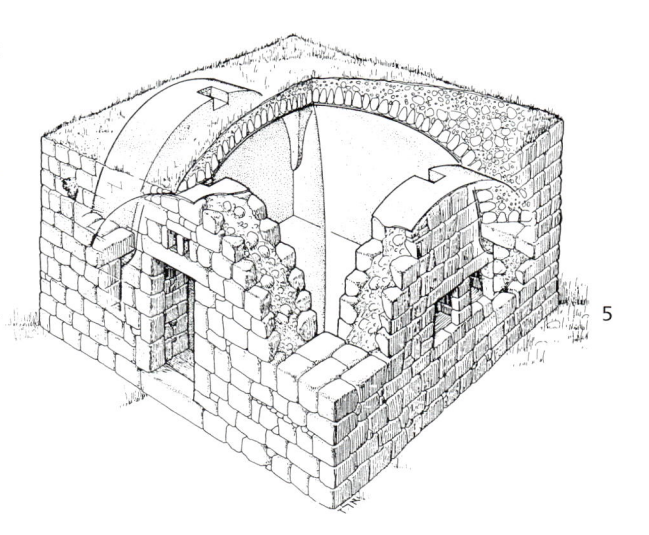

3. Former splendor: The Mashaiyoff House (1906) had delightful inner courtyards, covered arcades, and fruit trees, which have, as in most of the buildings in the Bukharan Quarter, deteriorated over the years.

5. Meter-thick stone walls and a cross vault supporting the domed stone roof are characteristic elements in rural Arab residential construction. Typically, a family built its own house, assisted by the other villagers.

The overriding realities in rural construction around Jerusalem were topography and the inherent limitations of building with stone. The great disparity in elevation between a village's upper and lower sections (in Silwan it is 430 feet, or 130 meters, the equivalent of a forty-story building) means that the problems involved in building on steep slopes had to be solved. This brought the widespread use of terraced agriculture, for field crops as well as for orchards and vineyards. The terraces became integral to the villages' architectural identity.

Buildings generally come together in a dense cluster at the village's historical core, thinning out toward sparse linear construction on the fringes. The old center is a jumble of structures built atop one another along the length and breadth of the slope within a limited area, while new building takes place along the ridgeline. From afar the village center seems to be a stone monolith, but up close the separate units become apparent. Actually, the tight cluster consists of small blocks, inhabited by extended patrilineal families and usually grouped about an inner courtyard (the *hosh*, similar to that of the Old City's Muslim Quarter), which had a few fruit trees growing in it. Clan feuds, together with fear of thieves and other trespassers, prompted such security measures as stone fences, locked gates, and façades unbroken except by small upper windows.

The village well or spring was a social center and meeting place, particularly for women and children. Since a Muslim may pray anywhere (other than on Fridays), social and religious life did not revolve around the mosque. In some villages, such as Lifta, a small building, without a minaret, served as the mosque. Every village or group of patrilinear families set aside a *madafah* ("guest house") to put up

1. Small, picturesque clusters of stone dwellings on hilly slopes form the typical Palestinian Arab village. The deserted village of Lifta, at the western entrance to Jerusalem, is a veritable architectural and technological preserve of rural Arab construction.

visitors, relatives, or others. Shops being nonexistent, most commerce proceeded by barter. An area for burying the dead was reserved at the village edge, although some families interred the deceased in their own courtyard.

Muslim religious and social principles affected construction. Thus, a wall common to two buildings, courtyards, or fields was deemed to belong to the owner whose property stood on the higher ground. No door opened onto a neighbor's courtyard or to a private alleyway. To ensure the Muslim woman's privacy, windows were usually placed—and trees planted—so that they did not overlook the house or courtyard next door. A house was normally built in a way that would not prevent the runoff of rain water into a neighbor's cistern.

A distinguishing quality of Arab rural building was, and remains, its harmonious blending with the landscape. This derives from values of modesty and conservatism, simplicity of design, functional apertures, and a human scale of construction employing stones of a similar size. Building with stone encouraged the use of elementary geometrical forms, with variety achieved through the placement of windows and the utilization of arches, domes, and diverse shades and dressings of stone. Rural building is based largely on vault construction. The low, horizontal abode was not diminished by monumental structures, and even the needlelike minarets, thrusting vertically from the broken silhouette of stone cubes, seem an innate feature of the Arab village landscape.

The Arab rural house, with its meter-thick walls, vaulted structure, small apertures, dirt floor, and low ceiling resembled in many ways the simple houses built in ancient times. The typical dwelling contained a living area above the lower level reserved for livestock as well as for the storage of grains and agricultural implements. The square structure enclosed some 178 square feet (25 square meters) of usable space with a height of 16.4 feet (5 meters). The upper living space, where the entire family cooked, ate, and slept, occupied about 75 percent of the total area. Bedding was stored in wall niches during the day.

2. The location of the windows on this affluent urban Arab house in the Musrara neighborhood creates an intriguing geometrical effect.

3. A striking example of opulent Arab urban construction is the 19th-century mansion of the Aga Rashid Nashashibi. This *liwan* house, characterized by a large central room flanked by smaller rooms on either side, is today the Ticho House Museum in downtown Jerusalem.

4. Not far from the Aga Rashid mansion is the even more ornate Navon Bey House, featuring a central gable, stylized roof pillars, and corner pilasters.

1. The imposing entrance to the former villa of Isma'il al-Husseini in East Jerusalem (1897), now Orient House (headquarters of Palestinian activity). The stylized plaster latticework with colored glass in the center of the gable, common in Islamic architecture, is known as *gamariya*.

2, 3. Stones richly decorated characterize Arab urban construction in the late Ottoman Period.

Basic household artifacts included water jars, cooking utensils, a few wooden stools, and oil lamps for illumination. As in the Old City, the dome vault was crucial in terms of construction, acoustics, and cooling properties in the summer heat. Roofs, usually accessed by external stairs and a ladder, were also used to dry fruits and vegetables and as a place to sleep on hot summer nights.

Decorative elements in the Arab rural house were generally religious in nature. Verses from the Koran, sometimes together with the name of the householder and the year of construction, were engraved on the stone lintels. Wealthy villagers liked to embellish the keystones of window and door arches with rosettes or geometrical designs.

In some dwellings, ceramic plates ornamented with floral motifs might be inserted above apertures or in the dome vault during construction. However, as in the Muslim Quarter of Old Jerusalem, *hajj* paintings honoring the pilgrims' return from Mecca constituted the most popular form of decoration.

Rural Arabs usually built their houses with their own hands, guided by the local professional builder-cum-"architect" but also aided by relatives and other villagers. Construction tended to be a prolonged affair, sometimes punctuated by lengthy intervals, in accordance with the family's financial means. A rich folklore, comprising ceremonies, proverbs, and traditions sprang up around house construction, signifying the very great importance the rural dweller attached to this process. The building of a new house (or the purchase of a completed house) is still considered one of the three most important events in an Arab's life, after marriage and the birth of a son. Completion of the roof would be marked by a celebration that included a festive meal, community singing, greetings, and gift-giving.

To keep evil spirits away from the house, villagers would propitiate them by making sacrifices. After digging the foundation, they slaughtered a sheep above the ditch so that its blood would repulse the spirits. Christian Arabs invited a priest to bless the foundation and sprinkle it with holy water. Another sheep was slaughtered on the completed roof. Muslim Arabs turned the beast's head toward Mecca, while Christian Arabs daubed a cross on the door lintel with the blood of the sacrificial animal. The sacrifice would be repeated when the family moved into the house, this time with the blood smeared around the door.

There were houses in Jerusalem that remained uninhabited for years, following disasters suffered by the families that had lived in them. The belief was that the "local spirit," denied the sacrifices due it, had taken one of the family members as a substitute. Some warded off the evil eye by placing a silver coin wrapped in a green leaf under the first foundation stone (green and silver were thought to be sacred colors). Others stuck an olive branch at the center of the freshly completed dome, assuming the olive to be a blessed tree construction. Until the 1870s, the few Muslim structures in the nascent New City were mainly religious in purpose—such as mosques or graves of revered men—but they did include *khans* as well as summer houses belonging to residents of the walled city. After 1870, Arab building, primarily to the north of the Old City, intensified, although from 1911 to 1918 some fifty houses were also built in the south and its branches tokens of good fortune. As in the Muslim Quarter, some households hung various objects above the door against the evil eye, such as blue beads, garlic, egg shells, a horseshoe, cactus, and the *hamsa*, a representation of the palm of the hand. Some families hung a white flag outside the house when they moved in, symbolizing hope that the owner would have a long life and unbroken peace with his neighbors.

Muslim building outside the walls lagged considerably behind Christian and Jewish (today's Baka). Smaller groups of Muslim houses went up in the Mamilla neighborhood opposite Jaffa Gate (usually with a ground-floor shop and apartments above), the Ethiopian Quarter, and Musrara across from Damascus Gate. A few wealthy *effendis* built mansions along Jaffa Road (see also "Affluent Arab Neighborhoods" on page 162). During this later period, all the Arab construction in the New City was residential, except for a few schools.

One reason for the almost total absence of Muslim public buildings outside the walls was

4, 5. Like a vision from the "Arabian Nights," the grandest residential building erected in the Mamilla neighborhood near the Old City—by the Clark family from the United States (1898)—displays horseshoe windows, interlocking red and white stones, and a serrated roof balustrade that are hallmarks of Islamic architecture. Long abandoned, the building will be renovated as part of the Mamilla Project, underway since the early 1990s.

1, 2. The elegant houses built in the late 19th century by the Nashashibi family on Ethiopia Street in central Jerusalem have large rooms, imposing entrances, and stylized windows with colored glass.

the failure of the Ottoman authorities to provide community services, which left the Arab population to make do with the public facilities available within the Old City. Moreover, they received some of their health and educational services from the Christian institutions. Indeed, before 1918 no master plan existed for the city's development, and no regulations governed the road system, public areas, permissible height of buildings, and so forth. Nevertheless, a building permit (*firman*) was required from the local Ottoman authorities, and in some cases from Constantinople. The Turks levied a building tax on construction beyond the walls, although not in the Old City.

Just as in the first Jewish neighborhoods, Arab building took place within convenient walking distance of the Old City, meaning the Muslim Quarter and the Haram al-Sharif. However, unlike Jewish building outside the walls, which was organized along social and institutional lines, Arab construction remained entirely private or carried out by patrilineal families. It proceeded by stages, which began when two or three families from the same extended family moved out of the Old City, with others gradually following. This gave rise to separate and unconnected "family neighborhoods," which lacked common community services. Most of the families in question—Husseini, Nashashibi, Nusseibeh, Dajani, and others—belonged to the local educated elite, owned land and capital, and held positions of influence in the political, municipal, and religious spheres.

While on the exterior Arab urban houses displayed a broad range of architectural forms—again, owing to the absence of building ordinances—their interiors followed the same basic plan. The major element was a large central room, known as a *liwan*, which functioned as a living room and guest-reception area. Flanking the liwan on both sides was a room, or series of rooms (depending on the size of the liwan and the house) that served as bedrooms, dens, or women's quarters (since the Arab way of family life dictated the division of the dwelling into male and female wings). In the "classic" model of the liwan house, the two opposite walls of the central hall were so placed as to take advantage of the day and night breezes. In many houses, projecting or recessed porches attached to the outer wall, in some cases with an arcade, underscored the presence and importance of the liwan.

A fine example of the liwan houses built in the late 19th century and the early 20th is the home of Aga Rashid (Nashashibi) located off Jaffa Road in downtown Jerusalem and now the Ticho House Museum. In its original form, the two-story structure resembled larger buildings in which the liwan was a composite of two domed rooms with a two-room wing on either side. Although various additions were built over the years, the original core is still easily discernible. The Nashashibis erected similar houses in the nearby Ethiopian Quarter, mainly after 1892. Their roofs, flat rather than domed, utilized rails as a structural element, then in plentiful supply following the completion of the railway line to Jerusalem, which made building materials readily available to the city.

Simplicity and modesty were the hallmarks of the urban house favored by Arabs in the late Ottoman era. Arched niches cut into thick walls were used to store everyday utensils made of clay or copper. The broad window sills served as sitting areas as well as storage for bedding underneath. Simple cotton mattresses stood piled up in a corner of every bedroom, waiting to be spread on the floor, or on simple wood stands, at night. The living room usually contained a wood or stone rack about 10 feet (3 meters) long on which mattresses, a carpet, and cushions could be placed next to one of the walls. Other living-room furniture consisted of low wood or straw stools and a large round copper table resting on a damascened wood frame with short legs.

In wealthy homes, like those built by the Nashashibi family on Ethiopia Street, the floor was made of marble or finished with colorful carpet-patterned tiling. The decorative wood ceilings emulated affluent homes in Damascus and elsewhere in the Ottoman Empire. Some of the panes in liwan windows might be set within a stylized wood frame and colored in intense shades of red, green, yellow, and blue. The walls remained bare, except perhaps for a print of verses from the Koran. Toward the end of the Ottoman Period photographs of family members might be hung high on the walls in descending order of importance, with the grandfather at the apex of the pyramid. More traditional Muslims, however, did not display family photographs, preferring to obey the religious ban on the public exhibition of a human image. Some families hung carpets with simple designs on the walls. The bedding was stored in special damascened wood chests.

One of the grandest Muslim buildings of the period survives at 26 Nablus Road north of the Old City, where it now functions as the ultraprestigious American Colony Hotel. The place was built from 1865 to 1876 by a wealthy merchant, Rabah al-Husseini, who lived there in high style with four wives and a large ret-

3, 4. A prime example of the splendor of some Arab houses in late-19th-century Jerusalem is the former Rabah al-Husseini mansion (now the American Colony Hotel). The inner courtyard and the sumptuous wood ceiling are a local Jerusalem example of opulence more usually found in Syria or Turkey.

inue of servants until his death in the 1890s. Originally, the structure, which stands on a 2-acre plot surrounded by a stone wall, had two stories, a basement, and a large cistern. A small foyer at the entrance led to large halls on the ground floor, which in turn gave access to a square, flagstoned inner courtyard—an unusual feature in Arab houses outside the Old City walls. The building was leased, and subsequently sold, to members of Jerusalem's American Colony.

At Rabah al-Husseini's house, staff and guards occupied the ground-floor rooms, which also housed a flour mill for domestic needs. The owner and his wives resided on the resplendent upper story, which contained a living room with a painted wood ceiling with a central, colorfully decorated and gilded dome. A portico crowned by a similar ceiling, a feature very characteristic of Ottoman wood construction, extended around part of the second story.

In both construction techniques and form, Arab urban architecture in the second half of the 19th century was fundamentally a continuation of rural architecture. The cubic houses, straight-angled and of modest deportment, followed the same basic plan, complete with thick stone walls, cross vaults, and round-headed double windows. This direct continuation—it would be misleading to speak of "influences" or "sources of inspiration"—resulted from the inherent limitations of building with stone, from a particular style of life, and from customs practiced by the period's Arab populations, rural and urban alike. Not until the turn of the century did new forms of design and technology come into play, among them tiled roofs and iron rails supporting balconies and ceilings.

The façades of Arab urban dwellings combined traditional local elements with foreign features. A major influence in the 19th century came from Europe's Neo-Classical architecture, in the Italian Renaissance style, which encouraged grand staircases, fluted pilasters, and elaborately dressed stone. Still, rural building and most urban construction undertaken by Jerusalem's Arabs in the fifty-year period beginning in 1870 constituted an authentic local product.

EUROPEAN CHRISTIAN BUILDING:
1860-1918
Monumental Institutional Architecture
The Power Struggle

Beginning in the mid-19th century, the European Powers and their Christian constituents vied for dominance in the emerging New Jerusalem; moreover, they succeeded in helping to forge its physical image. In contrast to contemporary Jewish building, geared to create an intimate community texture, or the Muslims' scattered family-tribal clusters, European Christian construction, riding the high tide of imperialism, produced large compounds as well as monumental structures and offered services that others could not match. The Christian communities, in an effort to extend their influence by winning the hearts and minds of the natives, looked for an alternative to the Old City's desperate physical conditions, the result of generations of Ottoman neglect. Politically too, the narrow, cramped lanes of the Old City did not lend themselves to the kind of architectural expression that could satisfy the overweening ambitions of Europe. However, the empty spaces amid the boulder-strewn hills along historic routes leading to Jerusalem, mainly from the north and west of the Old City, offered possibilities to architects intent upon giving full play to their masters' grand conceptions.

The Great Power rivalries that had spurred construction in the Old City eventually spread to the New City. Germans, French, British, Russians—all sought to gain hegemony in the Holy Land for strategic, religious, or colonial purposes. And the shortest, surest way to achieve that goal lay in effecting a religious presence, running associated humanitarian projects, such as hospitals and schools, and providing lodgings for the thousands of pilgrims—pawns in the interpower struggle—who flocked to the city. Like the Jews and the Muslims, but for other reasons, Europeans used pilgrims as justification for their drive to build sites near the Old City and its sacred places. Naturally they focused on the Christian Quarter and, for Catholics and the Eastern Orthodox, the Church of the Holy Sepulcher. Since many of the new Christian institutions outside the walls developed in a crescent-shaped area northwest of the Christian Quarter, the Great Powers pressured the Ottoman authorities to facilitate access to them by breaching a new gate in the Old City wall. Finally, in 1889, Sultan Abdul Hamid II consented. The result, aptly enough, has ever since been known as "New Gate."

Christians also targeted Mount Zion, the Mount of Olives, and the village of Ein Karem, all identified with the origins of Christianity. Almost as popular were the remains of the Crusader regimes. But more practical considerations, such as the price and availability of land, could play a part as well, especially for the German Protestants and the Anglicans, who were less concerned about proximity to the Old City. Sites then considered "remote," given the trackless, rocky spaces around the the Old City and the animal transportation available, were acquired, for example, by the German cleric Johann Schneller and the British Consul James Finn. As in the Old City, the new European Christian buildings were usually set within a compound enclosed by high stone walls and iron gates, for reasons of both security and the effects of imperial distance. The self-contained "minitowns" of the Old City look small beside the vast new compounds, with their outsized cisterns designed to collect runoff rainwater (receipt of a building permit was conditional on their construction) and their monumental architecture.

The grandiose structures, many featuring a cloister and an atrium, recall European buildings. In the Great Powers' competition for preeminence in Jerusalem, where the ability to impress both "locals" and visitors was vital, architectural design assumed paramount importance. Beyond size, mass, and height, what counted in a building was its evocation of well-known structures in the home country—although this also had to do with the simple fact that the architects generally came from Europe. Thus, the plan and façade of the Dormition Church on Mount Zion echoes Worms Cathedral, the Cathedral of the Holy Trinity in the Russian Compound recalls the Cathedral of the Assumption in Moscow, and so forth. Most of the new structures exemplify the eclectic architecture then fashionable in Europe, although some buildings incorporate indigenous architectural motifs, a function of stone-based technology, or else they make a statement by integrating ancient archaeological finds into new structures.

The German Colony

German interest in the Holy Land was fired by the reports of travelers who had visited there. That romantic ardor was complemented by the realpolitik pursued by Otto von Bismarck, Germany's imperialist "Iron Chancellor." In Palestine, the Germans operated, at first within the Old City, through the actively missionary Protestant Church. When, around 1860, the Ottoman government began allowing European Christians to build outside the walls, German Protestants were the first to establish philanthropic and other institutions for the local population. The visit made to Jerusalem in 1898 by Wilhelm II and his Empress gave a tremendous boost to German construction in the city. While in Jerusalem, the Kaiser dedicated the Lutheran Church of the Redeemer in the Old City and founded the Augusta Victoria Fund, named for the Kaiserin, which set about raising money to build a huge German hospice on Mount Scopus.

Germany did more building in New Jerusalem than any other European Power. Whether by Protestants, Templers, or Catholics, German construction was crucial to the New City's development and physical appearance. "Germanization" could be felt as well in improved health and welfare services, a system of high-quality vocational education, expanded tourism, and increased pilgrimage, better transportation, the dissemination of European culture, and a boom economy.

Of all the Great Powers, only Germany spawned a community of believers who settled in the Holy Land and built a full-fledged residential quarter in Jerusalem. The "German Colony," established by the Templer sect, was the New City's only European Christian neighborhood. (The residents of the "American Colony," north of the Old City, rented or purchased Arab buildings.) The German

1, 2. The German Colony in southern Jerusalem was planned by the Templers, a Christian sect, in the second half of the 19th century as a typical "street village" (*Strassendorf*), evoking the group's South German origins. Their modest houses had red-tiled roofs, were surrounded by stone walls and pine trees, and formed a straight row along the street.

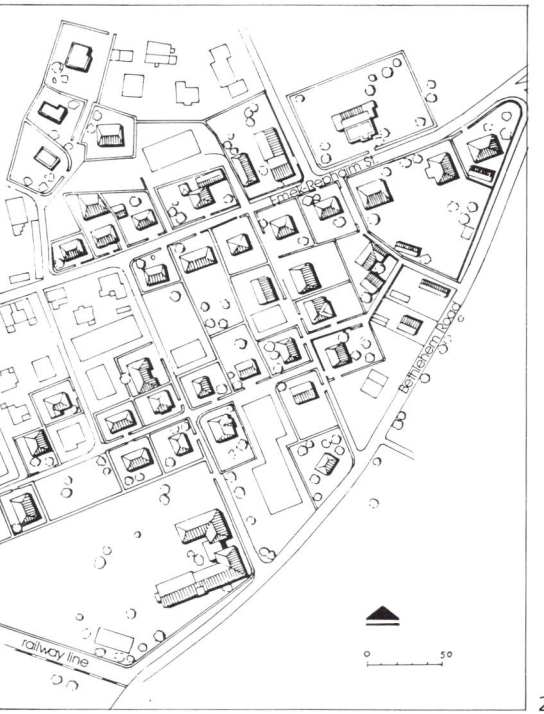

1-3. Although there are only about fifty original Templer buildings in the German Colony, the neighborhood's charm stems from the human scale of the houses and the rural atmosphere evoked by their red-tiled roofs, gardens, and green shutters. One of the grandest houses (2) was designed by its architect-owner, Friedrich Ehmann, and built in the early 20th century.

Colony's planning and construction blended rural German elements with Middle Eastern ones. The neighborhood gave a major impetus to the development of southern Jerusalem.

The name "Templers," which has nothing to do with the Templar Knights of the Crusades, signifies a "divine temple" to be built by a community of believers. Founded in South Germany in 1854, the modern-day Templers migrated to the Holy Land to fulfill ideals of early Christianity, to escape religious persecution, and to satisfy their economic needs. Fourteen years later, the first group—farmers, artisans, and small merchants—settled in Haifa and Jaffa, as well as at Sarona, now the site of the Israeli army's General Staff headquarters in Tel Aviv. A few took up residence in and around the Old City of Jerusalem. In 1873, four years after Prussia and Turkey signed an agreement permitting Germans to acquire land in Jerusalem, the Templers bought a large, fertile tract in the Emek Rephaim area from residents of the nearby Arab village of Beit Safafa.

Following initial economic hardship, the *Deutsche Kolonie* developed more extensively once the Jaffa-Jerusalem railway line had been inaugurated in 1892, with a station at the edge of the neighborhood. The visit to Jerusalem, and even to the German Colony, made by the Kaiser in 1898 heralded the renewal of the Templers' ties with the Fatherland. The local German population was then at its height of about four hundred, its members employed mainly in construction, commerce, industry, and service trades. Local Germans also contributed to the development of architecture and construction engineering in turn-of-the-century Jerusalem. The Templers achieved their greatest prosperity in the early stages of World War I, when some of them became principal suppliers for the German and Austrian troops stationed in Palestine. However, this period ended abruptly in 1918 following the British conquest, which forced almost all Palestinian Germans into exile in Egypt, whence they would eventually be allowed to return. But their story finally ends with World War II, when the Templers, as aliens in British Palestine, found their property confiscated and themselves exiled in Australia. Not only had some Templers joined the branch of the Nazi Party in Jerusalem; the party leader actually resided in the German Colony.

The distinctive quality of the neighborhood known as the German Colony stems primarily from its rural character. The layout mimicked that of a typical German *Strassendorf* ("street village"), including narrow streets lined with red-tile-roofed houses surrounded by low stone walls and pine trees. The "first generation" of standard, simple one- and two-story structures erected in the last quarter of the

4. Biblical verses, engraved in Gothic script above the entrances of some houses on Emek Rephaim Street, attest to the piety of the Templers and their deep attachment to the Holy Land, particularly Jerusalem. Friedrich Aberle built his house in 1874, according to the headstone in the arch.

5. A 1970s plan by the Jerusalem Municipality to preserve the German Colony's rural character prevented large-scale modern construction in the neighborhood.

6. The German Colony's most important public building was the Gemeindehaus, used for assemblies and worship. It was erected in 1882 with the help of donations from friends of the Templers in Palestine and abroad.

19th century remained, overall, the model for later construction. At least some of the original houses were built with the aid of local Arab workers. Moreover, local influence is evident in the interior plan, which recalls the liwan house with its large central room extending the entire length of the structure, with smaller rooms on either side. For the Arabs, as we saw, the liwan functioned as a living room and guest room, but the Germans, with their very different way of life, tended to make the central room narrower, more like a wide connecting hall.

The German Colony gained its first house in 1873. Built by the miller Matthaus Frank (1846-1923), it is still standing, at 6 Emek Rephaim Street. Frank had originally purchased the land on which the entire neighborhood would rise for his father-in-law, who planned to farm it. When the latter died on his way to Palestine, the Templers bought the tract and subdivided it. The two-story Frank house, behind which the owners erected a steam-driven flour mill (known as the "Old Mill" to distinguish it from the "New Mill" built later at a different location within the German Colony), stood on a 1.25-acre plot, five times the average size. The house displays both "Germanic" elements, such as a gable and a round window on the front façade, and local technology in the form of thick stone walls supporting cross vaults.

The Frank property hosted a large vineyard and two underground cisterns, in addition to a pair of open pools in which neighborhood children could swim. Next to the property stood the colony's *Sportplatz*, a facility that reflected the Templers' great love of sports. It served the recreational needs of schoolchildren as well as those of athletes from the various German colonies in Palestine.

German Protestant Buildings

The public institutions built by German Protestants were enclosed in large compounds, their sizes ranging from the 2 acres occupied by the Jesus Hilfe Leprosarium to the 25 acres reserved for the Schneller

121

1-3. South German Baroque is the style of most buildings of the former Schneller Syrian Orphanage (now an Israeli army base), built in the late 19th century and the early 20th. The main structure (1) and "Blindenheim" (3), a home for the blind, as well as others, stand around inner courtyards.

Orphanage. Building sites were selected according to functional need and the cost of land. Protestant (including Templer) dwellings and public buildings displayed modesty and simplicity in both their interior plans and their exterior façades. If the starkness of this construction stands in dramatic contrast to German Catholic flamboyance, it resulted not only from different religious sensibilities but also from the fact that the Protestants generally built earlier than the Catholics, before the country had begun seriously to develop.

The German Protestants favored two basic types of public structure. One was a two- or three-story courtyard building, symmetrical in form with a principal entrance at the center and rooms ranged about the flagstone-paved courtyard built over a large cistern. The second was a simple rectangular or square building also of two or three stories, this time characterized by a corridor giving access to rooms on either side and stretching the entire length of the edifice. Some Protestant structures, notably those designed by the architect Conrad Schick, incorporated European academic elements with local variations. One reason for the "local" flavor was the local residence of the German-born architects and their intimate knowledge of the city. Besides Schick, these included Ferdinand Palmer, a cleric who, like Schick, arrived in Palestine in 1846, and two other Templer architects, Theodor Sandel, who designed Jewish buildings as well, and Hermann Imberger.

The Schneller Syrian Orphanage emerged as the crowning achievement of German educational-philanthropic endeavors in 19th-century Palestine. It was founded in 1860 by Father Johann Ludwig Schneller (1820-96), six years after he arrived in Palestine for the purpose of devoting himself to educational and charitable work among the Arab population. Father Schneller bought the land for his orphanage from the Arabs of nearby Lifta, after which the compound developed by stages, with no overall plan. The imposing central building, a three-story structure erected about a narrow rectangular courtyard, housed the institution's community services, among them the central kitchen, dining room, library, and most of the classrooms. On the second floor was a magnificent church hall capable of seating five hundred people, who listened to an organ paid for by various communities in Germany. The building's main façade was in the South German Baroque style symptomatic of the period. In the impressive architectural space of the inner courtyard, an arcade forms a covered porch linking the rooms on the upper floor served by a curved staircase.

The Schneller compound's home and school for the blind—a splendid symmetrical structure—came into being in 1903, thanks to a large contribution from a German nobleman. Designed in the South German Baroque manner, the building featured a bell tower with a bronze dome resting on four stylized columns rising from the gabled roof. Father Schneller attached particular importance to this building, for with this facility he could accommodate the many parents who had pleaded with him to teach their blind children a useful profession so that they would not have to become beggars. This was at a time when eye diseases were rampant in Palestine.

Schneller's avowed purpose was "to transform the local inhabitants in the spirit of the Scriptures," a goal that could not be achieved "by teaching alone but first and foremost by work." Hence his strong emphasis on vocational education. For his wards, Schneller built modern workshops, in some cases utilizing bricks and roof tiles manufactured on the premises. For the staff, he erected a series of houses near the compound, each with two to four flats. Simple rectangular structures with red-tiled roofs, they resembled the houses in the German Colony.

In 1868, the Talitha Kumi Orphanage for Arab girls, designed by Conrad Schick, opened its doors on a 6.5-acre plot of land northwest of the Old City. Run by the Diakonissen Sisters, a charitable order based in Kaiserswerth, Germany, the new institution expanded the overcrowded one the order had operated since 1853 in the Old City. The site of the Talitha Kumi Orphanage—its name, from Mark 5:42, referring to Christ's resurrection of a dead girl—was selected for a whole range of perceived topographical and climatic advantages.

The main entrance to the Talitha Kumi Orphanage featured a keystone relief of a dove bearing an olive branch, symbolizing both peace and the Diakonissen Sisters. The style of the building, with its extensive use of pilasters, would be widely emulated in the architecture of New Jerusalem. However, the horizontal stone strip marking transitions between floors derived from Arab construction. The windows, with their form and size dictated by technological limitations, may have been the building's most immediately obvious architectural elements, but the most arresting feature was the roof, its masonry domes, bell tower, chimneys, winding stairs, and raised observation platform producing a brilliantly inventive sculptural composition.

In its fifty years of operation, Talitha Kumi permitted a thousand girls to get an education comparable to that offered by schools in Germany. The sisters did not pressure Muslim girls to convert, knowing the difficulties they would subsequently encounter in their society, and indeed only a few became Christians. Today, all that remains of Talitha Kumi are the upper façade emblazoned with the name of the institution, a chimney, and a typical gothic window, preserved when, in 1980, the build-

4, 5. The symmetry that characterizes most European Christian construction in Jerusalem is also the hallmark of the German Jesus Hilfe Leprosarium (1887), designed by architect Conrad Schick, as shown on a postcard (4) of the period.

6, 7. Dove of peace, symbol of the Diakonissen Sisters, whose efforts in education, health, and welfare greatly improved the condition of Jerusalem's Arab population in the later 19th century. The hospital founded by the order in central Jerusalem (1892-94)—its tower typical of German construction of the period—is today part of Bikur Holim Hospital.

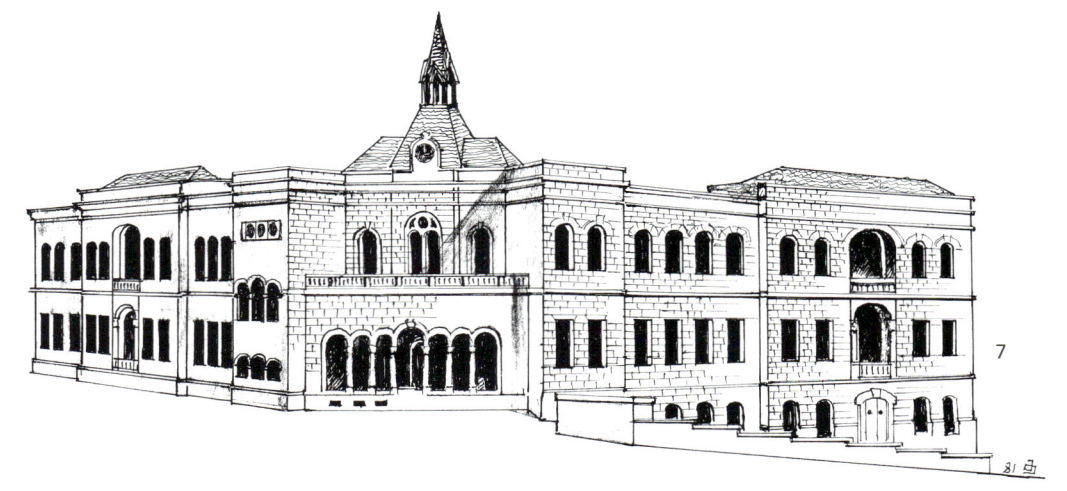

1-3. Conrad Schick (1822-1901) built Thabor House for his family in the 1880s. The entrance to his "house of dreams" suggested a miniature version of a medieval German fort (3). Schick fused European architectural elements, local Oriental construction technologies, and archaeological finds, which he inserted in the walls. The German-born architect and scholar also wrote on the archaeology of Jerusalem.

ing was demolished, despite public furor, to make room for a commercial-residential development. This "three-dimensional documentation" site stands in front of Hamashbir Latzarchan, Jerusalem's first department store, near the site of the former orphanage.

In an isolated area northwest of the German Colony there survives one of Jerusalem's loveliest buildings. Incongruously, it housed, as it does today, victims of a brutally deforming disease. Conrad Schick's Jesus Hilfe ("Help of Jesus") Leprosarium, built in 1887 on a 2-acre plot, stands walled off at the center of a thick pine grove near the Jerusalem Theater complex in the upscale Talbiyeh neighborhood. The square, two-story building embraces an inner, paved courtyard whose enclosed arcade opens into the rooms. Meter-thick stone walls support the cross vaults over the basement and ground floor. An innovative feature was the lavatories in a separate, two-story structure connected to the second floor of the main building by a 16-foot (5-meter) iron bridge.

Conrad Schick arrived in Jerusalem from Germany in 1846 at the age of 24, and for the next 55 years, until his death in 1901, he was the city's most renowned architect. In the 1880s Schick built his home and private chapel in a dense grove of pine trees behind a high stone wall at 58 Prophets Street in the city center. A devout Protestant, he named the building Thabor House, after Psalms 89:13, where the Lord's creation is praised. This self-taught *Baumeister* gave free reign to his imagination and shunned academic rigidity. His ability to blend European features with local motifs and techniques is well exemplified in his home. The entry gate, with a small lookout turret above, recalls the fortified portal of a medieval German castle. The plan of the main house suggests both Arab dwellings and residences in the German Colony. The exterior alludes to architectural elements ranging from Greco-Roman (a palmette) and Biblical times (the "horned altar") to rural German churches (the layout of the windows).

No house in Jerusalem carries the imprint of its designer and builder more powerfully than Schick's, now occupied by the Swedish Theological Institute and protected by municipal ordinances. One of Jerusalem's finest buildings, Thabor House will continue to justify its description as a "house of dreams."

German Catholic Grandeur

In contrast to the Protestants, whose structures reflect their declared mission to serve the local population, German Catholics built religious institutions and hospices mainly for tourists and pilgrims. German Catholic architecture in Jerusalem came forth replete with national, religious, and historical symbols that evoked German power and energy, reflecting the imperialist ambitions of the "Wilhelmine Era" (1888-1914) as much as the Catholic penchant for grandeur. By the same token, these structures display few local elements.

The Dormition Church and Monastery—designed by the German architect Heinrich Renard (1868-1928), well known for his work in the Rhineland, and administered by the Benedictine Order—was consecrated in 1910 on Mount Zion, where Mary, mother of Christ, reputedly died (hence "Dormition," meaning "eternal sleep"). Here too the Last Supper is believed to have taken place and the tomb of King David installed, which makes the site sacred to Jews and Muslims as well as to Christians. While designing the Dormition complex, Renard used photographs and large panoramas to ensure a suitable relationship between the new structure, the Old City wall, and the minaret of the Nebi Daoud Mosque adjacent to the royal tomb.

The awesome Dormition Church is marked by a rotunda structure and a Romanesque style that evokes Worms Cathedral overlooking the Rhine. The great 112-foot (34-meter) height of the interior generates an expansive feeling, reinforced by the six niched altars (donated by Catholic communities in Germany and Austria) surrounding the main space and the mosaic floor inlaid with traditional symbols. The crypt contains a sculptural representation of the dormant Mary, while six female figures from the Old Testament people the mosaic lining the great dome. The organ, situated above the entrance, is flanked by staircases leading, via corner towers, to an open gallery that encircles the rotunda roof and offers a spectacular view of the city. An inner passage links the church with its related monastery.

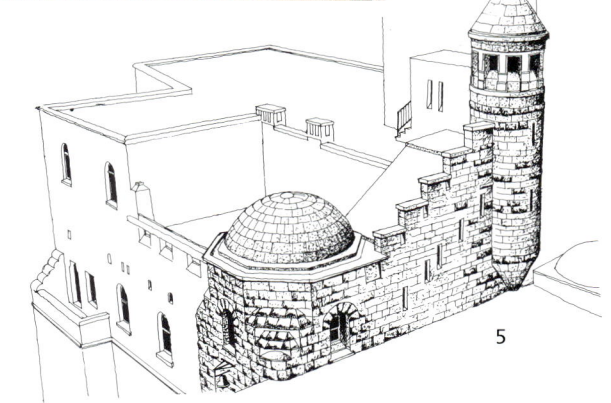

4, 5. Dominating Mount Zion just south of the Old City, the German Catholic Dormition Church and Monastery (consecrated 1910) uses a Neo-Romanesque style to evoke German cathedrals and underscore the presence of the German national identity (*Deutsche Eigenart*) in Jerusalem.

1. Great Power rivalry in Europe for influence in Jerusalem led Kaiser Wilhelm II (1859-1941), who visited the city in 1898, to initiate several large building projects. The domineering Augusta Victoria Hospice, built from 1906 to 1910 on Mount Scopus, epitomizes German imperialism.

2. The arcade around the inner courtyard of Augusta Victoria is covered with cross vaults and paved with stylized colored tiles. Most of the building materials were brought from Germany.

3. Modeled on a medieval castle, Augusta Victoria Hospice is strategically—and breathtakingly—located, overlooking the Old City and the Temple Mount to the west and the Judean Desert and Dead Sea to the east.

Unlike another Catholic architect, Robert Leibnitz, who designed the Augusta Victoria Hospice, Renard not only incorporated local architectural elements into the church's design: he also grasped the decorative potential of Jerusalem stone. The conceptual synthesis this produced obtained its most striking effect in the Neo-Romanesque bell tower, which is abutted by a stepped roof in the turn-of-the-century *Jugendstil* (Art Nouveau) manner as well as by a traditional masonry dome. Teutonic taste dominates the church, which was indeed erected as a monument to Wilhelm II. Among those present at the Easter consecration were the Kaiser's son and daughter-in-law, who, along with a host of German aristocrats, clerics, and pilgrims, came especially for the occasion—as well as for the dedication of both the Augusta Victoria Hospice and another Renard building, St. Paul's Hospice opposite Damascus Gate. Nowadays, apart from its spiritual functions, the Dormition Church serves as a popular venue for concerts of medieval and Baroque music, which blends harmoniously with the architectural setting.

It was Wilhelm II himself who initiated the construction of the Augusta Victoria Hospice, following his visit to Jerusalem in 1898. Named for the Kaiserin—who chose the site—it is the incarnation in stone of German imperial hauteur and desire for prestige. From its domineering location astride Mount Scopus, overlooking the Old City on one side and the Judean Desert and the Dead Sea on the other, to its impractical "Neo-Crusader" style and its panoply of religious and nationalist symbols—the German eagle, Crusader knights, an armor-clad Wilhelm, and a statue of the eponymous Empress—Augusta Victoria epitomizes monumental architecture in the service of Great Power politics in Jerusalem at the turn of the century. Designed by Robert Leibnitz, a Catholic architect who spurned local traditions, the hospice was built at tremen-

4. St. George as a Crusader knight with the slain dragon at his feet, protects the main entrance to August Victoria, nowadays a United Nations hospital.
5. The German eagle keeps watch by the stairs leading to the church hall at Augusta Victoria, named for the Kaiser's wife.

dous cost, ostensibly as a shelter for German visitors and pilgrims and as a vacation site. In fact, the building constitutes a colossal monument to the burgeoning German Empire and the great Kaiser, its construction marking the climax of the Wilhelmine Era in Jerusalem.

The main building, with its allusions to medieval German fortresses, was the central structure in a 20-acre compound purchased only after the Ottoman Sultan had interceded. The adjoining church terminated in a 200-foot (65-meter) bell tower and observation point. For inspiration, Leibnitz looked to Romanesque structures in Germany, while also utilizing the era's latest technology. Thus, Augusta Victoria had an electric generator and modern, sanitary plumbing, which included European-standard baths and lavatories, the first of their kind in Jerusalem.

Despite difficulties caused by the site's

1, 4. Monumental French architecture is exemplified by Notre Dame de France Hospice (late 19th century), across the street from the Old City wall. The building has a pronounced Renaissance symmetry, though the church and bell tower (designed by architect Père Étienne Boubet) are Neo-Baroque.

2, 3. Neo-Renaissance symmetry and a uniform spacing of windows are the hallmarks of St. Louis Hospital, built by French architects Guillemot and Planche opposite the Old City wall from 1879 to 1896. The flanking wings are decorated with stylized Baroque pillars.

2. Part of a cluster that includes Notre Dame de France Hospice, St. Louis Hospital was constructed in the years 1879-96 from plans by Guillemot and Planche, who combined Renaissance symmetry with Baroque pilasters. This was the first Catholic institution to be established adjacent to the Old City's Christian Quarter.

remoteness, bad roads, severe winter weather, an initial shortage of water, the need to import cement, and all the elements of the interior, the complex project was completed less than three years after the cornerstone had been laid.

Brief too were Augusta Victoria's days as a hospice. When war broke out in August 1914, the German-Turkish military forces commandeered the complex for their staff headquarters. After the British captured Jerusalem in 1917, they transformed Augusta Victoria into a residence for the British High Commissioners to Palestine, which it remained until 1927, when the building suffered severe damage during an earthquake. Today, Augusta Victoria, which belongs to the World Lutheran Federation, serves as a hospital for the United Nations Relief and Works Organization, most of whose patients are Arabs from East Jerusalem.

The French

Beginning in the mid-19th century, the French became allies of the Ottomans, which made France the preferred European Power in Palestine. The Vatican, too, enlisted the French as its ally in disputes with the Greek Orthodox Patriarchate over control of the holy sites. France had acquired its advantageous religious-political foothold in Palestine by virtue of the role it had long played as protector of places sacred to Catholics, as well as of such organizations as the Franciscans' Custodia di Terra Santa, which for five hundred years (1333-1847) had taken care of Catholic interests and pilgrims. Besides hostels, the Franciscans ran a network of schools around the country for the children of Christian Arabs. In 1843, following England and Prussia, France opened a consulate in Jerusalem.

The establishment of the Latin Patriarchate in Jerusalem in 1847 proved a further boon to French Catholic interests in the Holy Land. The Latin institutions offered first-rate educational, medical, and charitable services, which prompted growing numbers of Greek Orthodox Arabs to convert to Roman Catholicism. Now a "building war" broke out as the French, seeking greater local influence, erected great edifices meant to compete with the Russians and the Orthodox communities. However, in the 1890s, when France and Russia became allies, which required that the French no longer oppose the Orthodox sects in Palestine, it was the Protestants—the Germans and the English—who gained local advantage.

Some French religious orders built in clusters, the most important of which—comprising St. Louis Hospital, Notre Dame Hospice, St. Vincent de Paul school and orphanage, and the Soeurs Réparatrices convent (severely damaged in the 1948 war and demolished in 1967)—was situated just outside the Old City's Christian Quarter. Other institutions, including Ratisbonne vocational school and St. Étienne, a Biblical research institute, stood to the west and north of the Old City. The French also built in Ein Karem. The St. Claire Monastery, where the nuns devote themselves to a life of seclusion and prayer, was, suitably enough, erected in a vast, isolated compound in southern Jerusalem. Some of the institutions had forerunners in the Old City, which caused the new locations to be chosen for their proximity to the Christian Quarter, the Church of the Holy Sepulcher, and the Crusader sites. In this

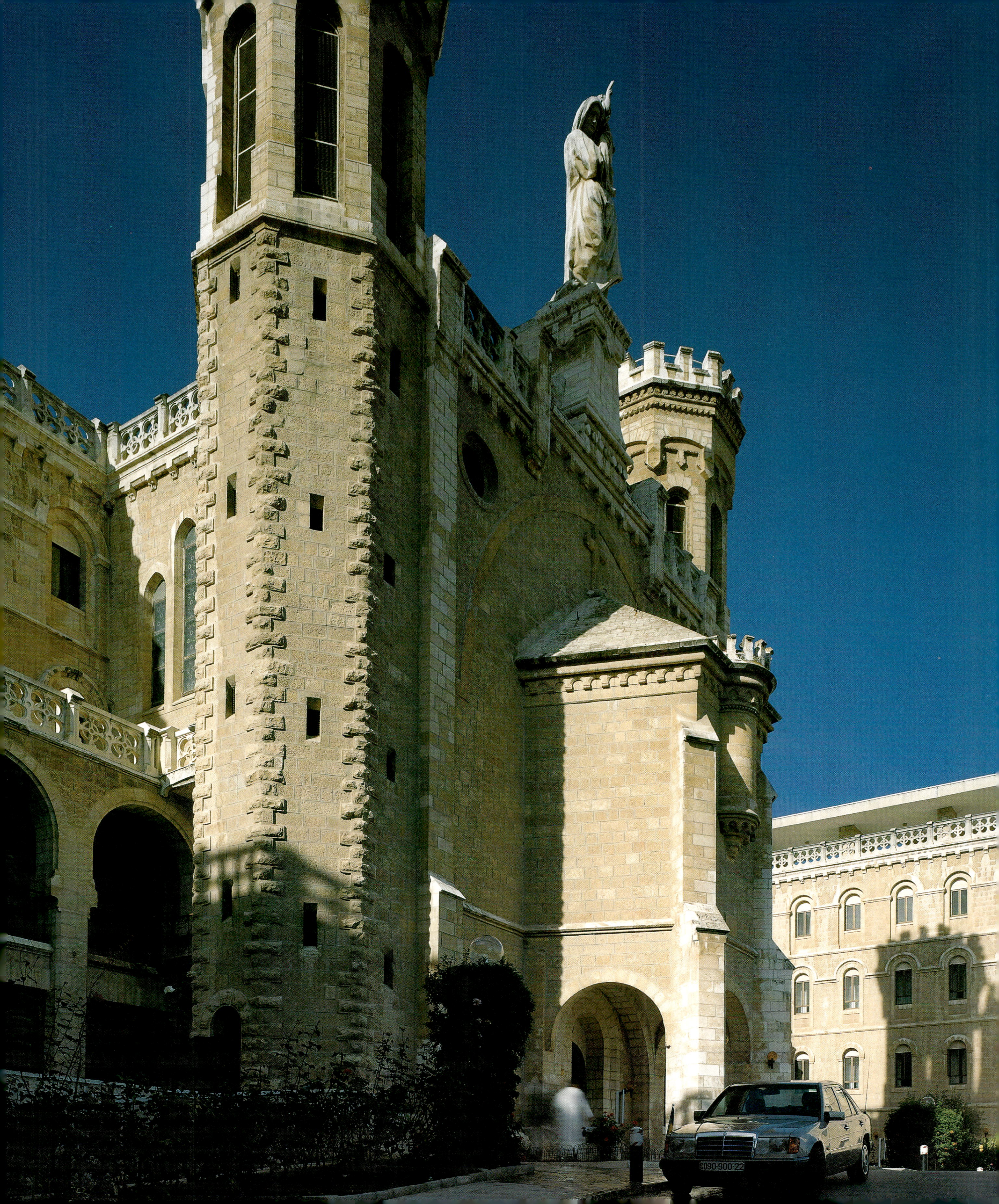
CD90·900·22

1, 2. Monumental symmetry in the Italian Renaissance-Baroque style marks Ratisbonne Monastery and Vocational School in central Jerusalem, built from 1877 to 1894. Note how the architect, M. Doumet, has set off the entrance and the flanking wings. A Madonna holding the Christ Child stands above the compound's water cistern and faces in, toward the building.

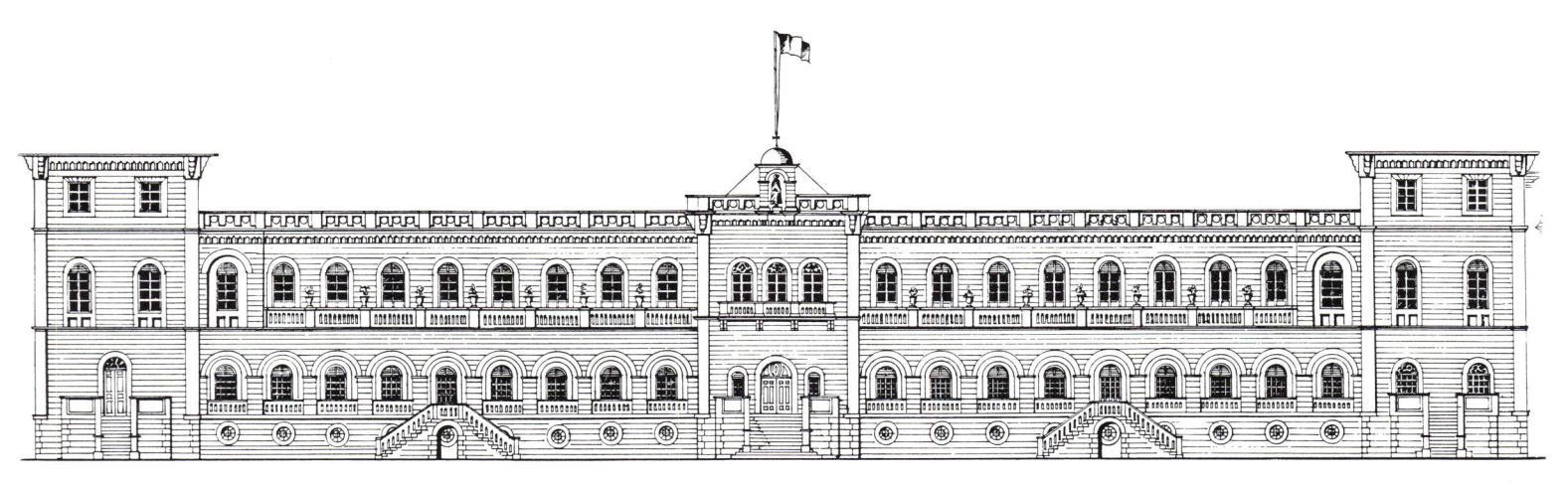

way, the French not only gratified history and nostalgia but also secured topographical advantages over the other European Powers (particularly the Russians). However, some of the smaller and less affluent orders made the cost of land the prime consideration in their choice of real estate.

The French compounds, all surrounded by high stone walls, had massive iron gates, a central building, cisterns, and service structures in the courtyard. The large projects, designed in whole or in part by French architects, intruded on the modest Jerusalem townscape. The main façades could run as long as 300 feet (90 meters) and boast accentuated entrances. As for the buildings' "serene" appearance, this was created mainly by the equidistant or balanced placement of arched windows. Meanwhile, the walls exhibited a mixture of styles, most of all Renaissance and Baroque, but with Neo-Gothic and Romanesque elements included as well. For some, French architecture in Jerusalem was generally rigid, formalistic, and rather overbearing.

St. Louis Hospital, the first Catholic institution built adjacent to the Christian Quarter, rose in stages from 1879 to 1896, on land purchased by Baron Marie Paul Amédée de Piellat (1851-1924). During a visit to the Holy Land in 1874, this aristocrat had been appalled by the conditions at the St. Louis Hospital in the Old City. The façade of the new building combines Renaissance and Baroque features, its harmonious symmetry "burdened" most strikingly by the two corner columns that embellish the flanking wings. "Crusader" motifs, painted by de Piellat himself, decorate the corridors and some of the rooms. As in many

French buildings of the period, St. Louis Hospital has no separate chapel and, for the sake of the patients, no bell tower either. In Israeli territory since the 1948 war, it is now an institution for terminally ill patients of all faiths.

Adjacent to St. Louis Hospital is the vast Notre Dame de France Hospice for Catholic pilgrims, which contains 410 rooms and took two decades to build, starting in 1884. Here too Renaissance symmetry reigns, in a central section joined by means of a covered colonnade to a pair of flanking wings. The hospice was a magnet for Catholics from all over Europe until the British conquest of Jerusalem, whereupon Catholic pilgrimage declined sharply. Since the southern wing was badly damaged in the 1948 fighting, the building underwent renovation. Rededicated in 1978, Notre Dame de France is once more a prestige hostel for pilgrims.

In 1894, Ratisbonne Monastery and Vocational School, which had previously operated in the Old City, became the first French Catholic institution to open in the New City, following seventeen years of construction. Atop the center of the main façade is a small bell tower sheltering a statue of Father Alphonse Ratisbonne, who with his brother Theodore (both Alsatian Jews and converts to Catholicism) founded the institution. The impressive façade is styled in the Renaissance-Baroque manner. In the thick-walled, cross-vaulted basement are large halls that were used for workshops, classrooms, a dining room, and a kitchen. The site, which also contains a guard tower erected by the Turks in the 1830s, was chosen for its vantage point over the Russian Compound as much as for its unobstructed view of the Old City. Moreover,

3, 4. Eclecticism reigns in the architecture of St. Étienne Monastery, which also comprises a biblical and archaeological institute, built from 1891 to 1901 in East Jerusalem according to a design by architect Boutaud. The church tower is Oriental in design, while Neo-Gothic flying buttresses reinforce the stone walls of the Romanesque church. An atrium surrounds the open courtyard, which has a water cistern at the center.

5, 6. Erected by stages from 1887 to 1923, the Convent of the Sisters of the Rosary in central Jerusalem consists of a U-shaped symmetrical Renaissance-style main building by architect Sansur and a large concentric church in the center of the main façade.

the large, level area appeared especially promising for monumental architecture. Ratisbonne, located on the edge of the prestigious Rehavia neighborhood, houses a French-Catholic monastery and seminar as well as private and public offices.

The Russians

From the mid-19th century until World War I, Russian activity in Palestine as a whole and Jerusalem in particular was motivated by Russian Orthodoxy's deep attachment to the Holy Land, reflected in large-scale popular pilgrimages. In addition, Russia granted protection to the local Greek Orthodox community, among which most of Palestine's Christian Arabs counted. Of course, the Russians themselves belonged to the Eastern branch of Christianity, the center of which was in Constantinople. The Russians' humiliating defeat in the Crimean War, at the hands of the French, British, and Turks—not to mention the failure of Eastern Orthodoxy to attract new adherents in Palestine by establishing educational and welfare institutions—led also to the decline of the local Greek Orthodox community and the waning of Russian influence in the Holy Land. To reverse this trend, the Russians set up a shipping line and promoted mass pilgrimage; moreover, they purchased land in Jerusalem and on it built monumental churches, hostels, and other structures. Until World War I, Russian activity was conducted through the "Imperial Russian Orthodox Palestine Society," a semiofficial agency based in St. Petersburg. However, this came to a virtual halt when the outbreak of World War I caused the Russian organizations in Palestine to be declared "enemy institutions," followed by the coup de grâce of 1917—the atheistic Bolshevik Revolution.

Russian building was eclectic, drawing on centuries of architectural styles at home and elsewhere, ranging from the Italian Renaissance to the Russian-Byzantine and from the Classical to the ornately Baroque. Many Russian buildings (like those of other communities) display elaborate, and costly, stonework. In the many structures earmarked for Russian pilgrims, the facilities differed radically according to the social class for which the hospice was designated. All the "heavy" items, such as furniture and cast-iron kitchen stoves, were imported from England, France, Germany, and Russia itself.

The Russians were the only European Power to build a truly vast complex of monumental structures in Jerusalem, a veritable "city within a city." The Russian Compound (as it is still known) stirred the envy—and admiration—of the other Powers. Its primary purpose was to provide lodgings and services to the masses of Russian pilgrims, who far outnumbered those from other countries. The Russian Compound effectively laid the foundations for the New Jerusalem outside the walls, and as such it was welcomed by the tiny Jewish community. The large minitown increased the sense of security felt by the first Jewish settlers in the new neighborhoods, spurring the establishment of additional quarters, among them Me'ah She'arim and the nearby Nahalat Shiva.

Built from 1860 to 1864, the Russian Compound became the first, largest, and most important of the Russian construction projects in Palestine. It was planned by a well-known architect, Martin Ivanovich Eppinger, on an 18.5-acre, strategically important site not far from the Church of the Holy Sepulcher. The virtually self-contained, triangular compound included the Cathedral of the Holy Trinity, the residence of the Russian religious mission, a hospital, the Russian Consulate, a women's

1. The emblem of the Imperial Russian Orthodox Palestine Society is engraved in the main façade of most of the Russian buildings erected in Jerusalem near the end of the 19th century.
2, 3. The Holy Trinity Cathedral in the Russian Compound (3) recalls Moscow's 15th-century Cathedral of the Assumption (2).

and a men's hostel, and, in time, a hostel for the nobility. The plan was based upon two main paths that converged at the church—the first and most important building and therefore situated at the center—with gardens in geometrical shapes separating them. Large cisterns were dug and a system for draining sewage and collecting runoff rainwater created by cutting channels into the bedrock. At times, even the two thousand available beds proved insufficient to meet demand, which increased to ten thousand pilgrims a year around the turn of the century. In peak periods, tents and huts had to be put up to accommodate the visiting throngs of pious Russians.

The Cathedral of the Holy Trinity, with its central nave, side aisles, and Renaissance styling, alludes to the late-15th-century, Italian-built Cathedral of the Assumption in the Kremlin. Fashioned of white limestone, the structure is adorned with eight small towers topped by green domes supporting gilded Russian Orthodox crosses. Lombardian bands embellish the façades as well as Renaissance-type "blind windows" flanked by Neo-Classical columns.

The Russian Mission Residence, the largest of the structures, is a two-story square building divided by two intersecting corridors that form four inner courtyards. A small, beautifully appointed private chapel served both mission members and important pilgrims, who also lodged in the building. The mission organized most of the Russian activity in Palestine, Syria, and Lebanon. It still occupies the majority of the southern wing, but since 1948 the rest of the building has been used by the Israeli court system, including, until late 1992, the Supreme Court.

Finally, the Grand Duke Sergei Hostel, built in 1886-90 and named for the brother of Tsar Alexander III, president of the Imperial

4-6. The hospice named for Grand Duke Sergei Alexandrovich had an imperial bearing and served pilgrims from the Russian aristocracy.

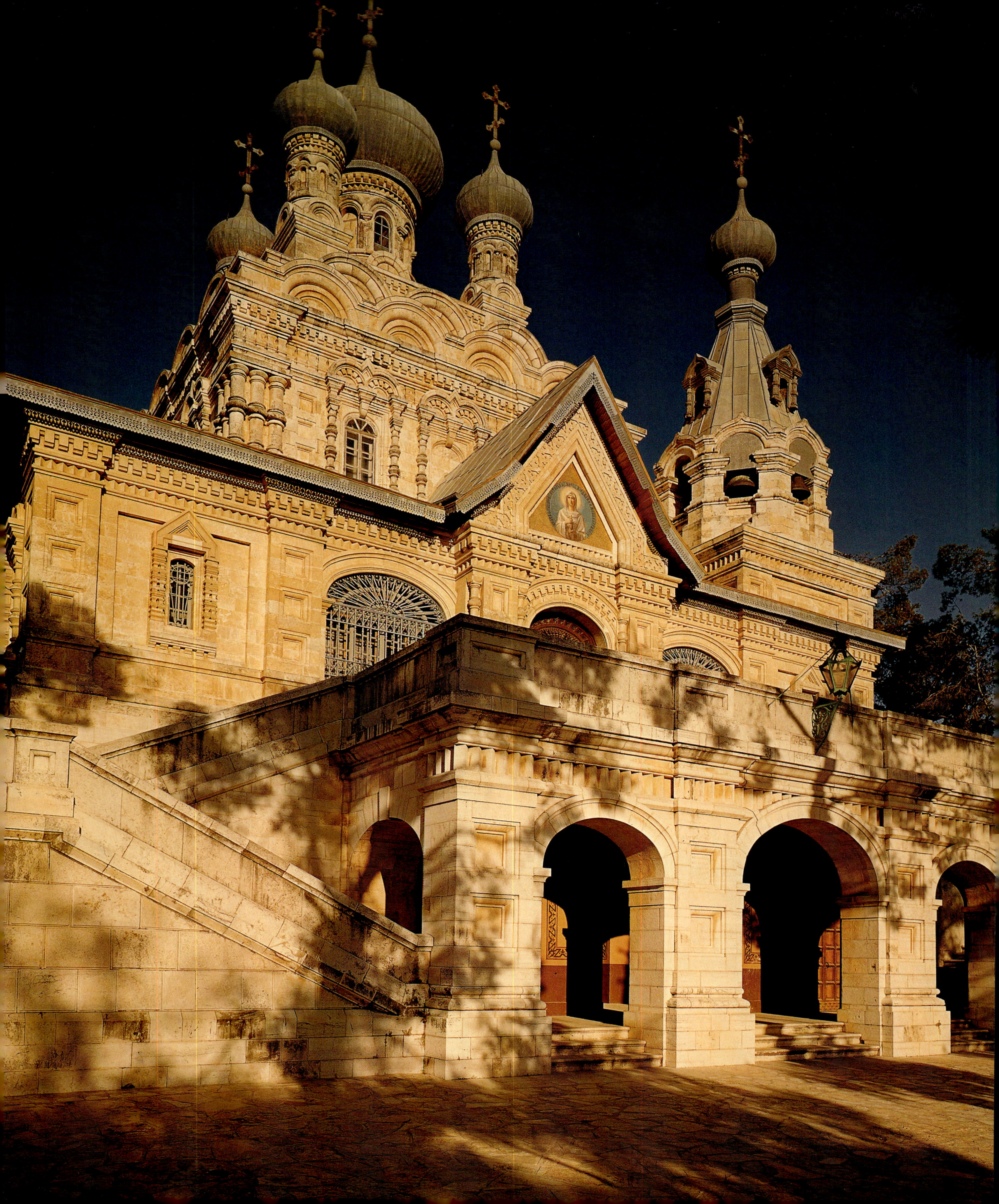

Russian Orthodox Palestine Society, catered to the needs of pilgrims from the aristocracy. Behind the symmetrical Renaissance façade, the twenty-five rooms offered elegant appointments and, in some cases, great luxury, with Persian carpets, heavy curtains, and lace bed trimmings. Two towerlike lavatory structures—the same type as those found at the Germans' Jesus Hilfe Leprosarium and in two of the early Jewish neighborhoods—stood in the courtyard and joined the second floor of the main building by way of a bridge. An ornate Baroque tower built above the chapel gave Grand Duke Sergei its signature "trademark." Today the hostel, which belongs to the Russian Orthodox Church, is used by the Israeli Ministry of Agriculture and the Society for the Protection of Nature. The Holy Trinity and the Mission Residence also belong to the Russian Orthodox Church, whereas the other buildings in the Russian Compound became property of the Jewish State by terms of a 1965 agreement.

Two Russian structures elsewhere in the city also deserve mention. One of them, a distinctive landmark on the Mount of Olives, is the Mary Magdalene Church, founded by Tsar Alexander III in memory of his mother, Marie of Hesse-Darmstadt. The structure, with its seven gilded onion domes, echoing those on the Cathedral of the Holy Trinity and, again, evoking Russian churches of the 15th-17th centuries, was designed by D. Greim, a major figure in 19th-century Russian architecture. Consecrated in 1888, it became, thirty-one years later, the burial place of Grand Duchess Elizabeta Feodorovna, murdered in 1918 during the Bolshevik Revolution. She had commissioned the art work in the church and been present at the consecration, along with her husband, Grand Duke Sergei Alexandrovich, himself murdered in the 1905 Revolution.

In Ein Karem, traditional birthplace of John the Baptist, stands a convent in the style and colors of a Russian village. Called Moskobiyeh by the local Arabs, most of the forty or so buildings, scattered over an area of 50 acres lush with pine and cypress, came into being during the 1890s. Here, the nuns live in small houses, of two or three rooms each, crowned by cross vaults supported upon the thick walls characteristic of Jerusalem. The bell tower, the relatively simple church, and the main dining hall at the center of the grounds all have red-painted exterior walls, while those of the private lodgings are in ochre, like houses in Russian villages.

1-3. Gilded onion domes identify the Mary Magdalene Church (1888) on the Mount of Olives, designed by architect D. Greim in a style typical of churches in Russia, such as the Ostankino Church (3), near Moscow, dating from the 16th century.

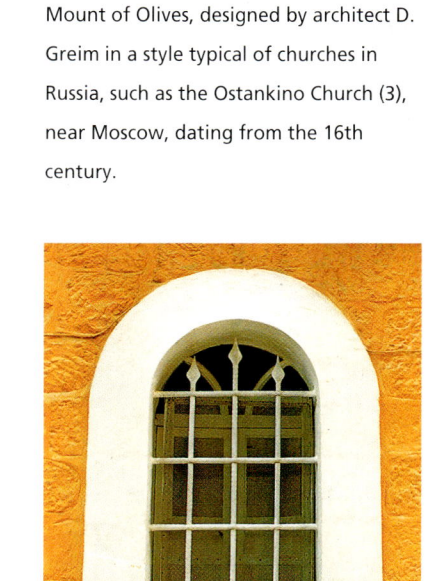

4. Window at the "Moskobiyeh" convent in the Ein Karem neighborhood (built in the 1890s). Ochre is widely used on buildings in Russia, though there construction is with timber, not stone.

1-3. Oxford in Jerusalem: St. George's College and Cathedral (built 1895-1912) emulate the English collegiate Gothic style of the 14th and 15th centuries. Architect Jeffery's overall design evokes New College in Oxford, while the bell tower is almost a dead ringer for its counterpart at Oxford's Magdalen College.

The English

British policy in Palestine from the late 18th century until World War I aimed to preserve Ottoman rule and thus prevent a conquest of the Ottoman Empire by another European Power. The local activities of the Anglican Church were carried out in the Old City largely by missionary societies whose ramified educational, medical, and religious services did much to win Great Britain sympathy among the Arab population. The British then turned those feelings to political advantage in the early 20th century as they consolidated their hold upon areas close to the strategic Suez Canal. However, the Jewish community, which London hoped would help further its interests in the region, did not appreciate the missionaries' attempts to convert them in accordance with millenarian beliefs.

There was no single identifiable "English style" of building in Jerusalem, perhaps because the individuals and institutions of Great Britain, unlike their continental counterparts, were not subject to the policies of a central national or established church authority. St. George's College might almost have been lifted from Oxford or Cambridge and placed on Nablus Road, close to the Old City, whereas the English Mission Hospital, with its connecting pavilions, exemplified colonial architecture such as could be found almost anywhere in the British Empire. Meanwhile, St. John's Ophthalmic Hospital, as the name suggests, recalled British structures on the island of Malta, where the Knights of St. John had governed for more than two centuries. Other buildings, notably the residence of Consul James Finn, conformed to local practice, displaying no distinctively English features whatever.

The St. George's College and Cathedral complex, situated about half a mile north of Damascus Gate, trained Anglican clerics for missionary work and served as a boys' and girls' school. Designed by George Jeffrey, the Government Architect in Cyprus, on commission from a missionary society ("Jerusalem and the East Mission"), the complex was dedicated in 1912, seventeen years after construction had first got underway. With its archetypically English name, St. George's evoked Eng-

136

3

lish collegiate Gothic of the late Middle Ages, particularly Oxford's New College, dating from 1379. The nucleus of the structure, which visitors reach after passing through a fine gate-tower, is a square atrium, or quadrangle, to which the buildings are attached. The structural material is local limestone, although wood was used in the church interior to enhance the acoustics. The most important structure was the Cathedral Church of St. George the Martyr, styled in the Neo-Romanesque and Neo-Gothic manner. The 1912 bell tower (109 feet, or 33 meters, high) recalls the tower at Magdalen College, Oxford.

Another missionary group, the London Jews Society, sponsored the construction of the English Mission Hospital (1901) on Prophets Street, one of the city's most prestigious areas at the turn of the century, when European consulates, hospitals, and other agencies clustered there. Proximity to key Jewish neighborhoods also made the location important for the missionary activists. The hospital had been operating in the Old City since 1844, but only after much cajoling, and even intercession by Britain's Deputy Foreign Secretary and Ambassador in Constantinople, did the Ottoman authorities issue a *firman* allowing the institution to expand to the New City. Designed by A. Beresford Pite, president of the Royal Institute of British Architects, who visited Jerusalem for the purpose in 1893, the English Mission Hospital consists of seven pavilions joined by a crescent-shaped corridor. The separation between the buildings, which Pite decided upon after scrupulously examining the terrain, produced superb light-ing, ventilation, and isolation, without affecting the convenient functional connection between the different wings. Funding for one of the pavilions came from the Birmingham-based Cadbury family, the chocolate manufacturers. The hospital's missionary activity infuriated leaders of the Jewish community, which for a time boycotted the facility, although some Jewish women evaded the edict by dressing as Muslims. Today, the structure houses the Anglican School, attended mainly by children of diplomats and United Nations personnel.

Very different were the residence and farmstead of British Consul James Finn, who arrived in Jerusalem in 1846, well prepared in Hebrew before setting out. Finn and his wife, Elizabeth Anne, were members of the London Society for Promoting Christianity Among the Jews, and they believed that Christian redemption would come with the return of the Jewish people to their homeland. In 1852 the Finns purchased a large plot, known locally as "Abraham's Vineyard," near the site of the future Schneller Orphanage. The modestly appointed two-story residence the English couple built there in 1855 had the form of a *liwan* house, with a large central hall and rooms on the sides. On the grounds Finn set up an agricultural enterprise, which at its height employed two hundred Jews a day and continued to operate for decades. The principle of education for productive agricultural work, which Finn endeavored to inculcate in the Jews, was quite similar to the ideas embraced by Schneller in his work with Arab children just across the way. Today the site is

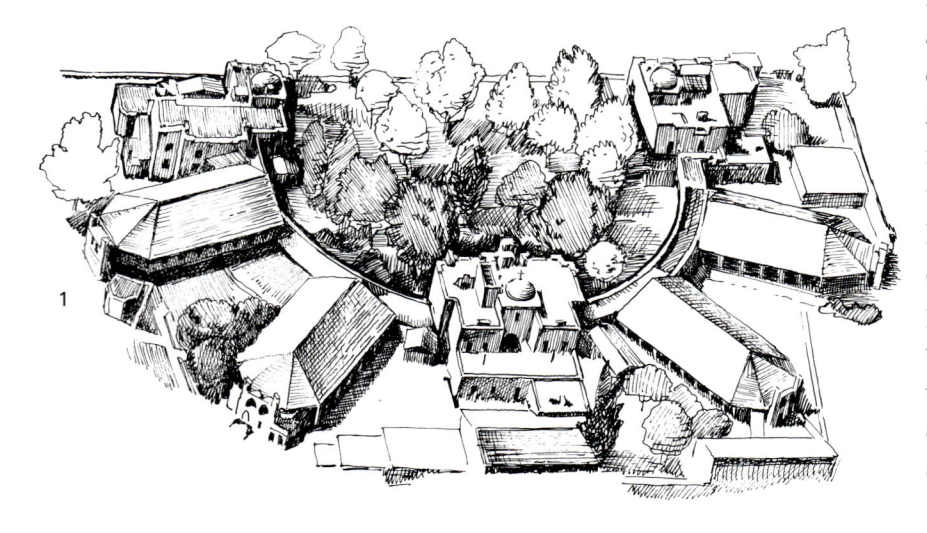

1, 2. The former English Mission Hospital was designed by architect A. Beresford Pite in the form of detached pavilions connected by means of a semicircular corridor, the whole surrounding a large garden. The style is quintessentially British Colonial. Of the seven pavilions, two were for male patients and two for female. Administration occupied the central building, while the pharmacy was on the right and the physician's residence was on the left.

host to an ultra-Orthodox Jewish girls' school, which renovated the main building in keeping with the original design. The new owners, however, took pains to remove a lintel stone engraved with a verse from the New Testament and substitute one bearing a verse from the Old Testament.

The Greek Orthodox and Others

The Greek Orthodox Church, the biggest and oldest of the Christian communities in Jerusalem, is also the principal real-estate owner among them. Its properties, acquired and built mostly in the late 19th century, include some thirty religious buildings in the Old City, land purchased mainly in southwestern Jerusalem, and commercial and other buildings in the New City. Two notable examples of Greek Orthodox construction are the Monastery of the Cross, built in the form of a walled minitown from the 7th century to the 19th and situated in a pastoral valley in western Jerusalem (traditional site of the olive tree used to make Jesus' cross), and a windmill, installed in the 1850s, to grind the wheat grown between the olive trees outside the walls. In 1987, the windmill was converted into an exclusive modern shopping center serving the prestigious Rehavia neighborhood.

Italy failed to take part in the race for influence in Jerusalem during the late 19th century. However, the two buildings that recently formed nation did erect—a hospital (now part of the Ministry of Education and Culture) and the Italian consulate (now offices), both outside the walls—display architectural features of a strongly nationalist character. The hospital in particular, built between 1910 and 1919, resembles the Palazzo Vecchio in Florence, and at the time it contributed much to the creation of Jerusalem's "European" skyline.

4. The Taphos ("grave" in Greek, and denoting the Holy Sepulcher), emblem of the Greek Orthodox Patriarchate, is engraved on the headstone of most of the buildings erected by the Greek Orthodox patriarchate.

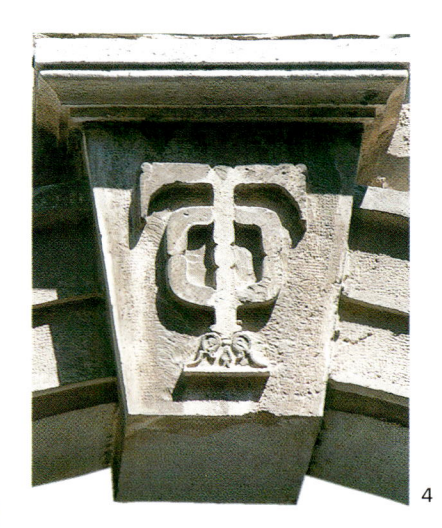

3, 5. The Greek Orthodox Monastery of the Cross, a walled mini-city, displays a variety of architectural styles, befitting its construction across twelve centuries. The perimeter wall and the church inside were built mainly in the 11th century, on Byzantine ruins. The exerior buttresses are later, and the Neo-Baroque bell tower dates from the 19th century.

1-4. Florence in Jerusalem: The Italian hospital built in central Jerusalem by architect Antonio Barluzzi recalls public buildings from medieval Italy, especially the Palazzo Vecchio in Florence (3).

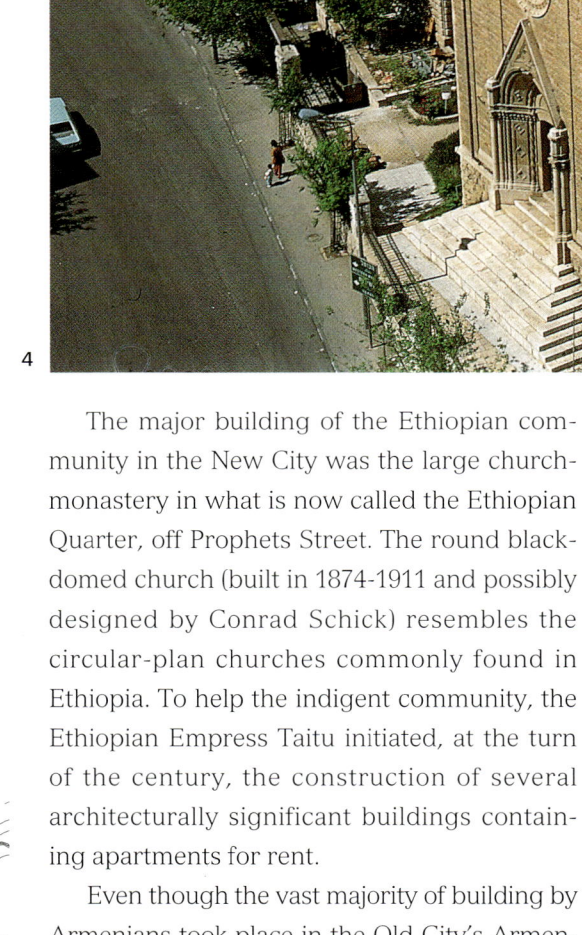

The major building of the Ethiopian community in the New City was the large church-monastery in what is now called the Ethiopian Quarter, off Prophets Street. The round black-domed church (built in 1874-1911 and possibly designed by Conrad Schick) resembles the circular-plan churches commonly found in Ethiopia. To help the indigent community, the Ethiopian Empress Taitu initiated, at the turn of the century, the construction of several architecturally significant buildings containing apartments for rent.

Even though the vast majority of building by Armenians took place in the Old City's Armenian Quarter, the community, one of the oldest in the city, also acquired large areas outside the walls, particularly northwest of Jaffa Gate and along Jaffa Road. Here, Armenians put up shops, offices, and apartments—all for rental purposes—employing a functional design enhanced by Neo-Classical decorative elements. Examples are the long, symmetrical structures opposite City Hall at the beginning of Jaffa Road, erected in 1900-02, and the former Hotel Fast, built in 1891 opposite the northwest corner of the Old City wall by the Armenian Patriarchate. Demolished in 1975, this structure has now been replaced by the Dan-Pearl Hotel.

5-7. Behind a high stone wall and a grand gateway (7) on colorful Ethiopia Street in the heart of Jerusalem is the Ethiopian Church complex from which the entire neighborhood derives its name. The circular-plan church, surrounded by monks' residences, was modeled on churches in Ethiopia, where the Holy of Holies is in a separate structure at the center of the church.

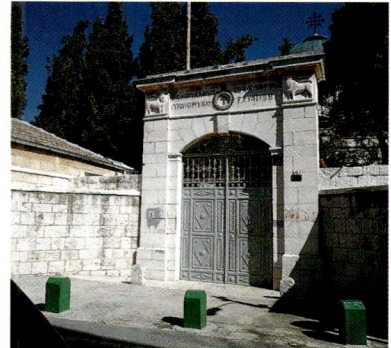

8. The Ethiopian Empress Taitu had this elegant residential building constructed in 1903 in central Jerusalem.

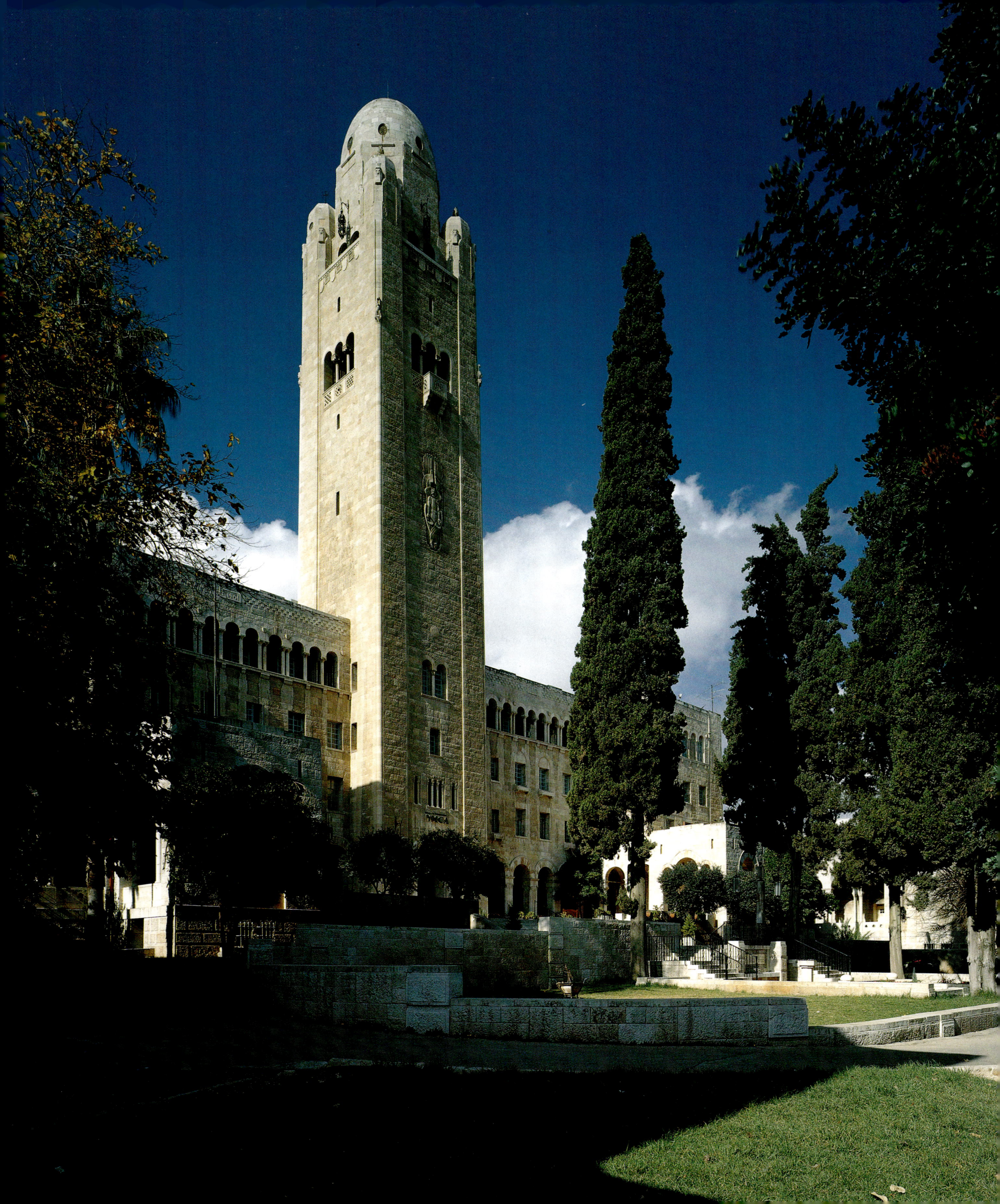

Building a New Jerusalem: The British Mandate
The Emergence of New Architectural Styles and Technologies

Urban Development and Public Buildings

Modern 20th-century Jerusalem began not in the year 1900 but in December 1917, when British troops, under General Edmund Allenby, entered the city following the forced departure of the Ottoman Turks and their German allies. It was a watershed in the ancient city's history. After hundreds of years, Palestine once again enjoyed recognition as a separate political entity. Its new rulers were committed by the Balfour Declaration of November 2, 1917, to "the establishment in Palestine of a national home for the Jewish people." Long a political backwater, Jerusalem now became a capital city for the first time since the Crusader era eight centuries before. The decision making this possible, taken by the British despite the inconvenience of the location for administrative purposes, would have enormous implications for the future development of Jerusalem and the struggle to preserve its distinctive character.

Four hundred years of Ottoman rule had produced slums and decaying markets in the Old City, while the new neighborhoods outside the walls, Arab and Jewish alike, remained isolated and woefully lacking in modern infrastructure. Ronald Storrs, the city's Military Governor, noted that when he took office Jerusalem could boast neither telephones nor automobiles. Its population had dwindled to 53,000 (31,000 Jews, 12,000 Christians, 10,000 Muslims), and its mood had turned grim, owing in large part to the loss of 20,000 inhabitants, dead of disease and starvation during the war years. Storrs' first concern was to make the debilitated city function, toward which goal the British Army supplied essential goods and opened military hospitals to the civilian population.

The special attitude of the British toward Jerusalem transcended the formalities of administration. These overlords knew the Bible and understood the roots of the city's spiritual and symbolic importance. Such awareness also underlay the special approach the British took to town planning and development. Until the arrival of the English, Jerusalem had been dominated by the Roman Catholic and Eastern Orthodox churches, all of them deeply conservative by nature. Now the Anglican Church, representing a more dynamic strain of Western Christianity, would leave its imprint. To the English, by and large, the triumph over the Turks signified the "Last Crusade," a victory that placed the Holy Land and Jerusalem firmly and eternally within the orbit of modern European Christianity.

Not only did the British upgrade the road and power systems; they also solved the generations-old problem of assuring a regular water supply. These among other improvements in the infrastructure paved the way for Jerusalem to grow. During the thirty years of British rule, the city's population increased threefold, to 165,000, and the built-up municipal area expanded apace, largely in the form of new Jewish garden neighborhoods. Meanwhile, the Jewish community itself undertook public construction to provide health, education, and social services. The building boom encompassed every sphere, from office buildings, commercial districts, modern hotels, and sports facilities to industrial plants and religious institutions. It also brought British military installations, including the large Allenby Camp in southern Jerusalem, and important memorial sites, notably the cemetery on Mount Scopus, the burial site of six thousand British Commonwealth soldiers killed in the

1. Thrusting 132 feet (40 meters) high above the main entrance, an impressive tower—one meter wider at the base than at the top—identifies the YMCA building in central Jerusalem (dedicated 1933). Architect Arthur Loomis Harmon's Eclectic Style fused Romanesque, Moorish, Muslim, Oriental, and Western architectural elements.

2. A bas-relief depicting a six-winged seraph from the Vision of Isaiah (Isaiah 6:2-3) projects from the YMCA tower. The 16.5-foot (5-meter) high work is made of seventy-seven stones and is an integral element of the building's main façade.

Middle East during World War I. While erecting relatively few individual buildings, the British administration did much to create the conditions for others to proceed; moreover, they enhanced the overall quality of life by means of public gardens and street lighting. Christian groups continued to build as well, although less intensively than in the late Ottoman Period.

The British laid the foundations for modern town planning in Jerusalem. Over a period of three decades they drew up five plans for the city, the conceptual basis of which was an ordinance issued by Storrs on April 8, 1918, forbidding all new construction within a 2,500-meter (1.6-mile) radius of Damascus Gate except by written permit from the Military Government. (In fact, this was merely a restatement of an existing Ottoman ordinance, the difference being that the British would actually enforce the rule.) The single most important contribution made by the Mandate to the city's appearance may have been another 1918 ordinance, this one banning the exterior use of tin and plaster (as well as other materials later added to the list) in construction, which effectively, if not formally, decreed the use of stone.

Cumulatively, the five master plans outlined what would and would not be permitted in zoning, density of construction, building rights, commercial areas, height of structures, and the use of materials. They also provided for preservation and the regulations governing it. The principle common to all the plans was the separateness of the Old City—the Holy City—and the modern secular city. From this fundamental concept would issue most of the other architectural and planning guidelines for Jerusalem. The British plans were inherently restrictive, their purpose being to prevent an overly rapid and uncontrolled development. They even set standards for sanitation and other interior facilities. Eventually, however, there would be a gradual transition from the ideological "naïveté" that marked the first master plan (drawn up in 1918 at Allenby's request by William McLean, the city engineer for Alexandria) to a more hard-headed, pragmatic approach ostensibly dictated by the city's rapid expansion. As reflected in the final plan (1944), prepared by British architect Henry Kendall, this would permit more construction immediately around the Old City and earmark many of the old Jewish neighborhoods for demolition. Still, most British planners strove to create a monumental urban environment, focusing on the Old City as befitted its sacred character.

The British approach to planning and building in Jerusalem and the importance it placed on the preservation of the city's unique physical character stemmed from a pragmatic grasp of the dynamics involved in modern urban growth, but also from religious sensibilities and the romanticism they fueled. Not only did Storrs found the Pro-Jerusalem Society (1918-22); he also nourished the English vision of a simple and modest historical Jerusalem. Given this, the Military Governor naturally found the monumental European Christian building undertaken during the late years of Ottoman rule decidedly ugly, an aesthetic judgment that may very well have been colored by Great Power politics.

The statutory basis for the orderly planning of Jerusalem was an ordinance of September 1921 that determined municipal zoning and set building limitations. It brought

1. The main residential neighborhoods built during the British Mandate Period, 1918-48.

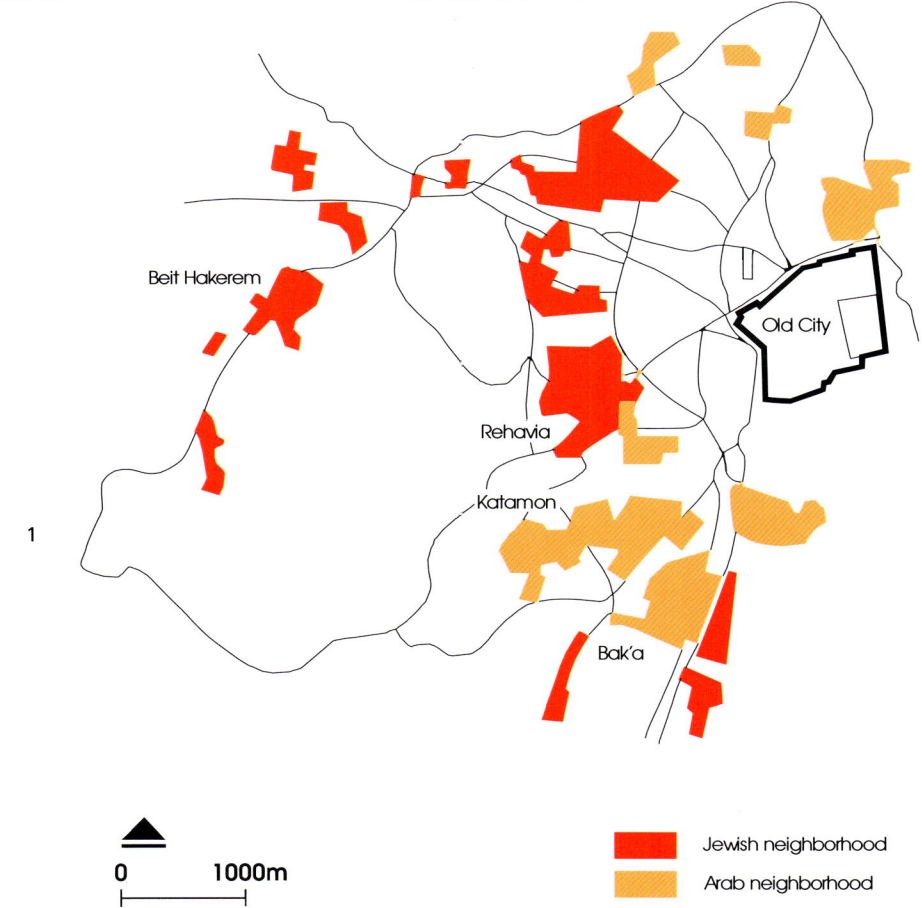

144

major British success in the preservation of the Old City and its immediate environs, in the establishment of the Hebrew University on Mount Scopus (dedicated in 1925), in the development of the Jewish garden neighborhoods and the affluent Arab neighborhoods, and in the creation of a new commercial district at the city center. As this would suggest, the British focused their planning efforts on the exposed hillsides of the New City, which they envisaged as a modern urban metropolis, a counterbalance to both the history-laden Old City and the first Jewish quarters outside the walls.

In the Ottoman period, a building's architectural identity was closely interwoven with ethnic, religious, and national criteria. Under the British this would change, thanks to enhanced security, a boom economy, higher standards of living, and the needs of immigrants pouring in from Europe. Equally favorable to change were new construction technologies utilizing reinforced concrete, metal, and glass. Monumental Christian building gave way to utilitarian secular structures more in keeping with the new era. Nothing better illustrates the trend than the Jewish garden neighborhoods—and, on a smaller scale, the affluent Arab sections—that became the major factor in the city's expansion and development beginning in the 1920s. These areas, made up of private dwellings, each standing on its own plot, with a small garden and relatively broad, tree-lined streets, were a sharp departure from the prewar style of congested Jewish neighborhoods and quarters.

Similarly, the period of the British Mandate saw the development of the downtown area—the "triangle" bounded by Jaffa Road, King George Street, and Ben-Yehuda Street, with its offices, banks, movie theaters, shops, restaurants, and cafés—which remains, in the early 1990s, the city's premier commercial area, although with its pristine luster somewhat dimmed. The rapid growth of the district occurred by virtue of substantial land purchases made in 1922 by Hachsharat Hayishuv, a company acting for the benefit of Jewish development in Palestine. The seller was the Greek Orthodox Patriarchate, which promptly reaped sharp objections from Muslim and Christian circles resistant to the sale of church lands to Jews.

Following parcelation and the purchase of plots by private and public entrepreneurs, both local and overseas, the city center came into being from 1926 to 1937, and then extended southward to present-day King David Street. Construction would generally be allowed right up to the edge of the lot, and demand, together with new technologies, induced the authorities even to permit some commercial building up to a height of eight stories. The result altered the Jerusalem skyline. On the ground, meanwhile, the chief characteristic became the "corridor effect," created by adjoining buildings with a continuous façade (albeit in a variety of architectural styles) erected along the edge of the sidewalk on both sides of a relatively narrow street. This hallmark of Mandate Period construction endowed the emerging downtown section with a "European" look. Key spaces could be defined by pairs of buildings that together created a kind of "gateway" to the center of town. Corner buildings, usually rounded, constituted another important element in corridor-type construction, their effect being to "close" a street corner and thus define an urban intersection. These and many other structures, both downtown and elsewhere, generally displayed the "International Style," the most prevalent of the main architectural styles symptomatic of the Mandate Period, with Moderne, "Return to the East," and Eclectic also favored.

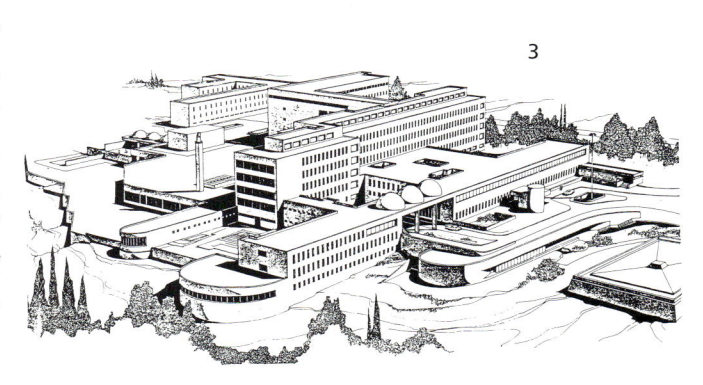

2, 3. Three "Oriental" domes atop the entrance to Hadassah Hospital on Mount Scopus (1938; architect: Erich Mendelsohn) provide a contrast with the predominantly straight-angled geometrical character of the complex and faintly echo the domed roofs in the nearby Arab village. Mendelsohn shunned the use of Oriental elements on his other buildings in Jerusalem.

Functionalism, asymmetry, unadorned façades, modern materials such as concrete, glass, and metal, and the subtle integration of certain local motifs—all distinguished the International Style as practiced in Jerusalem's New City. The style was imported to Palestine by Jewish architects from Germany and Central Europe who, after arriving in the late 1920s and early 1930s, adapted it to local conditions—climate, topography, materials, and technologies. Leading Jewish exponents of the style were Richard Kaufmann and the world-famed architect Erich Mendelsohn, who resided in Jerusalem during the years 1935-41. The British architects, Austen St. Barbe Harrison, who, from 1922 to 1937, served as chief architect for the Mandate administration, and Clifford Holliday, as well as the Christian Arab architects, Spyro Houris, Petassis, and Daoud T'lil, favored the more romantic Oriental styles.

In its Jerusalem version, the International Style is notable above all for its attempt to fracture monolithic masses into smaller blocks and units, often of different heights, thereby echoing the city's terrain of rolling hills. Arab rural building, with its stepped, "broken" appearance, and traditional Old City architecture also proved influential. A striking departure from the past was stone used as an overlay for the concrete construction so fundamental to the International Style in Europe. However, large glass windows, a defining feature in Europe and America, found very limited use in Jerusalem, for obvious climatic and technological reasons. The "strip window," frequently accentuated by a narrow concrete frame or similar device, provided the "streamline" effect, expressing the dynamic vision of progress at the conceptual heart of the new architecture. The flowing line was achieved, particularly on corner buildings, by the use of curved elements such as balconies.

Also adopted was Art Deco, a suavely streamlined, decorative style that in Europe and America triumphed as a popular alternative to the International Style. In Jerusalem, Art Deco showed up most often in variations on the straight line and the circle, as well as in the "rising sun" motif, as worked into window grilles, wrought-iron gates, and banisters used in combination with stonework.

To highlight the Oriental context of their works, some architects turned, once more, to local construction for motifs such as the dome and the arch. The three concrete domes at the entrance to Hadassah Hospital on Mount Scopus, designed in the mid-1930s by Eric Mendelsohn, represent a subtle modern echo of the Arab village of Issawiyeh, just across the valley, and a continuation of the domed roofs atop the National Library and the chemistry building at the Hebrew University. Unlike nearby Augusta Victoria Hospice, the project blends with its remarkable setting, which has civilization on one side in the shape of Old and New Jerusalem and on the other the awesome wilderness of the Judean Desert, which, in Mendelsohn's words, "leads straight to eternity." The courtyards, porches, and windows take optimal advantage of the spectacular views.

When it opened, in 1938, with three hundred beds, Hadassah was considered the last word in hospital design and an impressive example of International Style functionalism, its dominant straight lines broken, softened, or underscored by such architectural elements as a dramatic perch jutting over the desert landscape. Vertical alignment of the stone cladding stressed its essence as veneer. From 1948 until the reunification of Jerusalem in 1967, the hospital remained out of service, and the building deteriorated badly. Following a major renovation and modernization,

1. The semicircular "National Institutions" complex (1928-36; architect: Yohanan Rattner) combines the International Style with Classical elements. The leaders of the state-in-the-making orated from the representational balcony which sets off the main entrance.

carried out by architect Ya'akov Rechter, who preserved the original design, Hadassah Hospital reopened in 1979.

Another prominent International Style structure that had to be partially rebuilt—following the detonation of a car bomb planted by Arabs during the 1948 war—was the "National Institutions" complex at the edge of the affluent Rehavia neighborhood. Designed by Yohanan (Eugen) Rattner and erected from 1928 to 1936, the curved, triple-wing structure, with its large open courtyard for public assemblies, served as headquarters for the Zionist leadership of the "state-in-the-making." The use of straight lines gave it a functional yet fittingly dignified appearance. The modest character of National Institutions contrasted with that of other buildings put up at the time—the Muslim's Palace Hotel and the YMCA among them—by other ethnic or religious groups.

The Moderne Style in architecture refers to buildings erected since World War I that incorporate decorative elements typical of their era. Moderne, in contrast to the International Style, is not an innovative form, as can be seen in the Central Post Office (1934-38) on Jaffa Road, close to the Old City. Designed by Harrison in collaboration with Percy Winter, the Central Post Office is one of three representational buildings erected in the 1930s across from the Russian Compound (the others being the Generali Building and Bank Leumi, the latter formerly the Anglo-Palestine Bank). It is institutional and functional, a broad rectangular block with clear lines and a symmetrical, protruding main façade. The exterior is finished in different types of stone reminiscent of Mamluk construction (1260-1517). Combined with 1930s horizontal streamlines, the cladding creates an interesting and original old/new effect. The interior, thanks to its height and green-marble finish, smacks of colonial grandeur.

Separated from the Central Post Office by a broad staircase, the large Generali Building of 1936 (named for the Italian insurance company Assicurazioni Generali, which commissioned it) combines Neo-Classical elements with features of the Moderne Style in a design prepared by the Italian architect Marcello Piacenini. On the ground floor finished in rusticated stone, an arcade houses shops, leaving the upper stories for offices. Construction was carried out by the once renowned contracting firm De Farro, which also built Rockefeller Museum and City Hall.

During the Mandate Period, a host of motives—nostalgic, nationalist, religious—

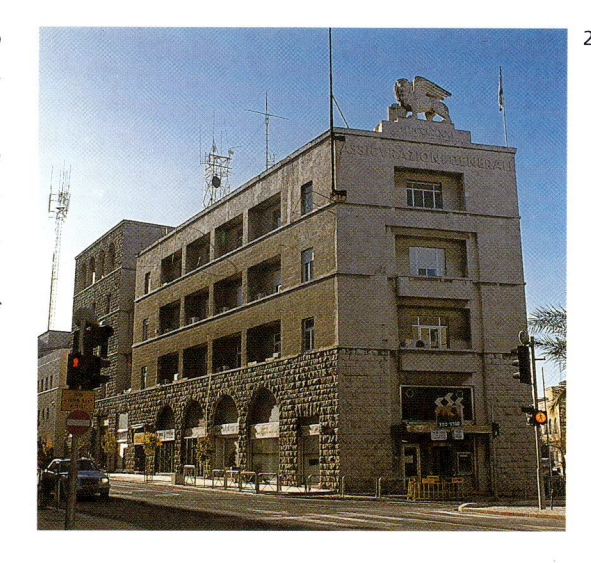

2. The winged lion atop the Generali Building (1934-36; architect: Marcello Piacenini) in downtown Jerusalem is the trademark of the Italian insurance company that commissioned the edifice.

3, 4. Main entrance façade of Jerusalem's Central Post Office (1938). Architect Austen St. Barbe Harrison used black basalt strips on the façades to emphasize the horizontal line characteristic of the International Style.

produced a distinctive building style that reflected not only ancient sources but also strong "Return to the East" sentiments. Romanticism, the style's principal motivating force, is most evident in British institutional construction, notably Government House. Here the design, with its prominent use of Middle Eastern motifs, expressed the emotional attachment of the English to Palestine and Jerusalem, to the Bible, and to the Crusader Kingdom. Among the architects working in this mode was an English Jew, Benjamin Chaikin, who designed projects for the Jewish establishment as well as for English-speaking families.

The dome, frequently a premier signifier of Middle Eastern building, appears in its most authentic form on Government House and Rockefeller Museum. However, on St. Andrew's Church of Scotland (a work of 1930 designed by architect Clifford Holliday) and on the Mount Scopus National Library (designed by architect Chaikin, together with Fritz Kornberg), the dome assumes a more modern character. Another common regional element, the arch, often serves to define doors, windows, colonnades, and inner spaces. English architects also conceived a great fondness for cross vaults, minaretlike towers, and Muslim decorative elements such as the octagon. Ceramic work as well caught the fancy of the English, who, in 1919, brought a celebrated Armenian artist, David Ohannessian, from Turkey to do restoration work on the Dome of the Rock. Ohannessian then opened a workshop in the city and produced the colorful glazed ceramics that adorn the fireplace in Government House and appear in other major British projects. Christian-Arab architects such as Spyro Houris and Petassis also exploited the decorative potential of ceramic tiles, primarily around doors and windows, in the luxurious villas they designed for their affluent Arab clients in neighborhoods like Talbiyeh and Sheikh Jarrah. Finally, Mamluk architecture provided an additional source of inspiration for the British. So successfully did Harrison and Holliday blend historical elements with local ones that a conscious effort must sometimes be made to accept their buildings as modern, eclectic creations with their own distinctive style.

One of the most striking of the eclectic creations is Government House, the official residence of the British High Commissioner, built from 1929 to 1933 in a magnificent setting on a 16-acre hilltop site in southern Jerusalem. The building was designed by Harrison, who in the course of three years drew up five alternative plans in an effort to satisfy the Colonial Office in London, which raised objections to the structure's size and cost. The end result is a felicitous interplay between local Eastern and imported European elements.

Monumental in character, but composed of "broken" and stepped units, Government House recalls buildings of the same period in England, at the same time that it also evokes

1-4. Modesty and simplicity characterize St. Andrew's Church of Scotland (architect: Clifford Holliday), which integrates Eastern and Western architectural features: a simple rectangular tower, white concrete domes, arches, colored windows, and Armenian ceramic tiles.

5-8. Government House in southern Jerusalem (dedicated 1933) makes impressive eclectic use of Muslim and Western architectural elements. Architect Harrison placed a sunken courtyard (6) by the main entrance façade.

ture on the grounds is a cemetery for pet dogs, dedicated by High Commissioner Arthur Wauchope in the 1930s.

The elaborate stonework at Government House and the intricate details of the interior design demonstrate masterful planning and execution. The impressive ballroom boasted large chandeliers and portraits of British monarchs in heavy gilded frames, as well as a memorably huge fireplace decorated with some of the elements of an Arab village such as Silwan, spilling down the northern slopes of the Kidron Valley, which Government House overlooks. Fittingly, Government House was constructed of stone quarried largely at the site itself. On its southern and most impressive side were a ballroom and lounge (with an adjoining billiard room), while above them an octagonal tower contained the High Commissioner's private apartment. In addition to the Judean Desert and the Dead Sea on one flank and Jerusalem itself on the other, the tower offers a view of the lovely sunken courtyards and gardens immediately below. At the center of the crescent-shaped formal garden on the eastern side stands an octagonal fountain of a type found in North African palaces. A rather more unusual fea-

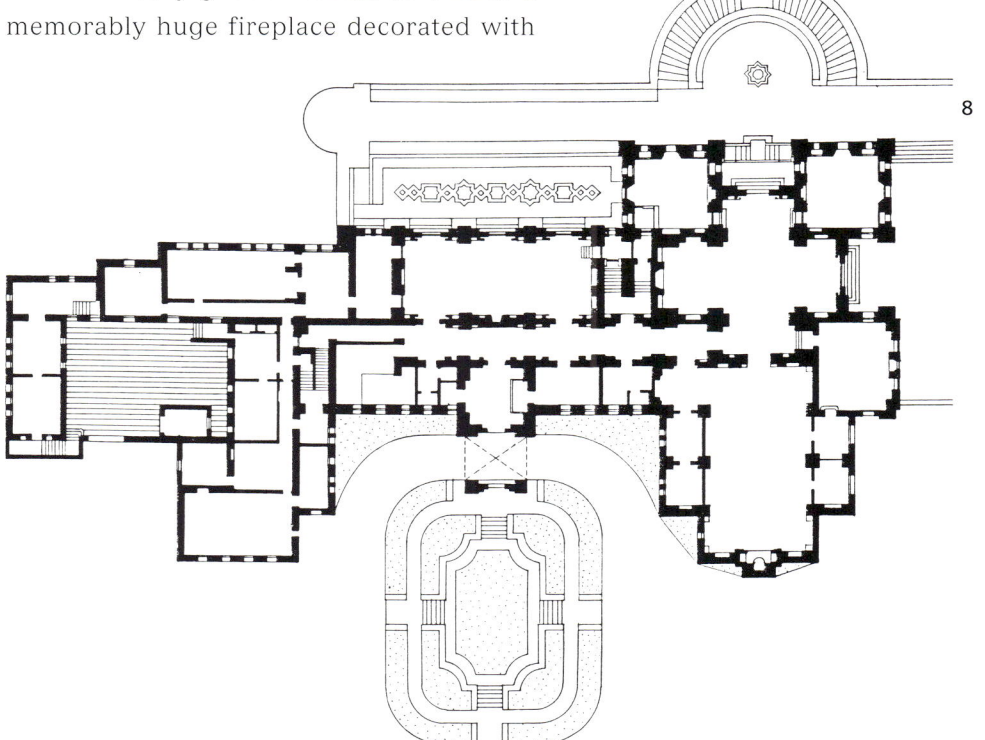

1-4. Innermost of the three courtyards that adorn Rockefeller Museum evokes the Alhambra in Granada. An octagonal tower (1) rises above the main entrance, and Armenian ceramic tiles decorate the fountain in the central courtyard.

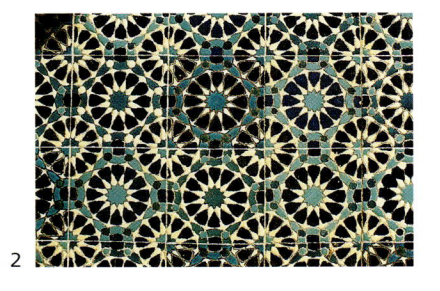

5-8. The main entrance to the YMCA building (5). The "zigzag" motif on the lamps is typical of the fashionable Art Deco style. Oriental Byzantine grandeur, incorporating decorative elements from Muslim art and architecture, mark the concert hall (7) and the entrance lobby (8).

Ohannessian's colorful Armenian ceramic tiles. Guests—mainly diplomats and members of the Jewish and Arab elite—danced to music played by a police or military band located on an upper gallery hung between the ballroom and the dining room. Since 1948 Government House has been occupied by the United Nations, which places it off limits to the general public. However, Israelis and tourists flock to the magnificent promenades that were constructed nearby in the late 1980s.

A Harrison creation that is accessible to the public is the fortresslike Rockefeller Museum, standing on an 8-acre plot opposite the northeast corner of the Old City. The museum, opened in 1938 and the only cultural institution built at British initiative during the Mandate Period, is named for the American oil tycoon John D. Rockefeller, Jr., who donated $2 million toward its construction. The focal point of the grounds is the inner courtyard, evocative of the 14th-century Alhambra Palace in Spain. Western and Eastern elements blend seamlessly in the museum's design. While influenced by contemporaneous public building in England, Harrison also took inspiration from monumental structures of the Elizabethan and Jacobean periods. Allusions, both structural and decorative, to Muslim and Oriental architecture also abound. Besides the courtyard, there are, for example, the pyramid-shaped buttresses at the outer corners of the tower.

In Rockefeller Museum, the construction technology combined the modern, in the form of reinforced concrete, and the traditional, meaning stone. As at Government House and the YMCA, execution and finish were carried out with meticulous care. Since the reunification of Jerusalem in 1967, Rockefeller Museum, dedicated to culture in Palestine from prehistoric times until the year 1700, has been administered by the Israel Museum.

The West Jerusalem headquarters of the YMCA (Young Men's Christian Association), which stands on a 7.5-acre plot, acquired from the Greek Orthodox Church, directly across the street from the King David Hotel, constitutes one of the city's finest buildings and probably the world's most spectacular YMCA center. It was designed by the noted American architect Arthur Loomis Harmon (while he simultaneously planned the Empire State Building in New York) and opened in 1933 after seven years of construction. The building consists of three principal structures—the main, central unit with its lofty bell-tower, a sports wing, and a wing for meetings and concerts. Connected by covered passageways, they create a harmonious architectural whole symbolizing the YMCA's triple commitment—to spirit, mind, and body—and alluding to the Holy Trinity. The eclectic design incorporates motifs from a range of cultures—Byzantine, Romanesque, and Muslim.

On the first floor is an exact replica of the room in London where George Williams and his colleagues founded the YMCA in 1844. The two upper floors function as an eighty-room hotel. The concert hall, which has a massive organ, is decorated in Byzantine style. Its immense dome contains twelve windows, representing the Twelve Tribes of Israel, the Twelve Disciples of Jesus, and the Twelve Followers of the Prophet Muhammad. Hanging from the dome, a splendid chandelier features the Crescent, the Cross, and the Star of David. Indeed, the entire building abounds with symbolic decorations expressing its central message of peace and harmony, grounded in a deep attachment to the Scriptures.

The "Return to the Sources" concept also played a role in the actual construction of the YMCA headquarters, a project on which Jewish builders and stonemasons worked alongside Christians and Muslims. For the altar in the small chapel beneath the main foyer, twelve rough, unhewn stones were used, collected from around the site of ancient Beit-El, near Jerusalem, to commemorate the altar built by Jacob (Genesis 35). For the Communion Room in the tower, architect Adamson, who was in charge of construction, received special permission to remove large stones from Solomon's Quarries (Zedekiah's Cave), traditionally believed to have been the source of the material used to build the First Temple. Adamson even went as far afield as Damascus and Istanbul in order personally to examine

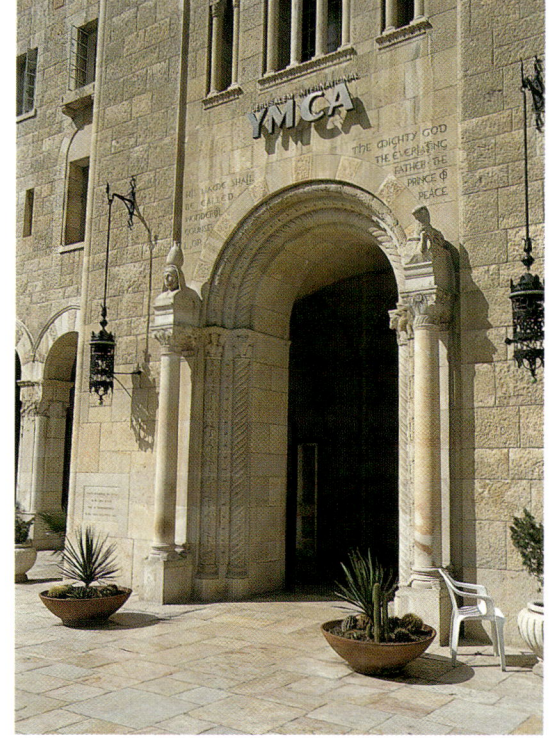

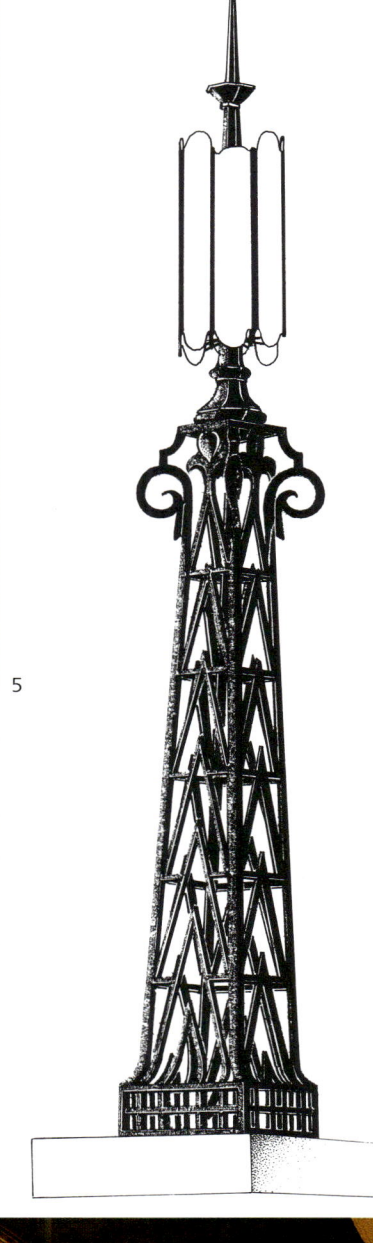

151

the original elements he wished to emulate. In Damascus he even succeeded in purchasing a magnificent old ceiling, which was dismantled and reinstalled. General Allenby dedicated the building on April 18, 1933, emphasizing its contribution to the improvement of relations among Jews, Muslims, and Christians.

An interesting attempt to create a Jewish national architecture—a bridge between ancient sources and modernity—was the Great Palestine Diskin Orphanage (1927) on the city's western outskirts, designed by Tel Aviv architect I.Z. Tabatchnik. Eclecticism, monumentalism, and Classicism all went into the design. With its pronounced symmetry and large scale, the building recalls some of the European Christian edifices erected in the late 19th century, such as Ratisbonne vocational school. Indeed, Tabatchnik drew quite consciously on that architecture, noting, for example, that the stately semicircular staircase on the main façade should be constructed "in a manner appropriate to a Christian building." Overall, however, he strove to produce an authentically "Hebraic" style inspired by ancient sources, specifically the Temple. Unfortunately, economic hardships forced the architect to abridge his original plan, which included a crenellated roofline to evoke the Old City wall and a structure echoing Absalom's Tomb in the Kidron Valley. The most impressive of the elements that survive are pillarlike palm trees, carved in stone at the corners of the eastern façade, almost to the full height of the building. The rising sun, a popular Art Deco feature symbolizing progress and vision, gives decorative shape to the door grille at the main entrance.

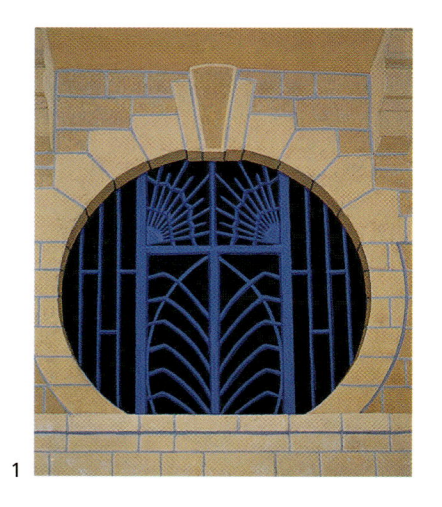

1-3. "Rising sun" motifs on a door of Diskin Orphanage (1927) symbolize vision and progress, while the stone palms carved into the corners of the building reflect architect I. Z. Tabatchnik's attempt to create an authentic local "Hebraic" architecture.

Some buildings from the Mandate Period seem to be an architectural continuation of the Eclectic Style that characterized the late Ottoman era. These are mainly, though by no means solely, Christian religious institutions, for certain Jewish and Muslim buildings—both public and private—also display a mixture of Greco-Roman, Renaissance, and later elements, notably Romanesque, Gothic, and Moorish. A striking feature is the use of columns styled according to the Classical orders (Corinthian, Ionian, Doric) to embellish doors and windows.

A prime example of the Eclectic Style is the former Palace Hotel, designed by the Turkish architect Nahas Bey, and one of the few Arab buildings of the time that was not a private residence. Erected at the initiative of the Supreme Muslim Council, the Palace opened in 1929. Architecturally, it is striking both for the sense of mass it exudes yet also for its fine details. Thus, the façades drip with decorative "stalactites" that evoke Mamluk and Moorish architecture. The festive mood of the exterior continues in the lobby, which soars to the building's full height, all of it irradiated from above by a large octagonal skylight.

Caught without the means to run a luxury hotel like the Palace, which boasted 145 rooms, 45 of them with baths, as well as 3 elevators and central heating, the Muslim authorities leased it to a leading Jewish hotelier, George Barsky, who for a time also ran the Hotel Fast. However, economic hardship and competition from the nearby King David Hotel, inaugurated in 1931, forced the Palace to close. The Mandate government then leased the structure for offices, and since 1948 the tenant has been the Israeli Ministry of Industry and Commerce.

The same architectural styles found in public and commercial construction also turned up, albeit on a different scale, in the many residential neighborhoods built during

4-7. Impressive use of the Eclectic Style on the former Palace Hotel (architect: Nahas Bey). The Arab inscription on the stone plaque atop the building notes the year (1929), and contains a verse from the Koran.

1-3. The sense of splendor in the King David Hotel, built in 1931, derives from the "Biblical" style of its public halls, produced by ornamentation borrowed from Assyrian, Hittite, and Phoenician cultures, and from Muslim art. Architect: Emile Vogt; interior decorator: G.G. Hufschmid.

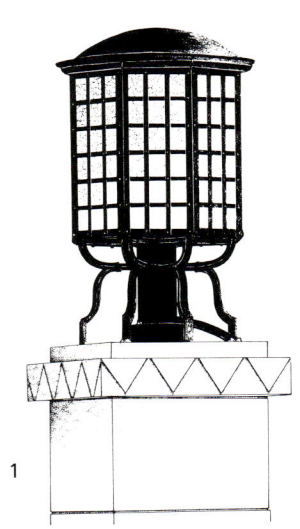

the Mandate Period. Indeed, the new districts dominated the city's expansion under the British. No fewer than fifty neighborhoods, two-thirds of them Jewish, were erected, reflecting the dramatic increase in population. Although one or two ultra-Orthodox sections virtually cloned the row-type perimeter quarters from the late Ottoman Period, something radically fresh came with six Jewish "garden neighborhoods" founded in the 1920s and, concurrently, with several affluent Arab neighborhoods established in southern Jerusalem.

Another group of neighborhoods, alike both architecturally and demographically, emerged in the city's northern section. Development began in the area about the Schneller compound, with the establishment of the Geulah neighborhood, so called for the Hebrew word meaning "redemption," since the land had been "redeemed" from two Christian missionaries, Schneller and the British Consul James Finn. Here, and in the nearby Makor Baruch and Sanhedriya neighborhoods, the streets had a uniform "European" look. The attached, facing three- and four-story buildings in the Geulah section created the same "corridor" effect as in the city center.

A major innovation in housing construction during the Mandate Period was the apartment house. Beginning in the 1930s, a large demand developed in the city for spacious flats in modern buildings similar to those fashionable at the time in Europe. The builders were mostly well-off Jews or Arabs who undertook the construction as an investment and let the apartments for income. At the same time there were also organized groups who built for their own use. The buildings generally stood two or three stories high and contained between four and twelve flats on both sides of a common staircase. Most of the apartment buildings were located in the city center and in the neighborhoods of Rehavia, Geulah, Talbiyeh, Katamon, and Abu-Tor. A few larger apartment houses, with several entrances, also went up at this time—notably Beit Hama'alot downtown—and offered the first passenger elevators in Jerusalem.

4-7. Built in 1930, the French Consulate building displays formal architecture marked by pronounced symmetry and the emblem of the French Republic on the main door (5). The Moderne thrust of the period is seen also in an Art Deco octagonal window. Architect: M. Favier.

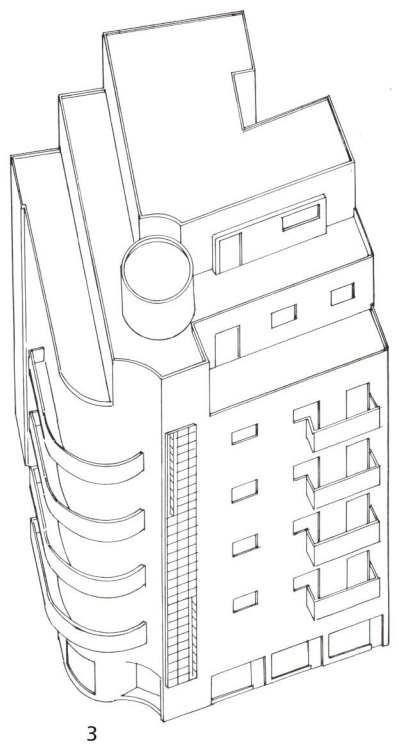

1-4. Flowing "streamlines" epitomize the International Style, seen in curved balconies and a vertical window that covers the entire stairwell. The large glass areas reflect the period's sense of technological progress. These two apartment buildings, Beit Hama'alot (1, 2) and Makower House (3, 4), erected in central Jerusalem in the 1930s, were designed by architects Alexander Friedman and Meir Rubin.

Jewish Garden Neighborhoods

These neighborhoods form the basis of Jerusalem's modern residential development, just as their planning rested on solid ideological premises. They were the expression par excellence of the "conquest" of Jerusalem by the Zionist ethos. The Beit Hakerem neighborhood (1922) rose in an area then quite isolated on the city's western edge, and properly so since it was intended to foster "pioneering." A contemporary description characterized it as "an urban settlement [based] on a new foundation, redemption of the land." The new sections represented a clean break, conceptually and physically, from the cramped, ghettolike traditional neighborhoods. The Jewish "urban pioneers" could thus pursue a lifestyle commensurate, in their eyes, with the spirit of the time. Land for the new neighborhoods was purchased by Hachsharat Hayishuv (Palestine Land Development Company), not only from churches but also from individuals, both Arabs and Christians.

For ideological reasons, construction was carried out mainly by groups of workers belonging to the newly formed Histadrut, the Federation of Jewish Labor. Fully planned before construction began, the neighborhoods all conformed to a basic design prepared by Richard Kaufmann, an architect well informed about similar neighborhoods in pre-World War I England and Germany. The essential pattern was a symmetrical road grid with a pedestrian boulevard at the center concluding in a public building. The scheme applied for Talpiot (1922), Rehavia (1924), Kiryat Moshe (1925), and Bayit Vegan (1928). Beit Hakerem, however, had two central axes. (Makor Hayim, the sixth garden neighborhood, built in 1924 in southern Jerusalem, also came from a plan created by Kaufmann but in a totally different format, and for various reasons this neighborhood did not develop like the others.) The large plots left room to grow a few staples behind the house. Each district had a few local shops as well as some community institutions such as a school and a synagogue.

Construction was supervised in some neighborhoods by local committees, to prevent things from getting out of hand. However, virtually every district fell victim to a common syndrome, in which scarce resources and tight credit undercut the initial boom and brought retreat. Indeed, from 1926 to 1928 a severe economic recession throughout Palestine forced a slowdown in development. Only Beit Hakerem and Rehavia A (the neighborhood's first phase) turned out almost exactly as Kaufmann had planned. Rehavia too enjoyed a degree of good luck, in the social makeup of its inhabitants—largely middle-class professionals—which could be accounted for by the quarter's proximity to both the National Institutions and the city center. Architecturally as well, Rehavia is the most interesting of the garden neighborhoods, its one-family houses and small apartment buildings displaying the characteristics of the International Style.

Rehavia A was the "classic" garden neighborhood, which rose on 30 acres of land bought from the Greek Orthodox Church, then strapped for funds because World War I had stanched the flow of cash from Russia. Decades later, Jerusalem planners were still emulating the original Rehavia model in both the scale and the character of such new neighborhoods as the post-1967 Ramot Eshkol. The symmetrical road grid, realized fully in Rehavia, facilitates access, which in turn per-

5. "Villa Leah" (Abcarius House), built in 1934 in the prestigious Rehavia neighborhood, displays a curved wing and concrete roofs, typical of the International Style. Architects: Dan and Raphael Ben-Dor.

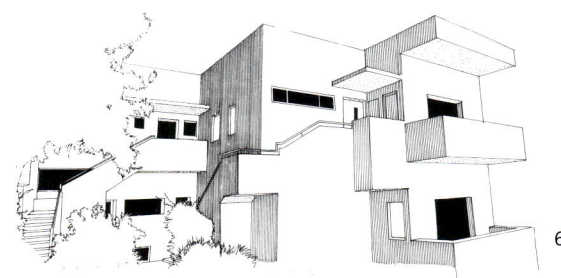

6, 7. An "urban kibbutz" is evoked by two cooperative housing projects in Rehavia. Me'onot Ovdim A (6) designed by architects Abraham and Zippora Cherniak, and Me'onot Ovdim B (7) by architect Dov Kutchinsky.

8. The concept of the symmetrical road grid was realized by architect Richard Kaufmann in his plan for the Rehavia A garden neighborhood.

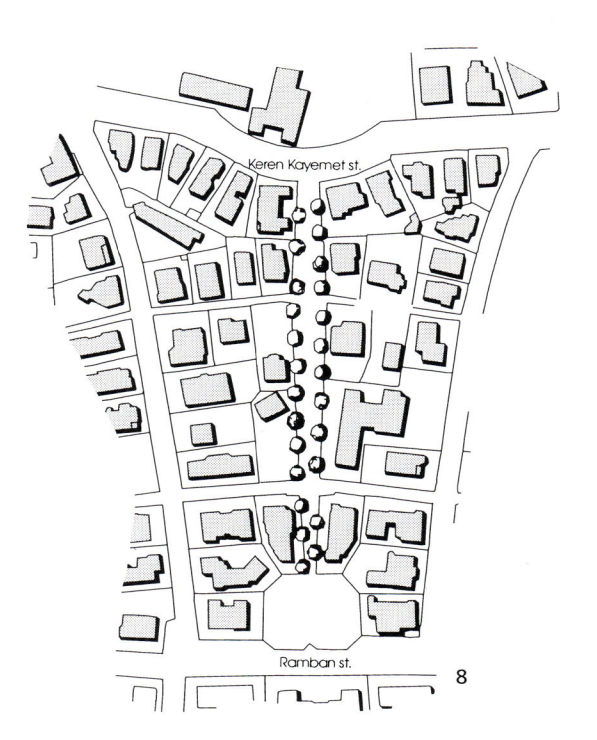

1-4. Curving lines with an accentuated horizontal thrust characterize International Style architecture in residential dwellings built in Rehavia and Talbiyeh in the 1930s.

2. The former Aghion House, designed by architect Richard Kaufmann, is now the official residence of the Prime Minister.

4. Entrance to a Talbiyeh apartment building. Architect: Zoltan Harmat.

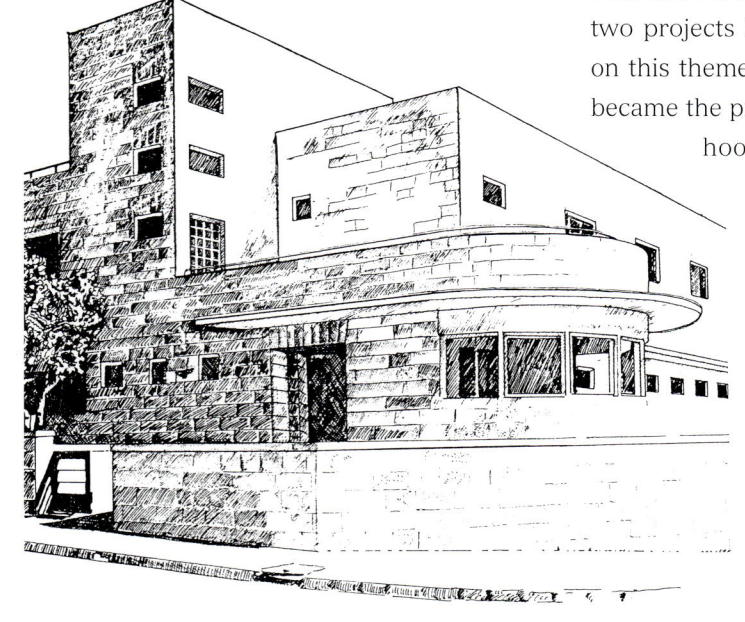

mits a high level of services. It also separates personal and public spheres, thereby enhancing individual privacy. Rehavia owed its "rural" appearance mainly to its overall garden-neighborhood plan and abundant greenery. Some of the houses were made of concrete finished in rough stucco, and many were built during the Arab Revolt of 1936-39, which caused a number of quarries to shut down, thereby reducing the supply of stone. At one end of the delightful pedestrian boulevard, the neighborhood's backbone, stands a public building, the Hebrew Gymnasium (high school) designed by Fritz Kornberg, and at the other a public garden. In the absence of its own power system, Rehavia A drew electricity from the nearby Ratisbonne school, which had a generator, and to solve the problem of transportation, the neighborhood ran its own one-bus line, at least for a while.

An interesting innovation in the design of residential construction during the Mandate Period occurred in the two "cooperative" housing projects—Me'onot Ovdim A and B—built in Rehavia, mostly for professionals in various fields and organized on socialist principles, rather like an urban kibbutz. Architecturally, this was embodied in a series of two-story dwellings, each containing a few apartments accessed by separate entrances from a common inner courtyard, an element drawn from the New City's first Jewish neighborhoods. Composed of cubelike structures broken by exterior staircases, the architectural proportions and design produced intriguing effects of light and shadow, which combined with the verdant inner courtyard to make the two projects highly successful. In a variation on this theme, trade-union or party affiliation became the pretext for a number of neighborhoods built toward the end of the Mandate Period (and after 1948 as well).

In Rehavia's later sections, most of the houses would be small apartment buildings, one of the factors contributing to the change of character the neighborhood experienced over time. In addition, rapid development of the New City as a whole, an exponential increase in automobile traffic, the invasion of commercial interests seeking office space, and the demolition of some of the original structures, including a few once inhabited by well-known personalities, have all done much to alter the original atmosphere and social fabric of Rehavia.

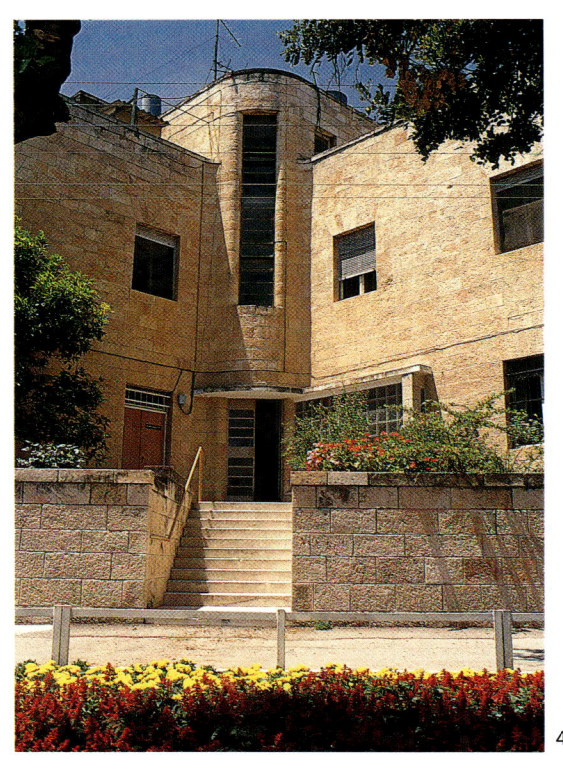

Even more than a neighborhood, Rehavia was a concept, and its story, like that of other Jerusalem quarters, is the story of the individual families living there. The special charm of the district, particularly during its first twenty years, came from the homogeneity of the constituent population. Rehavia was home to many professionals and savants from Central Europe—Germany, Austria, and Czechoslovakia especially—who came to Palestine in the 1930s following the rise of Nazi Germany. The immigrants hired the leading architects of the day and responded eagerly to new design ideas. The architectural map of Rehavia is equally a human map, and the large villas reflect, in addition to personal taste, a certain social and economic status. Those who were less well-to-do, many of them renowned professors such as Gershom Scholem and Hugo Bergman, built simpler homes. Modern-day Rehavia is becoming a "bourgeois" neighborhood without a defining cultural or class identity. Once known as a "Prussian island in an Oriental sea," where the Jerusalem intelligentsia sipped coffee at cafés and discussed—probably in German—the latest book, scandal, or political development, Rehavia in the 1990s remained, in some degree, a "nature preserve" for an all but vanished world.

A walk through Rehavia's tree-lined streets remains an aesthetic treat, its buildings forming a virtual catalogue of Mandate Period architecture. A handful of representative examples follows, beginning with what was probably the first house built in the neighborhood. It belonged to the architect Eliezer Yellin, who, with Wilhelm Hecker, designed a two-story structure in the form of "broken" cubes, highlighted by such motifs as Assyrian columns and a liberal use of arches on the main façade. Yellin's grandfather, Yehoshua, had been one of the seven founders of the Nahalat Shiva neighborhood, and his son, David, a well-known educator, would help found the Zichron Moshe neighborhood. The architect's wife, Thelma, a gifted cellist, organized chamber-music concerts in their home, and emerged as one of the period's leading hostesses.

Max Rosenbaum, a German-Jewish banker, gave Rehavia another "first," a terraced building. Designed in the International Style by architect Heinz Rau and completed in 1939, it had eight apartments.

5-7. The south-facing round glazed bay window on the Schocken Library (1933-36), designed by Erich Mendelsohn, provides illumination that the architect likened to the "light of Rembrandt." Mendelsohn also designed every item of the interior.

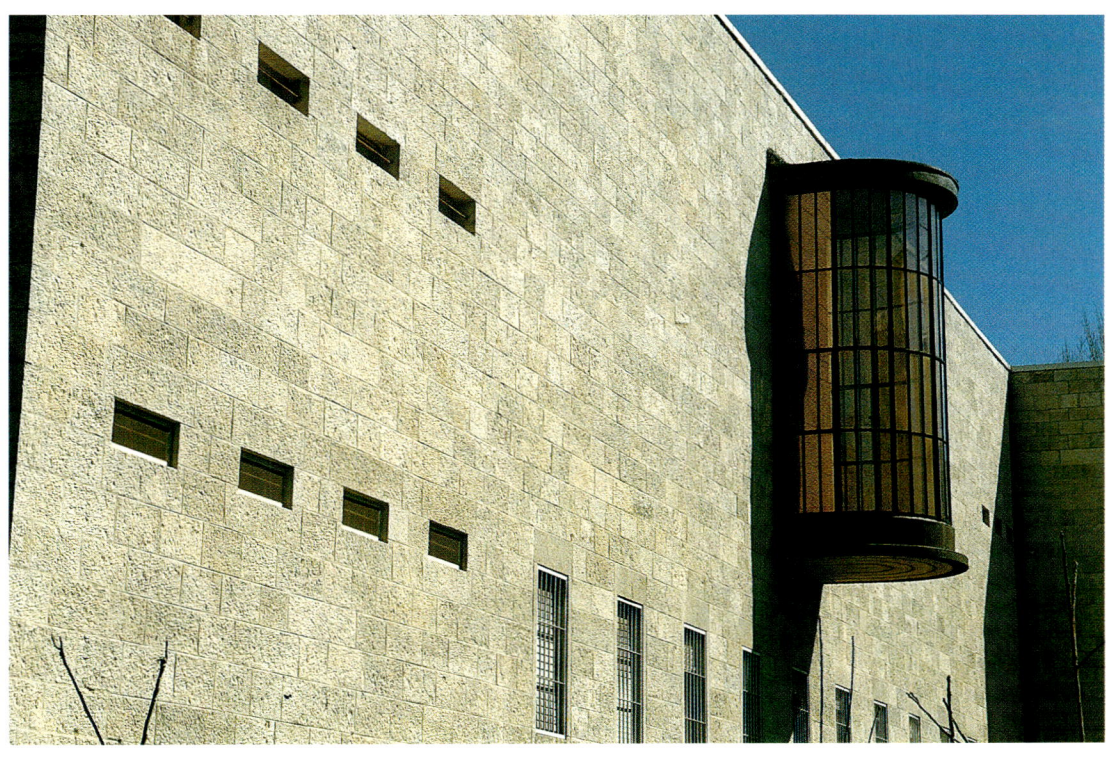

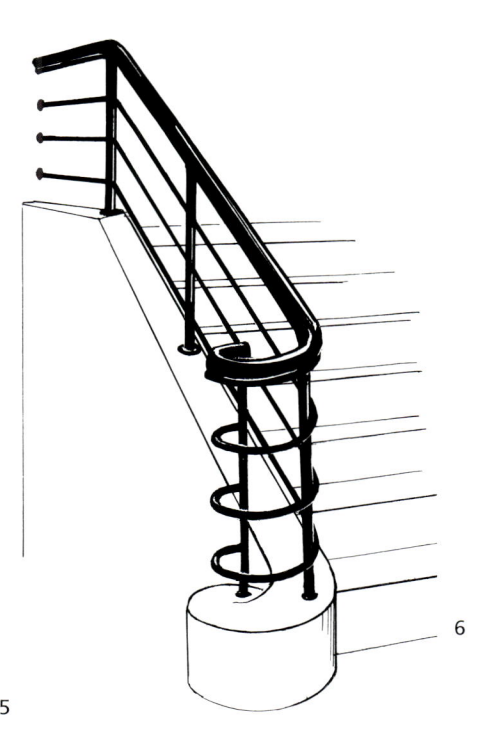

1, 3. Richard Kaufmann (1887-1954) designed the original Pomeranz House in Rehavia. The two upper stories were added in 1990 in keeping with the building's original character.
2. Typical apartment house in 1930s Rehavia.

The elegant Aghion Villa, which since 1974 has served as the official residence of Israel's Prime Ministers, was designed by Richard Kaufmann for a wealthy Jewish-Egyptian merchant. Completed in 1938, the building exemplifies the International Style, reflecting influences that range from Erich Mendelsohn to Frank Lloyd Wright and De Stijl. The local Orient can also be seen in the inner courtyard and garden. The Aghion family had lived in the villa only a short time, when, in 1939-40, they rented it to the exiled King Peter of Yugoslavia. The first Israeli Prime Minister to occupy the house, following its renovation, was Yitzhak Rabin, during his first term in office.

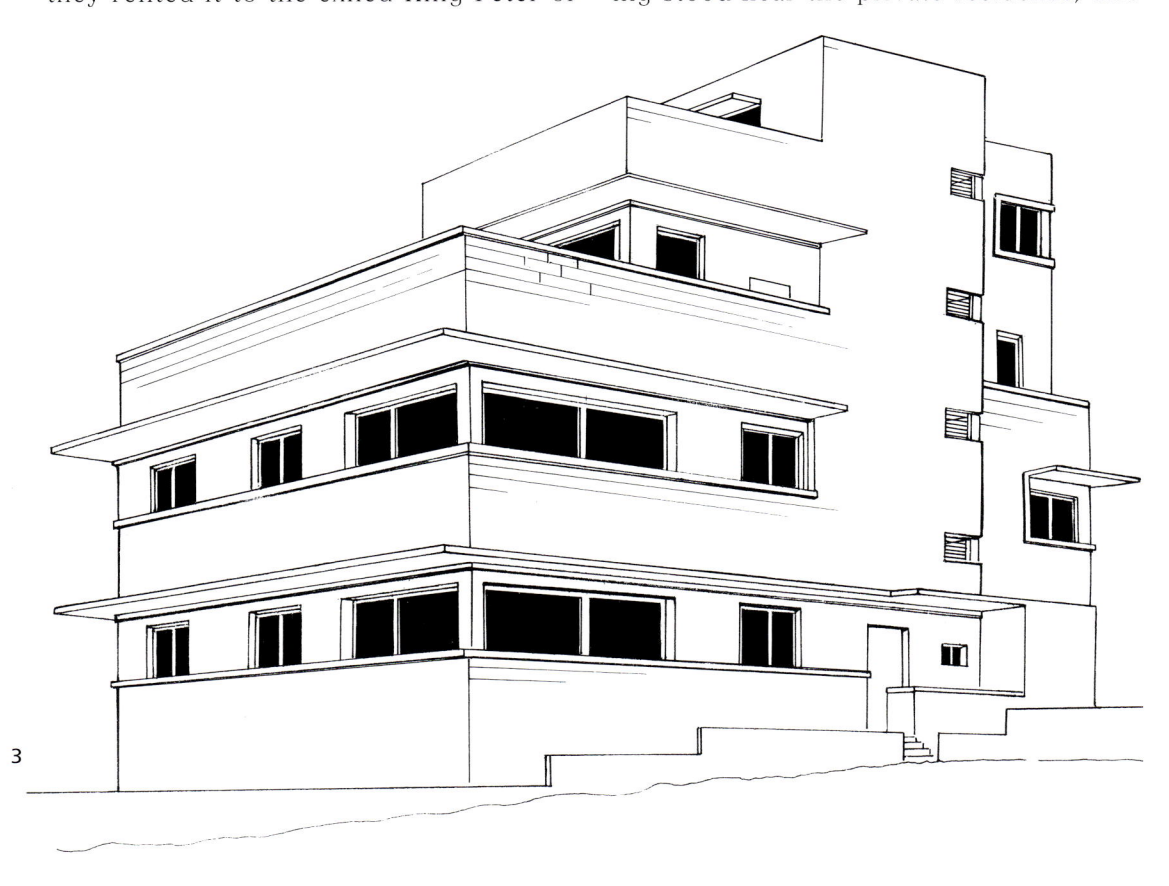

Directly across the street from the Aghion house is the Schocken Library and Institute for Jewish Research, designed by Erich Mendelsohn for Salman Schocken (1877-1959), whose family owns the prestigious Israeli newspaper *Ha'aretz*. Originally meant to house Schocken's private library, the building stood near the private residence, also designed by Mendelsohn (but since altered). Schocken lived there only briefly before emigrating to America in 1940, a few years after arriving in Palestine from Germany. Mendelsohn gave the library building a somewhat austere appearance, without the dynamic streamlining characteristic of his German projects. The most impressive architectural element is a dramatically rounded and glazed bay on the second floor, a faint echo of the dominant wing at the Schocken Department Store built in Stuttgart about a decade earlier, also from a design prepared by Mendelsohn. The bay has inspired a variety of symbolic interpretations, some of them taking it to be an evocation of the Muslim oriel or *Erker*, while others have seen the rounded spine of a book. Meanwhile, the feature performed the functional task of providing the library room with its only source of daylight. Mendelsohn designed every detail of the interior, from chairs to doorknobs.

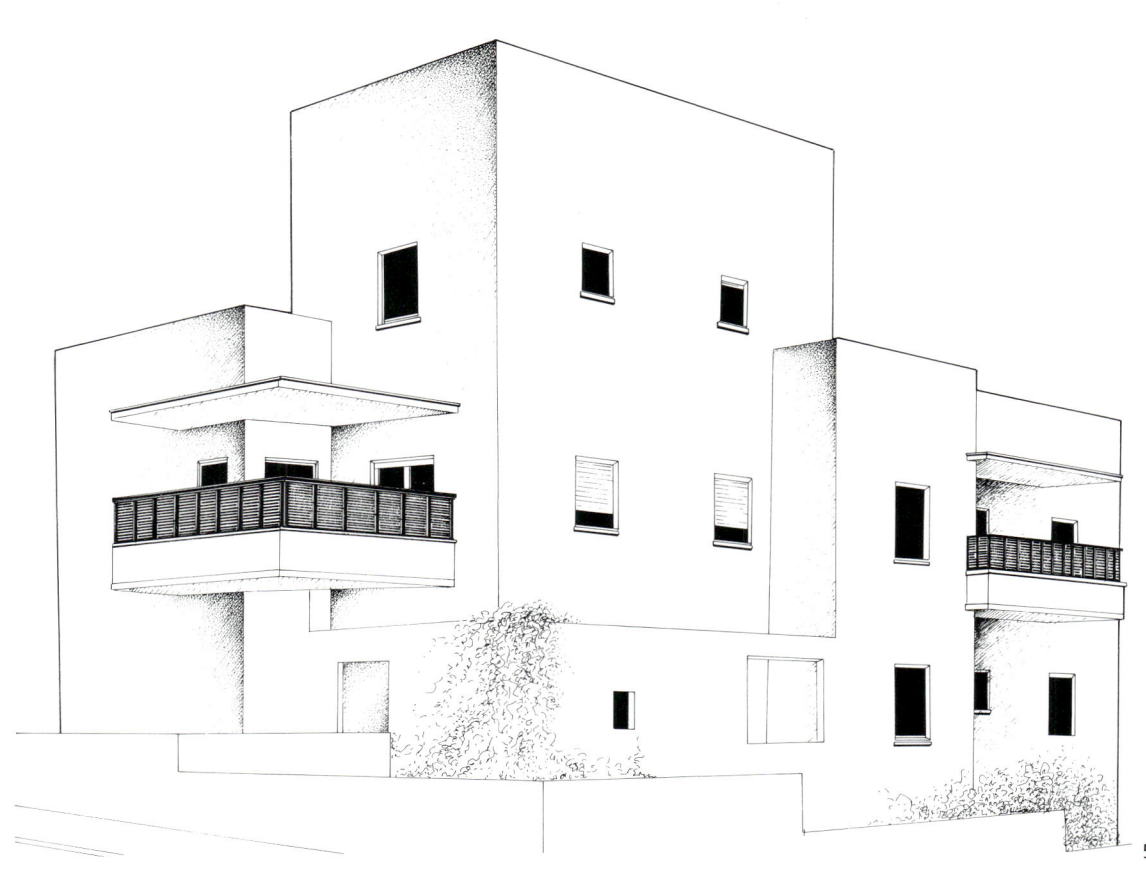

4. In the 1930s, architect Benjamin Chaikin designed the Rehavia home of Bernard (Dov) Joseph as a Mediterranean-style house, with a white plaster finish, wood balconies, tiled roof, and stylized grilles.

5. The proportions and the clean geomertric lines in the Rehavia home of Dr. Bonem (1935; architect: Leopold Krakauer) evoke buildings of the Dutch De Stijl movement.

6. Garden gates in Rehavia show geometric shapes and Art Deco motifs.

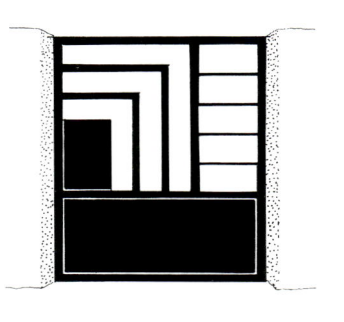

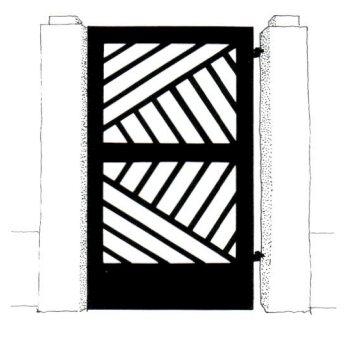

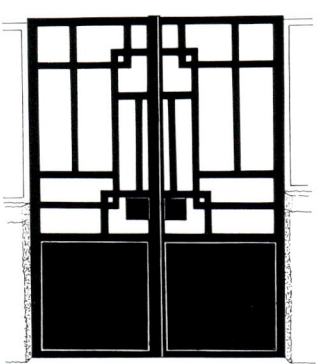

Affluent Arab Neighborhoods

Most of the luxurious single-family villas and apartment houses built in Jerusalem during the Mandate Period belonged to Christian Arabs, and the dwellings had a considerable impact on the city's physical texture. For the most part, Arab construction took place in four affluent neighborhoods in the southern sector—Talbiyeh, Katamon, Abu-Tor, and Baka—but also at the center of town, in Mamilla and north of the Old City. Arab residential building differed from its Jewish counterpart in overall neighborhood structure, which allowed public and community needs to go unaddressed, as well as in specific house plans and architectural elements. Most of the Arab buildings were of one or two stories, enclosed by fences, and surrounded by a private garden, all of which helped give the house its identity and shape the image of the street. The palm tree, symbol of fertility and repository of noble properties capable of warding off the evil eye, enjoyed a place of honor in many gardens, along with citrus, cypress, and fig trees. Many houses in Talbiyeh and Katamon had rose gardens, which made the properties much favored among British officials and officers. As in the Old City, a finely wrought iron gate and front door underscored the importance attached by the Oriental family to the transition from the public sphere to the private.

The basic house plan was still that of the traditional *liwan* model, meaning a very large central room flanked on two sides by other rooms. However, construction technology had improved since Ottoman days, with the result that reinforced concrete clad in stone became the preferred method of constructing private dwellings. Thanks to new building techniques, the liwan grew considerably grander. Most of the two- or three-story apartment houses put up in the 1930s had a central staircase on either side of which was a large apartment containing four to seven rooms opening to a liwan. Architecturally, eclecticism held sway. The fusion of Renaissance and Moorish elements together with Armenian ceramics and traditional Muslim motifs produced a distinctive style. As for the "Arab" version of the International Style, it featured elements not seen in the "Jewish" version, such as radio antennae mimicking the Eiffel Tower and stylized window grilles. Some houses had glazed porches enclosed with panes set in iron frames.

Talbiyeh, which may be Jerusalem's poshest neighborhood, displays the richest variety of Arab urban residential architecture dating from the British Mandate. Here the majority of houses came into being between 1924 and 1937, which makes them roughly contemporary with neighboring Rehavia. The plan of the quarter centers upon two main roads that intersect to form a splendid square. The grid-patterned streets that branch off the main roads also intersect to form rectangular tracts subdivided into large residential plots, each holding a single home or apartment house. As in the other Arab neighborhoods built at the time, no provision was made in Talbiyeh for public and community structures. The Rose Garden installed by the British at the edge of the quarter is delightful enough, but it does not directly relate to the neighborhood's over-

1-4. Ornate "carpet" floor tiles were popular in affluent Arab homes during the Mandate Period.

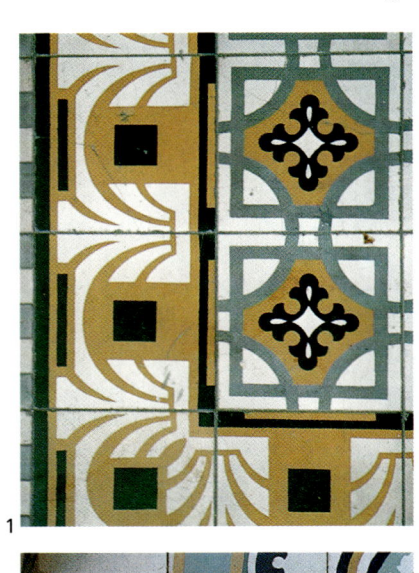

all plan. The absence of public buildings and a pedestrian walkway is particularly striking when compared to their presence in Rehavia. Still, Talbiyeh in the 1990s thrives as one of Jerusalem's most exclusive districts, its prestige guaranteed by a number of state and public institutions, including the President's Residence, the Israel Academy of Sciences, and the Jerusalem Theater complex.

Foreign diplomats also found the garden districts attractive, and since the early 1930s Talbiyeh has been home to various legations. Indeed, what is perhaps the most impressive house in the neighborhood, the villa of Constantine Salameh, constructed in the late 1930s, has housed the Belgian Consulate since 1948. Salameh also built two apartment blocks next to his residence around the square that bore his name (today's Orde Wingate Square), one of the most pleasant of New Jerusalem's urban spaces. Salameh had made a fortune in everything from construction to supplying fruits and vegetables to the British Army, and his residence, designed by the French architect M. Favier, epitomized the success and wealth enjoyed by certain Arab entrepreneurs during the Mandate Period. With its classical symmetry, fine stone detailing, clean, straight lines, and large, surrounding garden, the Salameh villa is a prime example of the fusion between Neo-Classical and Moderne architecture. The liwan plan, on which the house is based, allows for a double-height central hall erected about an octagonal marble fountain. The architect himself designed every item in the dwelling, from door handles to wood furniture, all in the Art Deco style.

Hana Salameh, Constantine's brother, built his villa in 1932 right across the road from the Aghion house. This Salameh represented General Motors in Palestine and Trans-Jordan. Although designed in the International Style, by the Jewish-Hungarian architect Zoltan S. Harmat, the villa has one unusual feature—a living room on the second floor reserved for Salameh's wife, a Muslim. Mme Salameh needed separate quarters in which to entertain her lady friends, while her Christian husband hosted his male companions in the large downstairs living room. After 1948, the building housed various foreign diplomats.

Among the most beautiful of the Arab buildings north of Damascus Gate is the Nashashibi Villa, built in the late 1930s and designed in a "Thousand and One Nights" style by the noted Greek Orthodox architect Spyro Houris. It counts as one of a number of

5. Iron doors, such as this one in Talbiyeh, enhanced many entrances in the affluent Arab neighborhoods.

6-9. Stylized wrought-iron garden gates reflect the importance and formality with which Arabs view the passage from the public domain to the private.

buildings that belonged to the distinguished Nashashibi family in the Sheikh Jarrah Quarter, known during the Mandate Period as the Nashashibi neighborhood. (The same family also had holdings in the Ethiopian Quarter.) Houris probably designed most of the city's "ceramics houses," so called for their lavish use of colorful glazed tiles.

Architect Houris, together with another leading Greek Orthodox architect, Petassis, designed and put up a series of structures in downtown Jerusalem, including one commissioned by a Christian Arab family from the town of Beit Jalla, near Bethlehem. Notable for its stylized doors and windows as well as for its ceramic embellishments, the al-Araj building, at 3 Heleni Ha-Malka Street, was meant to generate rental income, and, for a while, it did function as a hotel for a number of years during the Mandate Period.

In Jerusalem, the story of individual buildings reflects political events, as well as the physical evolution of entire quarters, no less than town planning affects urban texture. This is nowhere more evident than in neighborhoods such as Talbiyeh, Katamon, Baka, and other Arab sections of the New City. In 1948, political circumstances and the war that followed brought about the partition of Jerusalem. The Arab residents of West Jerusalem abandoned their houses, which were subsequently occupied by Jews who, in flight from the Arab Legion, had vacated their homes in the Jewish Quarter. For nineteen years, the two parts of the city developed in total separation from one another. In East Jerusalem, new residential buildings were built along the road toward Ramallah, similar in style to those built during the Mandate. Jerusalem has always occupied a special place in the political, social, and emotional relations between Arabs and Jews. Without delving into root causes, it is inevitable that parting, abandonment, and loss of property entail a heavy emotional burden, one that continually nourishes feelings of bitterness, frustration, and resentment.

1, 2, 5. Typical house and entrances in affluent Arab neighborhoods such as Talbiyeh, Baka, and Sheikh Jarrah during the Mandate Period.

3, 4, 6. Lavish "Arabian Nights" style architecture of the 1930s. The Jalad House (3) in Talbiyeh combines colored Armenian ceramic tiles with red and white stones on the roof parapet. The Nashashibi House (4, 6) in the Sheikh Jarrah neighborhood has an imposing entrance, glazed Armenian tiles, and lintels of red and white stone. Architect: Spyro Houris.

1, 2. Windows of various shapes ornamented with ceramic tiles made by the Armenian artist David Ohannessian add color to the façade of the 1930s Al-Araj House in central Jerusalem. Floral motifs in blue and turquoise are dominant on such tiles. Architect: Spyro Houris.

3. At the center of the roof balustrade on this lavish house in the Baka neighborhood is a stone plaque in Arabic bearing the builder's name and the date on which construction was completed.

4, 5. The opulent villa of the merchant and building contractor Constantine Salameh—since 1948 housing the Belgian Consulate—fuses Neo-Classical symmetry with the International Style. Architect: M. Favier.

6. Since the 1970s, old houses in both the Jewish garden neighborhoods and the affluent Arab neighborhoods—such as this one in Talbiyeh—have had new stories added.

7. An original one-family house in Katamon.

8. Many Arab villas built in northern Jerusalem after 1967 have ornate designs, with windows of different dimensions and shapes, tiled roofs, and stone dressed in a variety of sizes, textures, and colors.

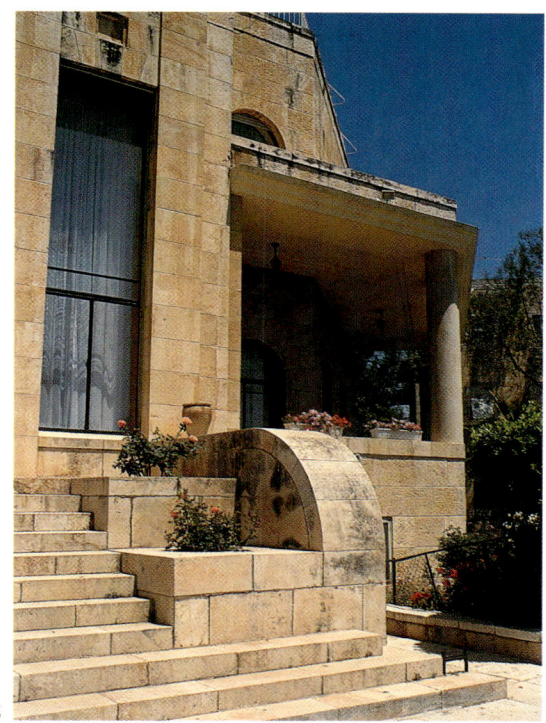

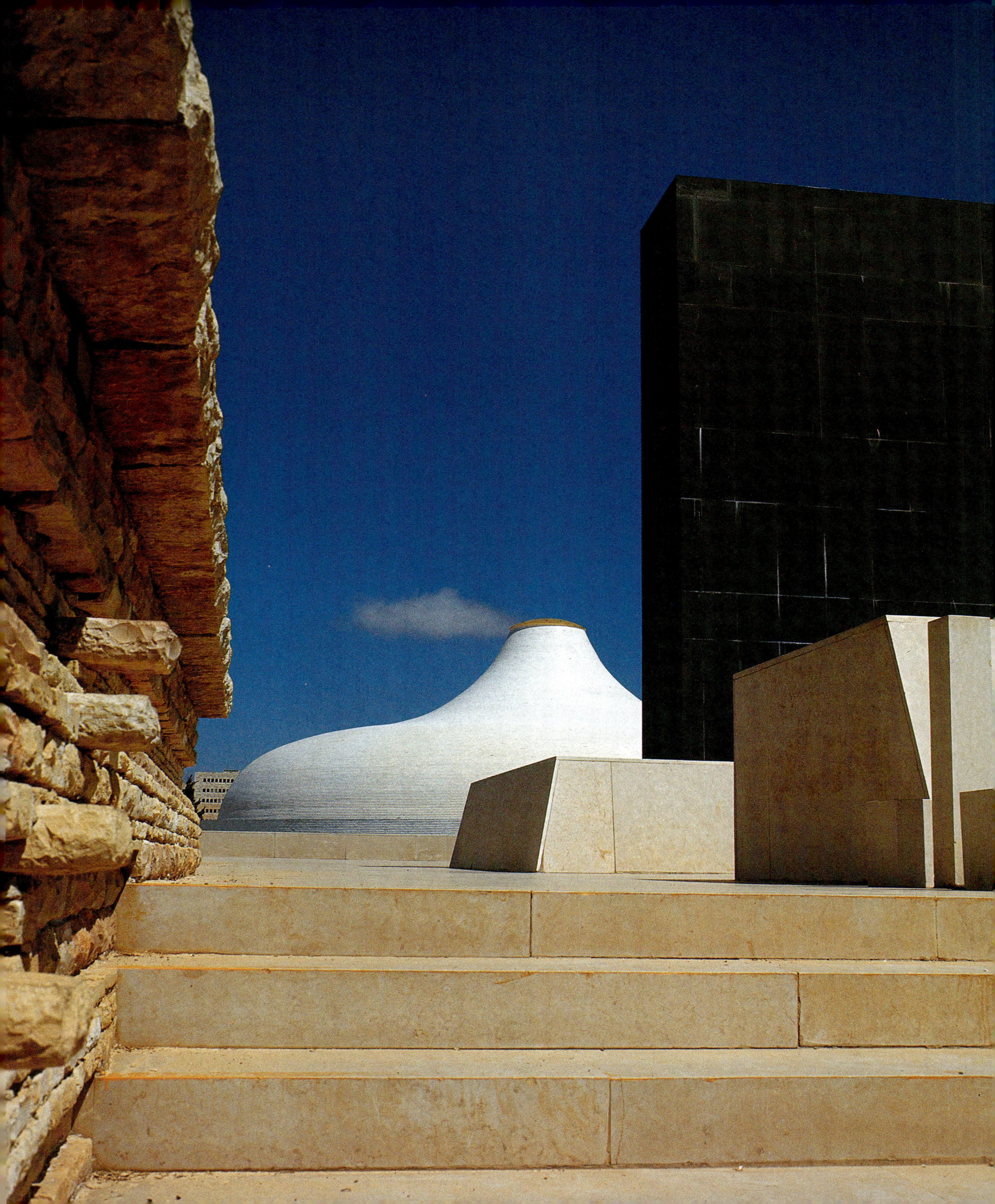

Modern Architecture: 1948-1993

From the International to the Neo-Oriental Style

Two major historical events, both spawned by war, contributed significantly to the evolution of modern Jerusalem's urban pattern and architectural texture. The first was the creation of the State of Israel in May 1948 and the partition of the city in the fighting that followed. The second was the reunification of Jerusalem in June 1967 during the Six-Day War. Under the separate and cumulative impact of those two great watersheds, although most intensively since 1967, Jerusalem experienced a development boom unprecedented in its three-thousand-year history. In 1948, for the first time since the Second Temple Period, Jewish construction in Israel could proceed without limitations imposed by a foreign power. The potential bore fruit in every realm: state and government institutions, residential buildings, commerce, service, and industry, not to mention religion, education, culture, health, and memorial needs. History's immanence was almost palpable.

The beginnings were inauspicious. In December 1949, when Jerusalem was officially declared the capital of Israel, the population of its western sector stood at 100,000 Jews (plus a few thousand Christians and others), separated by an intractable wall of hostility from the 65,000 residents of East Jerusalem and the Old City, who lived under Jordanian rule. Completely isolated, West (Israeli) Jerusalem lay at the end of what amounted to a cul-de-sac, without urban or rural hinterland. Some neighborhoods, battered from the fighting, suddenly found themselves on a volatile international border, harassed by sniper fire and occupied by new immigrants from North Africa, Turkey, and Persia. They degenerated into slums, while the city center stagnated.

During the 1950s, however, the huge influx of immigrants kindled a massive demand for housing, which in turn brought a wave of new construction, thereby increasing the city's built-up area by 50 percent. Virtually the whole of this expansion took place toward the west and southwest, for reasons both geopolitical and geographic, since Jerusalem, now a divided city, was a virtual enclave surrounded on the east, north, and south by Arab Jordan. To a considerable extent, new building took the form of vast and monotonous public-housing blocks similar to those already blighting other parts of the country. They rose in such neighborhoods as Kiryat Hayovel and New Katamon, joined in the 1960s by Kiryat Menahem, Talpiot, Shmuel Hanavi, Musrara, and others. At the same time, still-vacant areas in veteran neighborhoods like Rehavia and Beit Hakerem began to fill up with apartment buildings. Meanwhile, few private houses were erected.

Jerusalem architecture in the 1950s also reflected a rash of state needs, both functional

1. The war between the Sons of Light and the Sons of Darkness—good versus evil—is embodied in the contrast between the shining white dome and the black granite wall at the Shrine of the Book, Israel Museum (1965). Architects: Armand Bartos and Frederick Kiesler.

2. Dedicated in 1965, the Israel Museum was designed—by architects Al. Mansfeld and Dora Gad—as a cluster of modern cubelike pavilions which would enable the institution to grow cohesively, by stages, yet continue to blend with the hilly landscape.

3. The main Jewish and Arab neighborhoods built from 1948 to 1994.

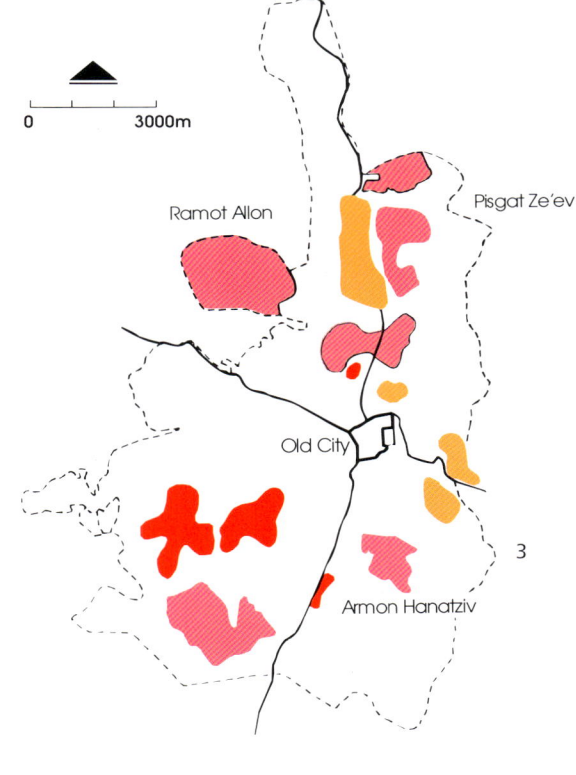

- - - - Municipal Boundary
- Jewish neighborhood, 1948-1967
- Jewish neighborhood, 1967-1994
- Arab neighborhood, 1948-1994

1, 2. The Knesset (Parliament) building (dedicated 1966) was designed by architect Joseph Klarwin as a modern version of Classical structures such as the Parthenon in Athens (1).

3. The small cubelike pavilions of the Israel Museum, situated above the Monastery of the Cross, suggest the scale of a traditonal Arab village.

4. The headquarters of the Bank of Israel, completed in the late 1970s and part of the Government Precinct in western Jerusalem, was one of the first buildings in Israel designed around an atrium. Architects: Arieh and Eldar Sharon.

and representational, all of them arising from the city's new role as the capital of sovereign Israel. At Givat Ram, on the western edge of the city, the Israeli authorities erected a series of buildings that embodied in stone the aspirations of a young/old nation in crucial realms of endeavor: the "Kirya" (governmental compound), the Knesset (Parliament), the Hebrew University, the Israel Museum, and Binyanei Ha'uma (Convention Center). Nearby Mount Herzl became a national memorial complex, which included the burial place of Theodor Herzl, founder of political Zionism, a military cemetery, and the Yad Vashem Holocaust Memorial.

170

While no one denied the symbolic importance of such structures, their architecture frequently became the subject of fierce debate centering on such questions as monumentalism, civic dignity, representational character, and solemnity. The bitter late-1950s arguments over the design of the Knesset, and later the President's Residence, were basically disagreements over the relationship between the Jewish state's democratic system and the desired shape of its official buildings. Was the Knesset no more than a "Greek temple"? Was the new architecture "totalitarian" and "overbearing," or was it in "harmony with the spirit of the country"? Modestly appointed structures that would capture the original Zionist ethos were not, it turned out, easily reconcilable with the stateliness that seemed required by the era of independence.

A key development in the 1950s and early 1960s was the transition, albeit gradual, from provisional solutions that reflected a primal, formative era to structures embodying the stability and permanence of a sovereign nation. Thus, the Knesset moved from temporary quarters in downtown Jerusalem to its new home, while the President's Residence changed from a modest wood structure in Rehavia to a specially built mansion in Talbiyeh.

5. The Billy Rose Art Garden at the Israel Museum was designed by Isamu Noguchi.
6. The Scroll of Isaiah is on display in the subterranean space inside the Shrine of the Book. The white dome evokes the lids of the clay vessels in which the Dead Sea Scrolls were found in the Judean Desert.

1. The flat concrete domes on the President's Residence (1972) are a modern version of Jerusalem's traditional stone domes. Designed by architect Abba Elhanani, the complex includes a ceremonial wing, the President's bureau, and the private apartment of the President and his family.

Religious construction occurred mainly in the ultra-Orthodox neighborhoods north of the city center. The Hebrew Union College building, sponsored by the World Movement for Progressive Judaism and sited close to the King David Hotel, sparked an early manifestation of the strife between Jewish Orthodox and secular residents. The period also saw the erection of two architecturally interesting synagogues, one on the Givat Ram campus of the Hebrew University and the other at Hadassah Hospital in Ein Karem. Construction for recreational and community activity came more slowly, and it served mainly to accommodate new immigrants. Tourism and pilgrimage were meager, since Jerusalem's major attractions had fallen into Jordanian hands, and thus meager too was hotel construction.

Urban development from 1948 to 1967 proceeded, to some degree, within the framework of comprehensive city planning, but it also became subject to many ad hoc decisions, made under pressure of circumstance. A master plan, drawn up in 1954, finally gained approval in 1959, after bitter opposition by builders and land owners who objected to the allocation of large areas for public use and to regulations that reduced building density. That plan, which underwent nonbinding modifications after 1968, remains in effect.

The architecture produced during the period of divided Jerusalem displays the International Style as practiced in the post-1945 era and imported for adaptation to Jerusalem's local needs and materials. In short, the Jerusalem International Style was primarily international and secondarily "Jerusalem," a monolithic architecture of residential blocks that bespoke nothing so much as anonymity. The basic form of many of the buildings was that of long, dull, trainlike boxes, some overlaid with cheap, uneven *wildbau* stone (nowadays used for bearing walls) that could be installed by unskilled labor. The latter part of the 1960s saw the widespread construction of prefabricated "bridge" housing: groups of massive, eight-story, aesthetically nondescript structures, built on steep terrain, each containing hundreds of small apartments, and linked to the street by narrow concrete bridges, extending from the middle of the building. These impoverished, tediously uniform, cheaply assembled monoliths, ungraced by elevators, virtually assured overcrowding, constant noise, and moldy walls in Jerusalem's cold, damp winters. The ubiquitous public-housing blocks of the 1960s resembled all too closely those being constructed throughout postwar Eastern and Western Europe. The stone veneer, required by city ordinance, did little to alter their "international" identity.

The International Style, which had played a dominant role in the architecture of the

Mandate Period, continued to do so, albeit differently, in the era of the divided city, particularly under the influence of the work of the French/Swiss architect Le Corbusier. In essence, it sought universal solutions with local nuances, utilizing a reductive, rigidly straight-angled geometry and minimal decorative flourishes. The Jerusalem version, as seen in both mass housing and public structures, incorporates three of Le Corbusier's major principles: free-standing ground-floor concrete columns (known as "pilotis") used to support the building, strip windows under flat roofs, and much exposed concrete. Many such buildings erected in Jerusalem during the 1950s and 1960s have infill walls of brick or rough stone. On many public buildings the infill walls might be covered with cut stone, albeit of a smooth, cheaper variety lacking the texture and "weight" of natural stone.

The Hebrew University's Givat Ram campus, built in the 1950s, is Jerusalem's largest showplace of buildings in the postwar International Style. The prime example there is the National Library building, a rectangular structure raised on pilotis to become a local, institutional version of Le Corbusier's renowned Villa Savoye, erected in 1929-31 at Poissy, France. Other buildings on the Givat Ram campus have large windows protected by "brise-soleils" that are both functional (protection against sun glare) and aesthetic (relieving the monotony of flat façades). Decoratively perforated concrete precasts and an overlay of colored ceramics (borrowed from contemporary Mexico) served the same purpose. Still, links with the past as well as with local building traditions continued to be a feature of Jerusalem architecture during this period. The familiar dome, as reinterpreted by architects Heinz Rau and David Reznik for the campus synagogue, was given a modern form and cast in concrete.

The Jerusalem Theater in Talbiyeh, the city's most important center of culture, provides an interesting example of the mixed use of stone and exposed concrete, which became highly fashionable during the 1960s and 1970s. The rounded, sculpturesque building

2. The stained-glass windows by Marc Chagall depicting the Twelve Tribes of Israel turned the Hadassah Medical Center in Ein Karem into a tourist attraction. The building, designed by architect Joseph Neufeld, has three windows on each side and evokes, thus, the tripartite entrance in ancient synagogues.

173

1, 3, 4, 7. The campus of the Hebrew University of Jerusalem at Givat Ram (1953-67)—low buildings set by a central axis alongside an open public space—is typical of international campus architecture in the 1950s. Most of the buildings are in the International Style. The administration building (1), by architects Karmi-Karmi-Meltzer, resembles the office building (2) designed by Lucio Costa, Oscar Niemeyer, and Le Corbusier in Rio de Janeiro (1937-42). The university synagogue (4), with a thin white dome supported by eight arches (architects: Heinz Rau and David Reznik) is a landmark in local modern architecture.

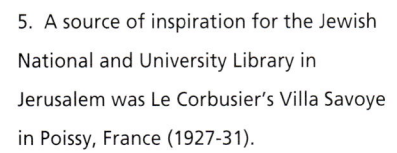

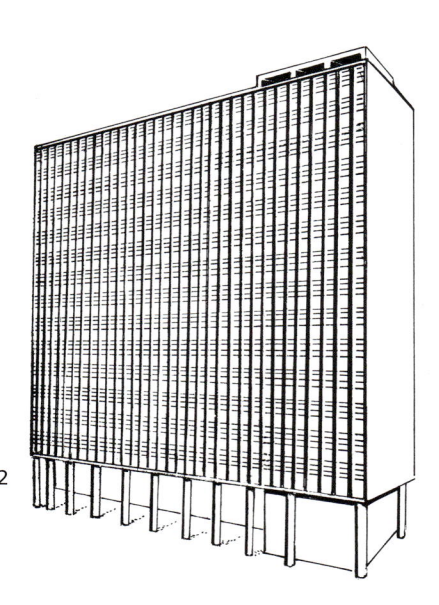

5. A source of inspiration for the Jewish National and University Library in Jerusalem was Le Corbusier's Villa Savoye in Poissy, France (1927-31).

174

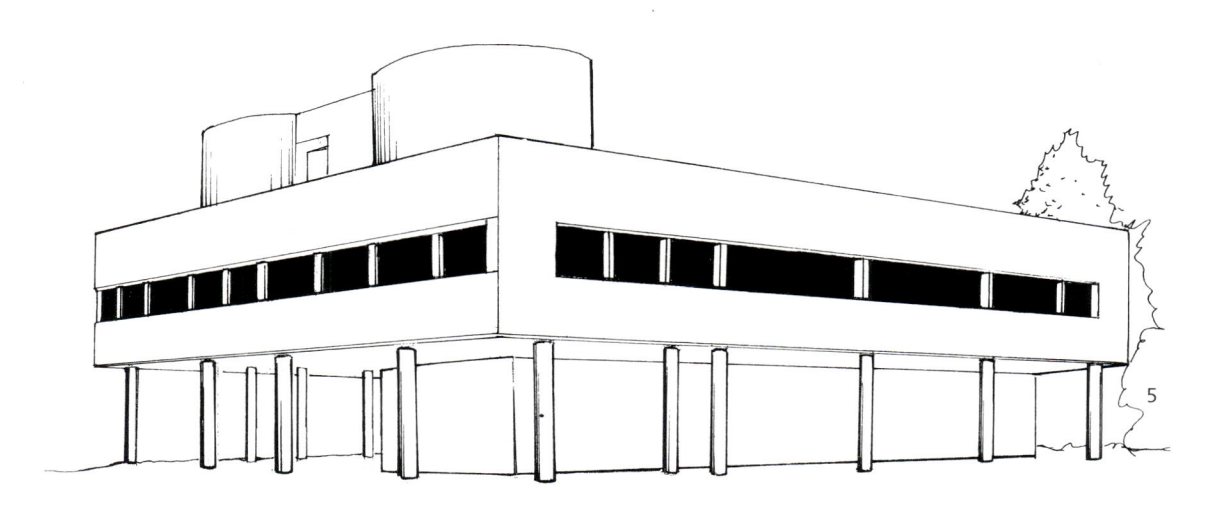

6, 7. Le Corbusier's "pilotis" transplanted to the National Library building. Architects: Alexandroni-Arnon-Yaski-Hebron-Nadler-Nadler-Powsner.

8. Simplicity and nobility are the hallmarks of Hebrew Union College (1963) in central Jerusalem, the local headquarters of the Movement for Progressive Judaism ("Reform"). Architect: Heinz Rau.

1. Construction in stone and exposed concrete contributes to the monumental sculpturesque effect of the Jerusalem Theater (1971) in the Talbiyeh neighborhood. Architects: Michael Nadler, Shulamit Nadler, Shmuel Bixon. The sculpture in the foreground is by Yehiel Shemi.

was designed by the architectural firm Nadler-Nadler-Bixon.

In the course of these years, there emerged in Jerusalem a form of architecture that suggested or recalled landmarks of world architecture, events in Jewish and Israeli history, or historical and religious symbols. As this would imply, it triggered a number of visual and emotional associations. The tragedy of the Holocaust is evoked abstractly, but powerfully, in the imposing black basalt walls and heavy concrete roof of the Ohel Yizkor ("Memorial Hall") at Yad Vashem, one of Jerusalem's most impressive buildings, designed by architect Arye Elhanani. Ancient history assumes striking physical form at the Israel Museum's Shrine of the Book, housing the Dead Sea Scrolls. The white dome alludes to the cover of the clay vessels in which the scrolls were found, while the stark contrast between the dome and the adjoining black wall symbolizes the "war between the Sons of Light and the Sons of Darkness," as described in the scrolls.

Evocative architecture is found as well in the tear-shaped Church of Dominus Flevit ("the Lord wept," Luke 19:37-44), designed by the Italian architect Antonio Barluzzi and erected in 1954 on the Mount of Olives. The Greek and Roman orders connote civic dignity, which accounts for their modern versions extensively used in the Knesset building. Less obtrusively, but more surprisingly, perhaps, the same motif appears on the façades of Heichal Shlomo (the Chief Rabbinate building) and the adjacent Great Synagogue, both designed by Dr. Alexander Friedman. The pyramid, memorial symbol since ancient Egypt and present in the Kidron Valley tombs of Absalom and Zechariah (Second Temple Period), inspired architect David Reznik's Yad Lebanim (Soldiers Memorial) complex in the 1970s.

References to landmarks in world architecture were common, among them the already-

2, 3. Holocaust commemoration architecture: powerful minimalism in the design of Ohel Yizkor at Yad Vashem Holocaust Memorial. Architects: Arye Elhanani with Arieh Sharon and Binyamin Idelson.

4, 5. Rocky monumental labyrinth of the "Valley of the Communities" at Yad Vashem perpetuates the names of the Jewish communities annihilated by the Nazis. Architects: Lipa Yahalom and Dan Zur (1983-93).

1. A complex of conservative, ponderous architecture, ornamented by a contemporaneous rendering of Classical columns: The Great Synagogue (dedicated 1982), topped by a modern version of the Tablets of the Law, and to its left the domed Chief Rabbinate headquarters (1953). Architect: Alexander Friedman.

2. The tear-shaped Church of Dominus Flevit ("the Lord wept") on the Mount of Olives was consecrated in 1954. Here, traditionally, Jesus looked down on Jerusalem and wept (Luke 19:37-44). Architect: Antonio Barluzzi.

mentioned mass housing that came forth as vastly overscaled, banalized versions of Le Corbusier's "Unité d'Habitation," a masterpiece built in 1947-52 for Marseilles. The row housing in London and elsewhere found an echo in the exterior stairs of town houses built in Jerusalem in the 1980s. The original complex of the Israel Museum, designed by Al. Mansfeld and Dora Gad in the late 1950s, is generally considered to evoke the indigenous shapes in the traditional Arab village. Yet, its overall appearance also recalls a more modern project—the "brick country house" conceived in 1923 by the famous German-American architect Mies van der Rohe.

After reunification in June 1967, Jerusalem developed exponentially. History itself seemed to accelerate in the city, where urban processes that otherwise might stretch over decades or centuries unfolded within barely a generation. The population more than doubled, from 267,000 in 1967 to over half a million in 1993, and the municipal area tripled. However, action often preceded comprehensive planning, or gave way to politicians with vested interests, and many problems remained unresolved. Besides physical considerations, planners found themselves having to cope with an extraordinarily pervasive, and intrusive, preconception—that of Jerusalem's ages-old image, harbored by millions everywhere, as a "holy" city, a visionary utopia of battlements and towers. How could the pressures—intensified by the worldwide media explosion and headline-grabbing events in the Middle East—to "preserve" the mythological Jerusalem be balanced against the prosaic, but equally compelling, fact that the ancient city was also a dynamic, thriving place whose inhabitants demanded efficient answers to everyday needs, aggravated by an outmoded infrastructure?

The conflicting expectations sparked heated public debates over the planning of the city, fueled, in the immediate aftermath of the 1967 border-expanding victory, by a "sky's the limit" euphoria that spawned overweeningly ambitious ideas for development. Two major spheres of dispute were the Jerusalem skyline, having to do most particularly with the proposal for a 22-story Hyatt Hotel on Mount Scopus, and the redevelopment or preservation of the Mamilla quarter opposite Jaffa Gate.

In the decades since independence the public-housing neighborhoods went through an evolutionary process. From the sprawling *ma'abarah* ("temporary immigrant camp") of the early 1950s, Talpiot evolved into the standard row tenements built on the same site in the 1960s. After the huge "bridge" buildings erected in 1960s Kiryat Hayovel came the Neo-Oriental courtyard housing in the post-1967 neighborhood of Gilo. In the 1980s, the traditional urban street in the northern Jerusalem neighborhood of Pisgat Ze'ev succeeded the "casbah" architecture of East Talpiot. A distinctive "Jerusalem style" developed. Immigrant absorption, security requirements, and economic hardship—hallmarks of the 1950s and 1960s—gave way in the 1970s and 1980s to expansiveness and the desire for higher standards of living.

Government policy aimed at preventing repartition of Jerusalem led to the construction of perimeter neighborhoods and a fundamental change in the city's structure. New neighborhoods at some remove from the urban center created political-physical facts, but they also entailed an expensive infrastructure across undeveloped areas separating the core from the new outlying districts.

Higher-quality housing reflected a shift from standardization, anonymity, and monotone appearance to diversity, privacy, and a more attractive architectural look. It is encapsulated in the difference between the two- or four-family "little boxes" of the early 1960s, with their 390-square-foot (35-square-meter) flats, and the villas of the "build-your-home" projects realized, for example, in the Ramot neighborhood during the 1970s and 1980s. Although erected only two decades earlier,

3. A curved tower is the central building at the Hadassah-Hebrew University Medical Center in Ein Karem, innovatively designed by architect Joseph Neufeld in the 1950s and dedicated in 1960. More buildings were added over the years to meet growing needs. The façades display a variety of materials, including red stone, red and white bricks, and decorative precasts of exposed concrete.

1. "Bridge" tenements, built in Jerusalem's western neighborhoods in the 1960s, were supposed to solve the problem of dense construction on steep slopes without the need for an elevator. A bridge connects the building's middle floor with the street. Designed by a Ministry of Housing Planning team.

2. Elevators are installed in the buildings of the ultra-Orthodox Har Nof neighborhood—planned by architect Ze'ev Schoenberg—under construction in West Jerusalem since the late 1970s.

3. Monotonous "train" tenements are common in Israel. They are the local version of the "Corbusierian" approach, as interpreted by the Ministry of Housing, mainly in the 1960s.

4-7. "Beehive" public-housing projects, of both the pentagonal stone-clad, prefabricated concrete walls type and as meandering zigzag structures, were built in Ramot in northern Jerusalem. Architect: Zvi Hecker.

8. An avant-garde "casbah" with external stairs for every apartment. This residential structure was built in the 1970s in the new Gilo neighborhood in southern Jerusalem. Architects: Arieh and Eldar Sharon.

the building-block-and-concrete tenements of the 1950s are light years distant from the quality of the courtyard and row houses in the Gilo neighborhood.

In the 1950s and 1960s the Ministry of Housing had been severely criticized for the lack of vision and imagination shown by its architects in planning and designing neighborhoods around the country. Consequently, when the post-1967 building boom ignited, the Ministry decided that Jerusalem, with all its importance and historical sensitivity, demanded a clean break from the boxy structures of the recent past. This brought an attempt to create a local-original building style on a large scale upon the rocky slopes around the inner city, and it produced some unusual architectural results. The most striking example of such avant-gardism is Zvi Hecker's "beehive architecture" in the Ramot neighborhood of north Jerusalem. The exterior walls of these residential buildings have an outward slant and are made of prefabricated concrete elements thinly clad in uncut stone.

The advent of a consumer society manifests itself in the stark disparity between a 1960s neighborhood like Ir Ganim, with its dreary, uninviting commercial center of three or four shops, and the 1970s Ramot Eshkol neighborhood, brightened by a large, modern shopping center.

181

1, 2. Post-1967 "build your home" neighborhoods capitalize on the yearning of city dwellers for a separate house and a green garden. The Ramot neighborhood in northern Jerusalem is considered the most successful of the new housing projects because of its strict adherence to architectural guidelines regarding height, roofs, stone, and environmental development. General layout: architects Nahum Meltzer and Nehemia Goraly.

3. Small, roof-tiled apartment buildings —this one is in Arnona, in southeastern Jerusalem—erected since the 1980s, are a reaction to earlier large-scale monotonous public-housing tenements and condominiums. Architect: Louis Klachko.

The developing city found one of its most dramatic expressions in a changing skyline. Various types of high-rise buildings—hotels (Sheraton Plaza and the former Hilton), office buildings (Clal Center, Migdal Ha'ir), and residential complexes (Kiryat Wolfson)—contributed to this development. Many of the post-1967 high-rise buildings have a stale, standardized look, even while towering massively above the city's traditional low profile. Architecturally, they reflect their counterparts in the Western world, only in a pallid, derivative manner.

Reacting to this monolithic heaviness, architects Ya'akov Rechter and Moshe Zarhi attempted to break it up in their work for the Jerusalem Hilton (now the Holiday Inn Crown Plaza) and the King Solomon Hotel. They designed the former as a tower rising from a

182

4, 7. An original local Jerusalem style, in the spirit of New Orientalism, emerged after 1967. It was a modern version of the Romantic-Oriental world of forms, with its plethora of gates, arches, protrusions, and recesses. Public-housing project, designed by architect Salo Hershman and built in the early 1970s in Gilo, on the city's southern edge.

5. Monumental stone architecture in a public-housing project in Gilo: a modern version of the traditional-romantic world of forms of the Old City. Architect: Meir Levi.

6. The commercial centers built in the new post-1967 perimeter neighborhoods —such as this one, in Gilo, from the 1980s— were designed so as to stress their civic status. Architects: Avraham Yaski, Ya'akov Gil, Joseph Sivan.

staggered base and the latter as a cluster of staggered towers of varying heights.

Industrial and other structures also demonstrate the transition from the uniform and the functional to the diverse and the aesthetic. The multipurpose modular, industrial structures built since the 1950s in Talpiot and Har Hotzvim, on the southern and western fringes of the city, yielded to a number of industrial "villas" whose very design, in glass and metal, projected innovative technology.

Jerusalem's Arabs, continuing the trend of earlier periods, erected few public buildings in the post-1948 era. After 1967, however, the Arab population grew rapidly, from 60,000 at reunification to 140,000 in 1990. The result mainly of internal migration from the West Bank and improved economic conditions, it generated a boom in private housing. Much of this construction has taken place in the rural-urban sections of the city, such as Beit Hanina and Shuafat in the north, as well as in nearby

1. Megastructure: The campus of the Hebrew University on Mount Scopus, which faces the Old City ramparts and central New Jerusalem, has a fortresslike façade, in a modern Brutalist manner. Overall plan was by architects David Reznik, Shmuel Shaked, Haim Katseff, and Ram Karmi.

2. At the center of the Mount Scopus campus is an open public space. The historic buildings of the pre-1948 period, such as the former National Library (with dome), were integrated into the modern fortresslike architecture.

villages once based on agriculture but gradually evolved into full-fledged urban quarters. Politics has been a driving force, bringing funds from the Arab states eager to offset the massive Jewish construction around the city and in the West Bank. The Arab population has developed a potent strategy of "clinging to the land" in order to create physical-political facts as a counterbalance to Jewish settlements.

Virtually all the Arab residential construction belongs to the single-family type, differentiated according to the economic circumstances of the builders. In many cases, these lavish villas, scattered along the Jerusalem-Ramalla road, display the pitched roofs, stone arches, and "majestic" external staircases favored in Amman during the boom years there (1972-82). Their plethora of styles derived in part from Western architectural magazines that caught the fancy of wealthy Arab families, just as they did some Jewish Jerusalemites. Indeed, a number of reciprocal influences can be detected. An Arab residential villa, for instance, may very well reflect the Jewish population's penchant for multilevel houses with sharply sloping tile roofs; meanwhile, many Jewish villas display Neo-Oriental elements.

Clearly, the post-1967 period witnessed a powerful thrust away from the International Style of the 1950s and 1960s, increasingly stigmatized as monotonous and limiting. In its place came efforts to produce a new, distinctively "Jerusalem style," which generally turned out to be an organic continuation of local traditions, including Oriental forms and designs. The new style would in part respond to public and professional criticism of the dreary, unimaginative sameness of Israel's cityscape, but in part it also tracked events in international architecture, which, like most fashions, reached Israel a decade late. In the early 1960s, many architects in the world, tired of International Style clichés, adopted the freer, more interesting constructions of "Brutalism," which depended upon optimal use of concrete to achieve greater richness of form and texture. The "Brutalist Style" found strong support in Israel.

Israeli Brutalism may have set off its most thunderous reverberation in the Hebrew University's original campus, on Mount Scopus, which was restored following the 1967 war and given the look of a "Neo-Crusader" fortress. The Mount Scopus megastructure is the most dominant, and domineering, expression of public-state construction in the post-1967 era. Its location reflects not only a political decision to prevent the city's repartition; it also constitutes the symbolic incarnation of a national and cultural yearning to rediscover the roots of the Zionist vision. The designers

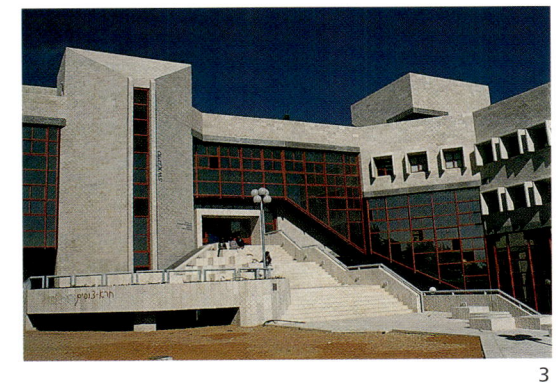

3. Jerusalem Post-Modernism combines glasss with red metal lintels and heavy sculpturesque stone construction. Bezalel Academy of Art on Mount Scopus (1990), designed by architect Gershon Zippor.

4. "Growing" out of the hill, the School of Education building at the Hebrew University on Mount Scopus is set off by a rough stone base. The building itself is clad with smooth cut stone. Architect: David Reznik.

of the new/old campus (master-planned by architects David Reznik and Shmuel Shaked, then detailed by Reznik, Ram Karmi, and Haim Katseff) decided that terrain and climate ruled out the possibility of buildings separated by green areas, such as had been realized on the Givat Ram campus. Instead, they opted for a compact structure closed in from all sides. Visually and conceptually, the campus was intended to be a modern echo of the Old City rampart below, creating meaningful correspondences between an ancient fortification and a modern structure surrounded by a wall.

The architectural form of the campus is that of an inward-looking fortress, a mélange of projections and recessions, sloping ramparts, domes, arches, periscopes, and turrets. The overall effect is of a single, continuous building;

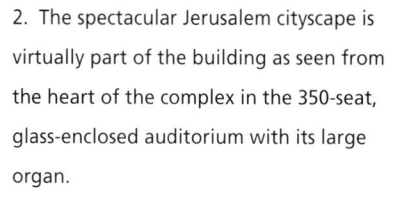

1-4. The terraced structure of the Mormons' Jerusalem Center for Near Eastern Studies (1986) on Mount Scopus blends with the hilly topography opposite the Old City. Architects: David Reznik and Franklin T. Ferguson.

2. The spectacular Jerusalem cityscape is virtually part of the building as seen from the heart of the complex in the 350-seat, glass-enclosed auditorium with its large organ.

186

only from close up does the distinctiveness of each separate structure become apparent. The concept is of a closed city huddled about open and closed plazas, with a wallscape turned to the world outside. The architects involved in the decade-long project took pains to preserve the original structures of the 1920s campus in the complex, ultra-sophisticated megastructure they created atop Mount Scopus.

Two other major complexes erected on Mount Scopus after 1967 are very different in character. The Jerusalem Center for Near Eastern Studies, an extension of the Mormons' Brigham Young University in Salt Lake City, rose in the 1980s on the western slope. Designed by David Reznik and Franklin T. Ferguson (from a Salt Lake City architectural firm), the Center has a stepped structure that

3, 4. The play of light and shadow is integral to the building's architecture. A barrel-vaulted corridor (4) connects the various sections in the building's upper area, and wood lattices (*mushrabiyya*) produce shadow-dappled walls in the garden.

1

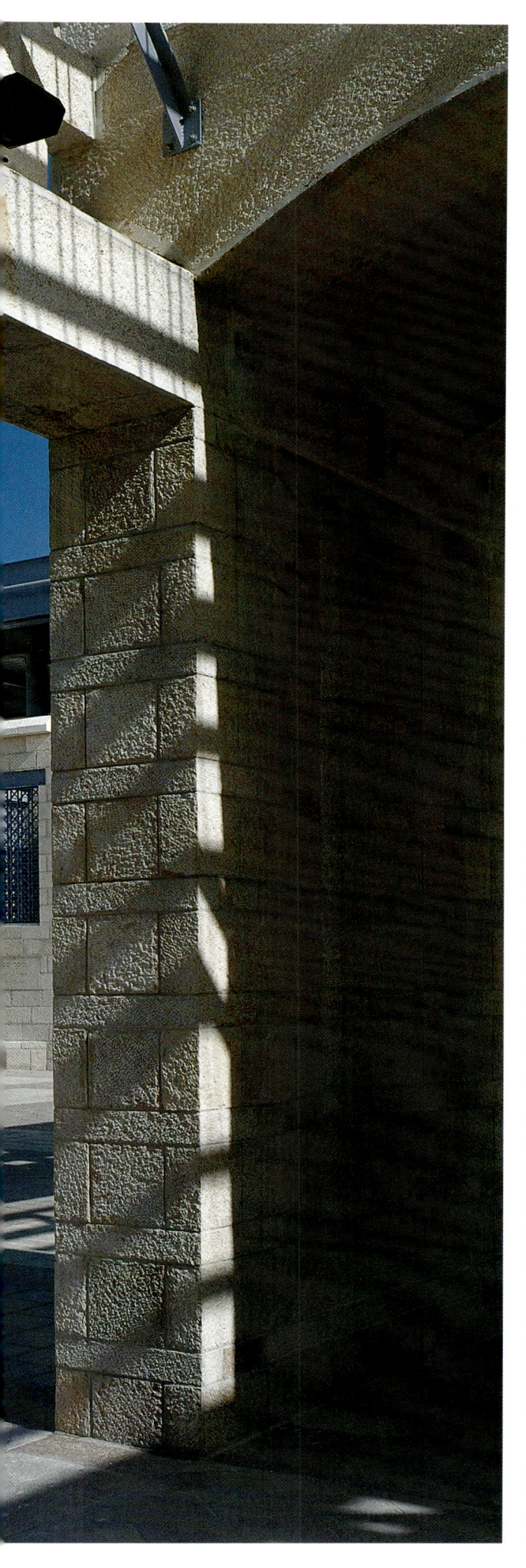

1-3. The City Hall complex, dedicated in 1993, is a modern architectural translation of traditional Jerusalem forms as seen in broad arches decorated with stylized *mushrabiyya* latticework, façades built of alternating rows of red and yellow stone, and an updated version of the traditional Jerusalem dome atop the council chamber. Designed by Canadian architect A.J. Diamond, with local architects Kolker-Kolker-Epstein, Bugod-Figueiredo-Niv-Krendel, and Meltzer-Igra.

blends with the surrounding topography. Its many inner courtyards and shaded, landscaped terraces imbue the building with a sense of expansive openness. The inevitable comparison with the nearby Hebrew University campus brings out the architectural quality of the Center, which, in its harmonious fusion of stone, marble, and wood, becomes a successful modern-day variant of the traditional world of Jerusalem forms.

The second major complex, the 550-room Hyatt Hotel, dedicated in 1987, was originally planned as a 22-story tower that would have dwarfed its entire surroundings and irrevocably altered the city's skyline. However, fierce public opposition forced a change in the design, with the result that architect David Reznik focused his plan on "broken" blocks around inner courtyards. The hotel's terraced structure, combined with the continuous rhythm of arches and stone walls, creates an interesting play of light and shade that shatters the monolithic character of the building, which rises, in graduated form, to a height of ten stories.

The quest for originality, shared even by the government, brought a revival of the Romantic-Oriental mode. Architects of the period were enthralled by the old mythological image of Jerusalem, a vision of picturesque towers, battlements, arches, and domes that tours of the Old City—the authentic item—could only confirm. In this sense, the original yet traditional Neo-Oriental style that evolved in the city after 1967 can be considered the Jerusalem version of Post-Modernism, then emerging on the international

1. The luxurious David's Village residential complex, opposite Jaffa Gate, epitomizes the Neo-Orientalist architecture that has characterized local building since the city's reunification in 1967. Architect: Moshe Safdie.

2. The 550 rooms of the Hyatt Hotel (1987) on Mount Scopus are built around a series of inner courtyards. Traditional stone construction is integratred with concrete and glass. Architect: David Reznik.

scene. However, native conservatism, as well as the charged history of the city and its stone edifices, obviated—at least until the mid-1980s—the lighter touches and the brighter materials that marked Post-Modernism elsewhere.

Critics of Jerusalem's revived Neo-Orientalism warned against the creation of "eclectic kitsch Disneyland" architecture. For these observers, the style could be little more than a simplistic translation of old, exotic forms into new materials and technologies. However, the critique fails to appreciate the prodigious impact of the encounter that a new generation had with the Old City following reunification in 1967. The powerful emotions released by this experience naturally sought an objective correlative in the symbols and markers of the past. Thus, it should hardly surprise that past styles would be copied, in some cases uncreatively and without a firm grasp of their original significance, resulting in a "nervous" architecture replete with structural distortions and a sense of dislocation. Since the mid-1980s, however, the urge to employ shapes from the past has moderated. Indeed, buildings erected in the early 1990s tend to be sedate in form, with fewer arches and more straight lines.

For an important example of Neo-Orientalism used in a subtle and sensitive manner, there is the City Hall Plaza, inaugurated in June 1993. This project, which changed the physical scale of the urban core, stands at the meeting point between East and West Jerusalem. It was meant to concentrate all the departments of the municipality—previously scattered about the city in dozens of different

3. For his conception of the Laromme Hotel (foreground), located next to Liberty Bell Park and opposite the Old City, architect Ya'akov Rechter drew on the typical Jerusalem courtyard with rooms around it. The dome (right) is the inflatable roof of the hotel's pool, which is covered in winter.

4. The campus of the Hebrew Union College was beautifully designed by architect Moshe Safdie (1986), around a series of inner courtyards of various sizes, with many arches and pergolas, fusing stone with exposed concrete, glass, and aluminum.

1-3. One of the most important and impressive modern architectural creations in Israel is the Supreme Court Building (dedicated 1993). An arcade sets off the north-south axis of the building facing the Knesset. The large openings to the judges' chambers are emphasized by a sculpturesque stone element. A strong horizontal thrust integrates the building into its environment. "It is an urban island," say the architects, Ram Karmi and Ada Karmi-Melamed, "contained by a wall that seems to grow from the earth as an organic extension of the hilly terrain."

buildings—in one central compound. Designed by A.J. Diamond, a Canadian architect, in collaboration with three local firms (Kolker-Kolker-Epstein, Bugod-Figueiredo-Niv-Krendel, and Meltzer-Igra), City Hall Plaza comprises a public square surrounded by two new office structures and ten renovated historical buildings, among them the former City Hall from the 1930s. The new buildings feature modern design and abound in evocations of the local Orient, including the use of reddish and yellowish stone in the *ablaq* style favored by the 15th-century Mamluks, *mushrabiyya* latticework, an aqueduct, and an entrance piazza with palm trees.

To create the new Supreme Court Building of 1992, in the National Government Precinct at Givat Ram, Ram Karmi and Ada Karmi-Melamed, a brother and sister team, regenerated forms and shapes from Jerusalem's historical and architectural past. Moreover, the architects garnered considerable praise for their remarkable ability to translate such abstract concepts as justice and equality, morality and law into a dignified architectural language expressing serene elegance through the refined use of monumental elements both inside and out. A pyramid motif recalls the ancient Kidron Valley tombs, while the inner courtyard echoes the analogous feature at the 1930s Rockefeller Museum, which in turn alludes to early Muslim motifs. Another example of toned-down Neo-Orientalism is the recent addition to Hebrew Union College, planned by architect Moshe Safdie and inaugurated in 1987. This design modernizes traditional forms, such as inner courtyards, arcades, and projecting oriels.

One of the focal points of construction in Jerusalem since the end of the 1980s has been Manahat, the city's southwest area. Development here reflects the change in municipal

4. The foyer leading to the five courtrooms is the largest and most impressive space in the building. Each entry (left) is designed as a gradual recession, as though hewed out of the stone wall.

5. Two copper pyramids projecting from the roof symbolize the historical link between past and present, between people and place. Like the ancient pyramids that are impervious to vagaries of change and fashion, the court rests on immutable principles. The far pyramid sets off the entry to the court library, while the forward one marks the western extremity of the entryway to the courtrooms.

planning, which emphasizes favoring the citizenry with an improved quality of both commercial services and facilities for sport and leisure. Thus, since the beginning of the 1990s Manahat has seen the arrival of three large architectural complexes, projects that have caused activity in the city to shift its center of gravity. They are the new Biblical Zoo, the Teddy Stadium for soccer, and the Jerusalem Shopping Mall, all located within a short distance of one another.

The new zoo, with its modern and advanced design, is inhabited by the animals that were formerly denizens of the old Biblical Zoo in the city's north. Architect Pasqual Broid's soccer stadium, while modern in its design and use of technology, integrates traditional stone construction with metal and plastic roofing. Finally, there is the Jerusalem Shopping Mall, the largest and most spacious in

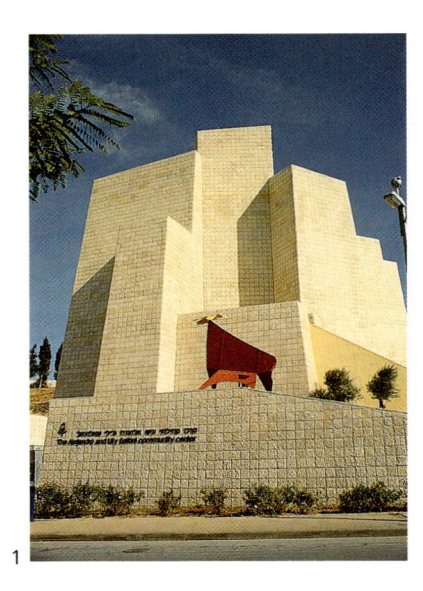

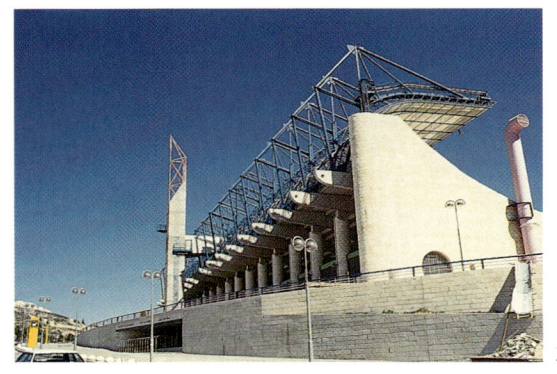

1. A deliberate antithesis to the boxlike apartment buildings of East Talpiot is the neighborhood's Saltiel Community Center. The cladding of the walls with small stone tiles emphasizes the stone's purely decorative function. The sculpture in front (*The Cow*) is by Alexander Calder. Architects: sculptor Mathias Goeritz, with Arthur Spector and Micha Amisar.

2. Post-Modernism combining Neo-Classical elements with Art Deco motifs, glass, concrete, stone, and bold colors marks one of the entrances to the Jerusalem Shopping Mall (1993). Architects: Avraham Yaski and Joseph Sivan together with promoter-builder David J. Azrieli.

3. The Teddy Stadium (1992; named for longtime mayor Teddy Kollek) combines the use of traditional stone with metal constructions, plastic roofs, and striking colors. Architect: Pasqual Broid.

4. Main entrance and one of the artificial lakes of the new Tisch Family Zoological Garden (New Biblical Zoo; 1993). Combining zoology, botany, archaeology, and educational activities, the zoo makes a major contribution to the development of leisure facilities in Jerusalem. Architects: Zvi Miller and Moshe Blum.

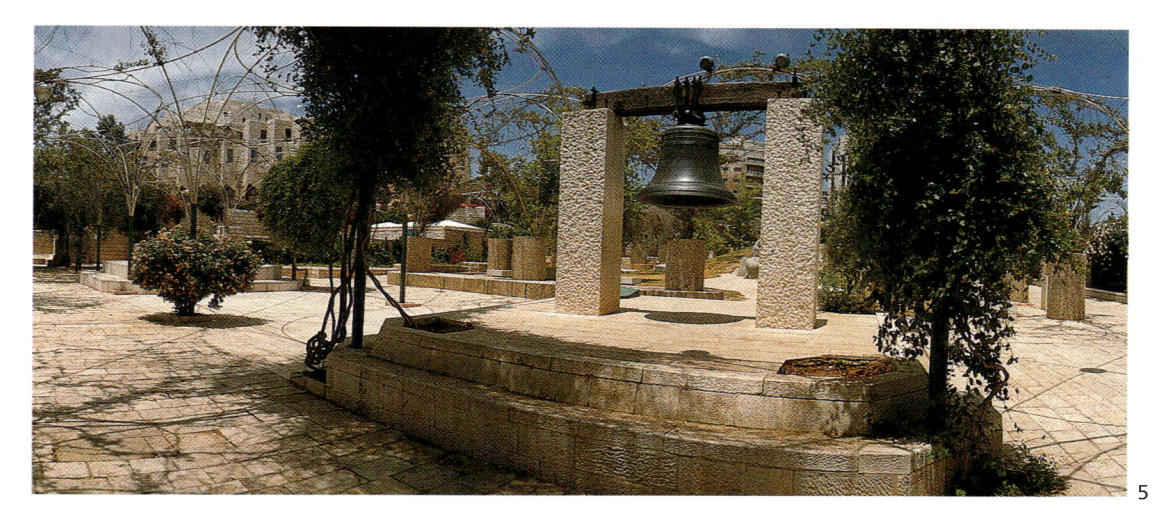

5-7. Jerusalem's modern urban and architectural development also comprises green areas with advanced leisure-time facilities that play an important role in enhancing the city's standard of living. Liberty Bell Park and the adjacent Bloomfield Park, were both designed by architect Ulrik Plessner. The core of Liberty Bell Park, which has a formal linear design of pergolas coverd with green vegetation, is a replica of the American Liberty Bell. Bloomfield Park features a round pergola supported by unfinished stone pillars beneath which are a fountain and pool. Together the two parks cover 25 acres of landscaped greenery and offer views of the Old City.

Israel (or indeed in the Middle East). Designed by Avraham Yaski, together with promoter-builder David Azrieli, it incorporates shapes and colors drawn primarily from the Post-Modernist repertoire, fusing traditional building with contemporary convenience.

The large perimeter neighborhoods built after 1967 at some remove from the inner city were the major, if not the exclusive, factor in the creation of "New Jerusalem." The renovations carried out within the Old City—mainly in the Jewish Quarter and on the wall and gates—and the building of the National Park around the walls contributed significantly to the city's changing face. The National Park dominated the "green revolution" waged during the early 1970s, a movement that produced other large-scale parks as well as pocket gardens scattered about the capital. This was a hard-fought campaign, in which the public, led by environmentally conscious groups as well as by Mayor Teddy Kollek himself, managed to scuttle plans for high-rises and highways in sensitive locations, particularly those affording views of the Old City. Two of the open, green spaces created in proximity to the wall—Liberty Bell Park and nearby Bloomfield Park, designed by architect Ulrik Plessner—are much favored by Jewish and Arab residents alike. Furthermore, both recreational facilities form part of the Cultural Mile that stretches from Jaffa Gate and the Tower of David to the southwest as far as the Jerusalem Theater complex in Talbiyeh.

Jerusalem's most derelict area in the aftermath of reunification was the former no-man's-land along the Israeli-Jordanian frontier within the divided city. Once strewn with mine

1, 2. Part of the "Cultural Mile," the most important section of the National Park around the Old City walls, accommodates many of Jerusalem's cultural centers and leisure facilities. View to the north shows, left of the amphitheater in Sultan's Pool, Mishkenot Sha'ananim, the Jerusalem Music Center, and Khutzot Hayotzer for arts and crafts.

2. Until the end of the Ottoman Period, Sultan's Pool was a water reservoir. Renovated in 1980, it is now the open-air Hassenfeld Amphitheater with a specially designed acoustic shell, made of modular elements, which is mounted before each performance and afterward dismantled. Architect: A. Rahamimoff.

3. Distinctive windmill containing an exhibition devoted to Sir Moses (Moshe) Montefiore is the landmark of Yemin Moshe neighborhood.

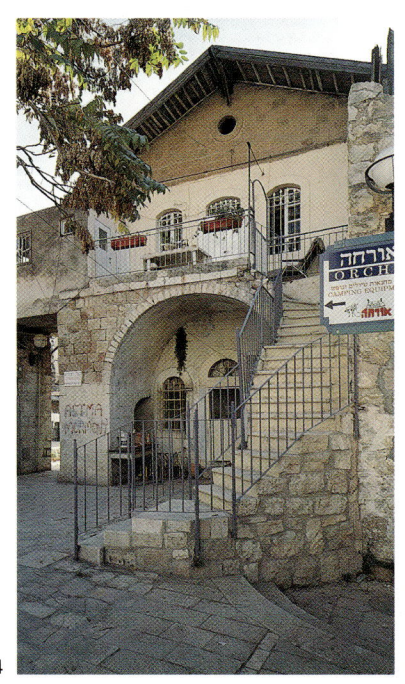

fields, barbed-wire fences, and wrecks, this area is now known as the Cultural Mile, the city's most attractive enclosure of gardens, leisure facilities, and cultural centers. Here, some twenty different types of activities unfold, enriching the life of Jerusalem, often in historic buildings revitalized and modernized mostly through the Jerusalem Foundation. Among the institutions along the Cultural Mile are Khutzot Hayotzer, an arts and crafts center, the Hassenfeld Amphitheater at the Sultan's Pool, Mishkenot Sha'ananim Artists Guest House, the Jerusalem Music Center, the Cinémathèque, and the Khan Theater.

Between 1948 and 1967 the 19th-century neighborhood of Yemin Moshe hovered on the very border between East and West Jerusalem, across from the Jordanian positions on the Old City wall. The residents were mostly new immigrants making do in the quarter's dilapidated houses. After 1967, architects Sa'adia Mandel and Gabriel Kertesz drew up a comprehensive plan for preservation, complete with detailed architectural guidelines. Subsequently, the neighborhood has gradually evolved to become one of Jerusalem's most beautiful residential areas.

Adjacent to Yemin Moshe, Mamilla too lay on the border of the divided city and on the edge of no-man's-land. The buildings in this neighborhood, some of them damaged from the 1948 war, would eventually come into use as garages, workshops, and substandard housing. In the post-1967 period Mamilla was the subject of a public debate over the scale its preservation should take and the form of its future development. Today, construction in the area is well advanced, as part of an overall plan conceived by architect Moshe Safdie. In the current phase, a large parking area is under construction across from Jaffa Gate, while simultaneously the first group of residential dwellings in "David's Village" is being completed.

The building style employed in this residential project displays elements of the indigenous Neo-Orientalism that has emerged in Jerusalem since the mid-1970s. It features terraced dwellings of two or three stories, located along and between narrow lanes, with inner courtyards, bridge structures, and a range of domes and arches in various types and sizes. But however traditional the effects, they depend upon the use of modern technologies and state-of-the-art materials.

The public continued to enjoy some of the most spectacular views in Jerusalem, thanks to the pitched battle fought in the early 1970s against construction proposed for the slopes of Government House ridge. Out of the struggle, moreover, came the splendid Haas and Sherover Promenades, which, following their completion in 1987 and 1989, quickly gained vast popular favor, offering as they did unrivaled views across the Hinnom Valley to both Old and New Cities. The Haas Promenade, designed by Lawrence Halprin and Shlomo Aronson to recall an ancient aqueduct, displays fine stonework and cast-iron lamps styled in the 1930s manner found in the YMCA building and nearby Government House, among other period structures. The Sherover Promenade, planned by Shlomo Aronson, continues elegantly along the valley's western ridge, affording magnificent panoramic views from vantage points defined by wood pergolas.

4. A major architectural effort was invested to preserve and commercially revitalize the buildings of the Nahalat Shiva neighborhood in downtown Jerusalem. Architects: Nahum Meltzer and Guy Igra.

5. Overlooking one of the most spectacular panoramas in Jerusalem is the elegant Gabriel Sherover Promenade (1989) in the city's south. Stone paving and stylized lamps help form a backdrop for performances in the promenade's amphitheater, set off by a picturesque pergola structure, with dressing rooms on the sides. Some 600 newly planted olive, carob, and cherry trees add to the unique atmosphere. Architect: Shlomo Aronson.

Until the early 1970s, planning authorities took a reverent attitude toward the Old City but failed to appreciate all the merits of preserving relatively "new" structures (a century and more old). The majority of the New City's 19th-century neighborhoods are decaying, although some have undergone successful revitalization or gentrification—most strikingly, perhaps, Nahalat Shiva, Jerusalem's version of "Soho."

In the heart of downtown Jerusalem, close to Nahalat Shiva, there is a mansion that was once slated for demolition but then given a new lease on life. Built, as already mentioned, in the late 19th century by Aga Rashid Nashashibi, the villa and its spacious garden became the home of Dr. Abraham Ticho and his wife in 1921. Dr. Ticho, a leading ophthalmologist, set up his surgery on the ground floor. The family quarters were on the second floor, where Mme Ticho, an artist renowned for her exquisite drawings of Jerusalem, also maintained her studio. Anna Ticho, who died in 1980, twenty years after her husband, bequeathed the building to the people of Jerusalem. Following renovation, carried out in a way to preserve the original flavor of the place, the Tichos' residence became a quiet sanctuary amidst the din of downtown Jerusalem. It opened in 1984 as a café, a museum for many of Anna Ticho's works, and a venue for chamber-music concerts.

The German Colony and the affluent Arab neighborhoods of the Mandate Period, south of the city center, are prime examples of a gentrification process that is altering sections of the city by means of "add-on architecture." This type of building is particularly important in preserving the architectural and environmental character of old neighborhoods erected from the late 19th century through the 1920s and 1930s. Two schools of thought have developed with regard to add-on architecture. The conservative-classical view is that the style of the additions must be consistent with the general format and architectural specifications of the original structure, playing down the difference between new and old. The sec-

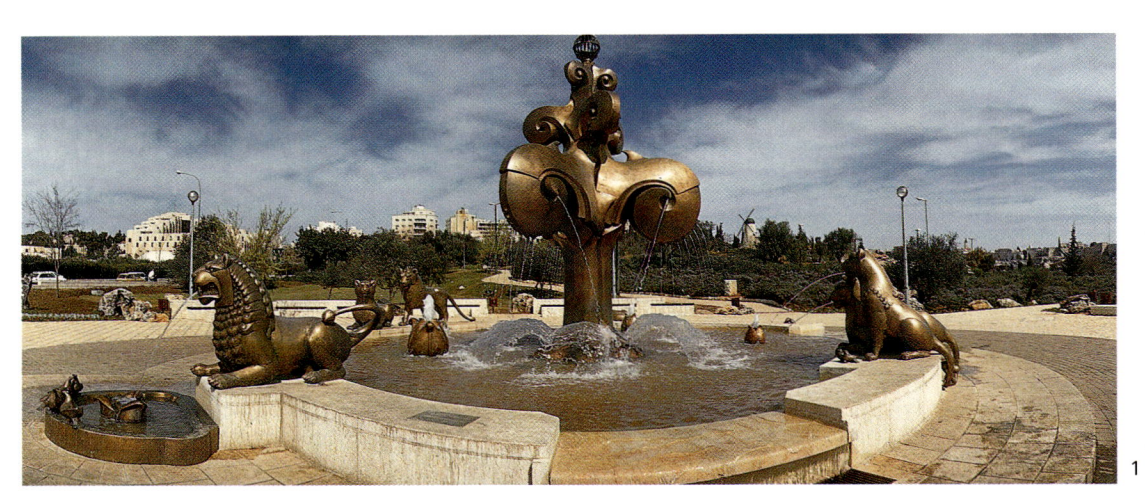

1. Outdoor sculptures, installed prominently in Jerusalem since 1967, play an important role in determining cultural-physical perspectives in the urban texture and create the effect of an "outdoor museum." *Lions' Fountain* (1989) by sculptor Gernot Rumpf in Bloomfield Park.

2. *The Golem*, or *The Monster* (1971), a popular activity-sculpture by Niki de Saint-Phalle in a public park in the Kiryat Hayovel neighborhood of western Jerusalem. The beast's tongues are red slides.

3. Some outdoor sculptures are the artistic equivalent of milestones at important intersections. By its size and sculpturesque geometry, *Faith*, by Alexander Liberman (1987), marks the transition to northern Jerusalem, near the Givat Shapira ("French Hill") neighborhood.

ond school takes the opposite tack, striving to emphasize the discrepancy between the original and the additions through the use of different forms, technologies, and materials. According to this approach, candor about the life of the building is better than concealment.

Since 1967, gentrification has been a gradual, but continuous, process in some of the long-established neighborhoods at the core of New Jerusalem. Architecturally and physically, this has taken the form of renovating and/or expanding run-down houses and building new ones on empty lots in a manner harmoniously blended with the established environment—with the scale, roof shape, stone type, and architectural detailing of the older structures. In the main, this is a matter of creating companionable infill for an existing urban texture.

Parallel to this gentrification, fueled by middle-class families moving into the old neighborhoods of the urban core, a program known as "Project Renewal" has been underway to renovate the public-housing blocks of the pre-1967 era. Run by the state and the Jewish Agency, with the assistance of Jewish communities abroad, Project Renewal attempts to break up the monotonous appearance of these monoliths. Equally important, the program endeavors to enlarge the small, cubelike apartments and thus reduce overcrowding, while also preserving the local community structure and persuading relatively established families not to abandon the neighborhood.

The nation's aesthetic consciousness has been raised as well by many outdoor sculptures, which, particularly since 1967, have added to the city's beauty and transformed Jerusalem into an "outdoor museum." In public spaces all over the city are now installed over one hundred works, by such world-famed sculptors as Henry Moore, Alexander Calder, and Jacques Lipchitz, as well as by leading Israeli artists, among them Yitzhak Danziger, Menashe Kadishman, and Yigal Tumarkin. A number of public buildings have also been enhanced by strategically placed works of art.

In addition, Jerusalem boasts a building best described as an architectural sculpture: the Saltiel Community Center in the East Talpiot neighborhood. Planned by Mexican architect Mathias Goeritz, together with Arthur Spector and Micha Amisar, the edifice comprises a cluster of construction blocks with different heights and upward-sloping walls. Stone squares, similar to floor tiles, dramatize the reality of stone used solely as overlay and not as structure.

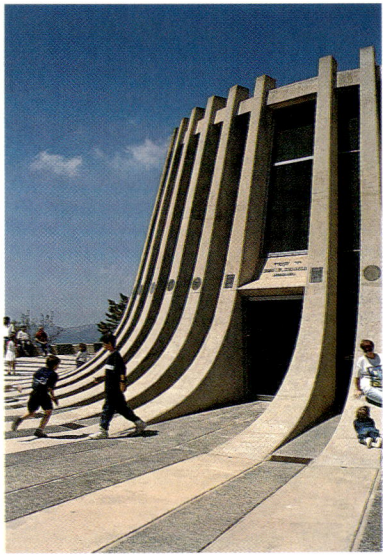

4. Standing on a hilltop on the edge of West Jerusalem is the Kennedy Memorial (1966). The structure, which commemorates the assassination of the United States President John F. Kennedy in 1963, suggests a tree that has been felled, or a volcanic eruption. Fifty paving strips that become concrete columns stand for the fifty American states. Architect: David Reznik.

5. For thousands of years pyramids, whether in Egypt or Jerusalem, have symbolized the ascending soul. The main entrance to the Hall of Remembrance at Yad Lebanim (Soldiers Memorial, 1977) is a split pyramid, with the names of the fallen engraved on either side. Architects: David Reznik with Arthur Spector and Micha Amisar.

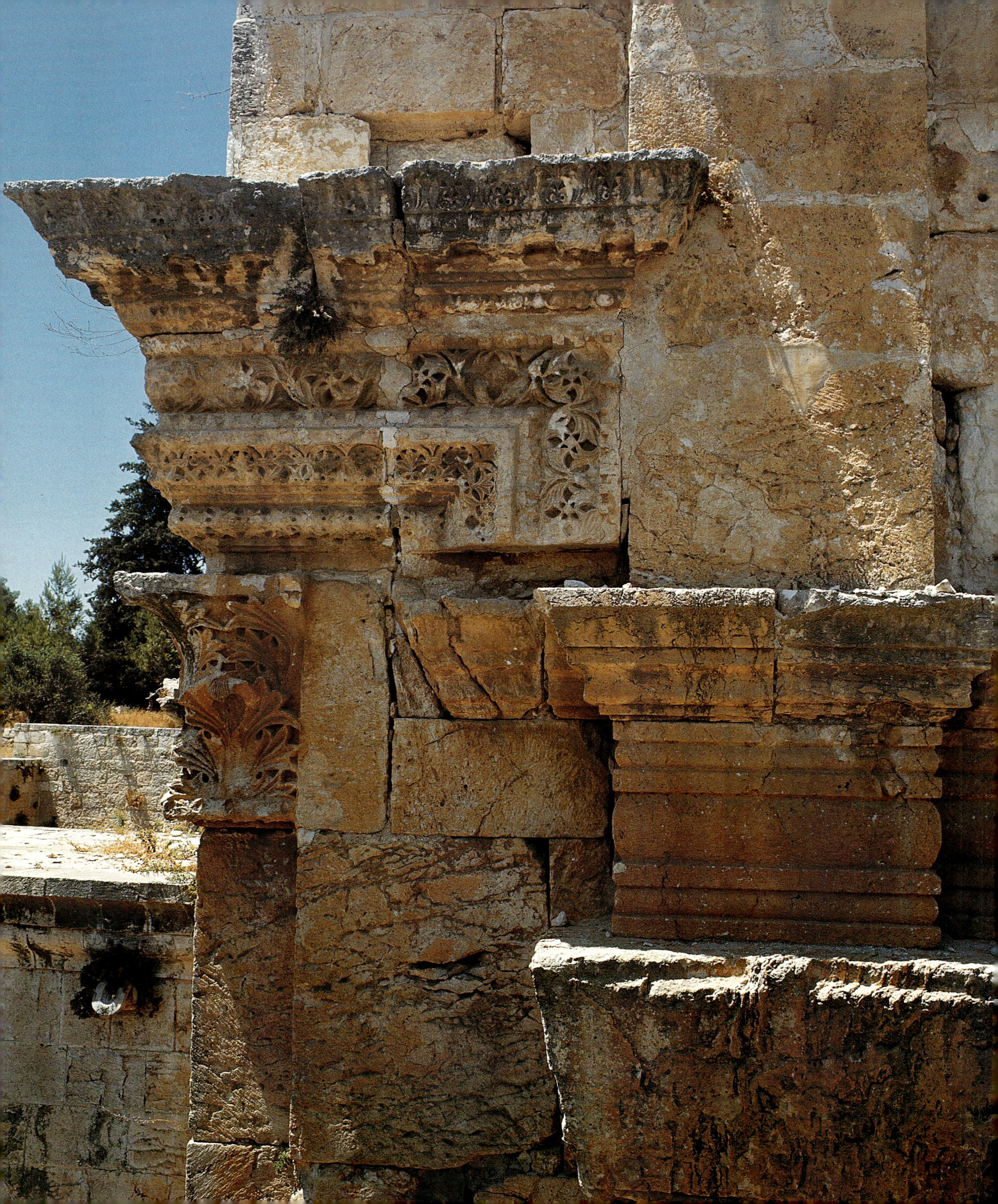

Epilogue
Stone: The Unifying Element

As demonstrated in the text and pictures seen earlier, the architecture of Jerusalem throughout its long history displays a multitude of styles, all of which share stone as the primary construction material. Stone has always been Jerusalem's "trademark," the common denominator of all building periods from the First Temple era to our own day. Just as London is red brick, New York is glass, and Sana, in Yemen, is clay, so Jerusalem is stone. Shortly after the British captured Jerusalem from the Turks in 1917, the new Military Governor, Ronald Storrs, decreed that no structure may be erected in the city using such materials as metal and plaster. More than any other law or regulation laid down in Jerusalem during the last seventy-five years, Storrs' historic ordinance has mandated stone-built architecture, thereby determining the face of the city. The English, with their own venerable tradition of conservation, and their grasp of the historic value universally attached to Jerusalem, understood the importance of preserving the city and its unique character in the modern era.

The majority of houses dating from the late Ottoman Period were constructed of stone, with thick double walls and a filler sandwiched between them. In Arab building there had been a widespread tradition of cross-vaulted structures, topped by stone-clad domes; however, by the end of the 19th century ceilings had gone flat, supported by steel rails and covered with tiles laid on a sloping timber roof. These technologies restricted the height of dwellings to no more than two or three stories; they also required that interior spaces have relatively modest apertures. Naturally, such limitations did not allow for much range in architectural design.

Beginning in the 1920s, cement and concrete became cheap and readily available, creating new possibilities for design. A resilient and strong material, concrete allows walls and ceilings to be fashioned quickly and efficiently. As builders in Jerusalem grew more sophisticated in their use of concrete, stone lost its importance as a structural element. In most of the houses erected in Jerusalem since the mid-1920s, the walls have a concrete back 8-12 inches (20-30 centimeters) thick and exterior stone cladding only about half that deep.

Industrialized building arrived in Jerusalem during the 1960s, when the Housing Ministry moved from low, scattered construction to massive, dense row-buildings. Instead of one- or two-story houses made of concrete, plaster, or *wildbau* ("rough-hewn") stone and containing four to sixteen apartments, the Ministry favored three- and four-story buildings with dozens of residential units. Heavy machinery came into use and with it more modern types of construction. As a result, some public housing and buildings were structured as exposed-concrete frames and infilled walls of prefabricated concrete with various overlays, none of them authentic Jerusalem stone.

In order to accommodate the strict ordinance requiring stone construction, and to hasten the growth of urgently needed public housing, while also controlling costs, builders have been allowed, since the 1970s, to employ prefabricated concrete walls faced with a thin layer of cut stone.

The transition from stone walls some 3 feet (1 meter) thick, built during the Ottoman Period, to the concrete wall, merely veneered in stone an inch (3 centimeters) thick, clearly illustrates the development from traditional building processes to the industrialized technologies of the modern world.

The history of Jerusalem is writ in stone. Like the rings that mark the age of the oldest living things on earth, the Giant Redwoods of California, the stones with which Jerusalem is built narrate the saga of the ancient city's three-thousand-year role in the evolution of the human spirit.

1. Jerusalem stone is the unifying architectural element in the city from time immemorial to our own day. Palaces and huts, fences, towers, walls, arches, vaults, and gardens—all were built of stone that was reused in each succeeding era. Detail from the Gate of Mercy ("Golden Gate") on the eastern side of the Temple Mount wall.

2. An Arab stonecutter plies his timeless trade: The type of cut, the design, and the color of the stone imbue it with the texture and hue that contribute mightily to the shimmering eternity of Jerusalem.

Bibliography

Abbreviation: PEFQSt (Palestine Exploration Fund, Quarterly Statement).

Amiran, David. "The Geographical Background," *The Saga of the Holy City*. Universitas Publishers: Jerusalem, 1954.

—-"The Development of Jerusalem 1860-1970," *Urban Geography of Jerusalem*, companion vol. to *Atlas of Jerusalem*. Massada Press: Jerusalem, 1973.

Amiran, D.H.K., Shachar, A., Kimhi, I., Karmon, M., Bandel, P. (eds.). *Atlas of Jerusalem*. Walter de Gruyter: Berlin-New York, 1973.

Amiran, H.K. David. "Jerusalem's Urban Development," *Middle East Review*. Spring-Summer, 1981.

Architecture of Islamic Jerusalem, The. Exh. cat., World of Islam Festival. London, 1976.

Ashbee, C.R. (ed.). *Jerusalem 1918-1920, Being the Records of the Pro-Jerusalem Council during the Period of the British Military Administration*. John Murray: London, 1921.

—- (ed.). *Jerusalem 1920-1922, Being the Records of the Pro-Jerusalem Council during the First Two Years of the Civil Administration*. John Murray: London, 1924.

Avigad, Nahman. *Discovering Jerusalem*. Blackwell: Oxford, 1984.

Azariya, Victor. *The Armenian Quarter of Jerusalem*. U. of Calif. Press: Berkeley, Los Angeles, London, 1984.

Bahat, Dan. *A Selection of Ottoman Structures in the Old City of Jerusalem*. Jerusalem, 1990.

—-. *The Illustrated Atlas of Jerusalem*. Carta: Jerusalem, 1990.

Beck, Haig (ed.). *UIA International Architect*, Issue 9, 1985.

Ben-Arieh, Yehoshua. *Jerusalem in the 19th Century—The Old City; The New City* (2 vols.). Yad Izhak Ben Zvi: Jerusalem; St. Martin's Press: New York, 1984.

Bourgoin, Jules. *Les Arts Arabes*. Morelet: Paris, 1873.

Briggs, Martin S. *Muhammadan Architecture in Egypt and Palestine*. Clarendon Press: Oxford, 1924.

Brlek, Metodio. *La Chiesa di S. Salvatore, storia e arte*. Franciscan Printing Press: Jerusalem, 1986.

Broshi, Magen. "Along Jerusalem's Walls," *Biblical Archaeologist*, Vol. 40, No. 1, March 1977.

Burgoyne, M.H. *Mamluk Jerusalem*. British School of Archaeology in Jerusalem, Scorpion: London, 1987.

Cana'an, Taufik. *The Palestinian Arab House: Its Architecture and Folklore*. Syrian Orphanage Press: Jerusalem, 1933.

Cassuto, D. "Four Sephardi Synagogues in the Old City," *Jerusalem Revealed, Archaeology in the Holy City 1968-1974*. Israel Exploration Society: Jerusalem, 1976.

Corbo, Virgilio. *Il Santo Sepolcro di Gerusalemme: aspetti archeologici dalle origini al periodo crociato*. Franciscan Printing Press: Jerusalem, 1981.

Couasnon, Charles. *The Church of the Holy Sepulchre in Jerusalem*. British Academy: London, 1974.

Creswell, K.A.C. *Early Muslim Architecture*, Vols. 1, 2. Clarendon Press: Oxford, 1969.

Dalman, Gustaf. *Arbeit und Sitte in Palästina*, Vol. 7, *Das Haus, Hühnerzucht, Taubenzucht, Bienenzucht*. "Der Rufer": Gütersloh, 1942.

Dash, Jacob, and Elisha Efrat. *The Israel Physical Master Plan*. Ministry of Interior, Planning Department: Jerusalem 1964.

Dickie, Archibald C. "Stone Dressing of Jerusalem, Past and Present," *PEFQSt*, 1897.

Eckardt, Wolf von. "Blending Past and Present," *Time*, March 12, 1984.

Efrat, Elisha. "Changes in the Town Planning Concepts of Jerusalem 1919-1969," *Environmental Planning* (Israeli Association for Environmental Planning Quarterly). Jerusalem, 1971.

Elan, Shlomo. *Deutsche Gebäude in Jerusalem*. Wertheim: 1984.

Erlik, Avraham. "British Architects in Mandatory Palestine," *TVAI*, Vol. 22. Tel Aviv, 1984.

Fletcher, Banister. *A History of Architecture on the Comparative Method*. Athlone Press: London, 1961.

Gilbert, Martin. *Jerusalem Illustrated History Atlas*. Steimatzky: Jerusalem, 1977.

Golani, Yehonathan, and Dieter Gershom von Schwartze (eds.) *Israel Builds 1970*. Ministry of Housing: Jerusalem, 1970.

Gonen, Rivka, and David Kroyanker. *To Live in Jerusalem*. Israel Museum: Jerusalem, 1993.

Goodwin, Godfrey. *A History of Ottoman Architecture*. Thames and Hudson: London, 1971.

Graham, John. "Jerusalem Post-1967: The New Neighbourhoods Gilo, Ramot and North Jerusalem," *UIA International Architect*, No. 9, 1985.

Hamilton, R.W. *The Structural History of the Aqsa Mosque*. Oxford U. Press: London, 1949.

Harlap, Amiram (ed.). *Israel Builds 1977*. Ministry of Housing: Israel, 1977.

Harris, Cyril M. (ed.). *Illustrated Dictionary of Historic Architecture*. Dover: New York, 1977.

Heinze-Mühleib, Ita. *Erich Mendelsohn, Bauten und Projekte in Palästina (1934-1941)*. Scaneg: Munich, 1986.

Hill, Derek. *Islamic Architecture and its Decoration AD 800-1500*. Faber and Faber: London, 1964.

Hyman, Benjamin, Israel Kimhi, and Joseph Savitsky. *Jerusalem in Transition: Urban Growth and Change 1970s-1980s*. Jerusalem Institute for Israel Studies; Institute of Urban and Regional Studies of the Hebrew University of Jerusalem. March 1985.

Israel Builds 1948-1968. Ministry of Housing: Tel Aviv, 1968.

Israel Builds: New Trends in Planning of Housing. Ministry of Housing: Israel, 1987.

Jäger, Karl. *Das Bauernhaus in Palästina*. Vanderhoeck & Ruprecht: Göttingen, 1912.

Jewish Quarter: Ruins and Restoration, The. Israel Information Center: Jerusalem, September 1973.

Johns, J.W. *The Anglican Cathedral Church of Saint James*. Jerusalem, London, 1844.

Keenan, N. "A Local Trend in Crusader Art in Jerusalem," *Jerusalem Revealed: Archaeology in the Holy City 1968-1974* (Yigael Yadin, ed.). Israel Exploration Society, 1976.

Kenaan, Nurith. "Local Christian Art in Twelfth-Century Jerusalem," *Israel Exploration Journal*, No. 23, 1973.

Kendall, Henry. *Jerusalem City Plan, Preservation and Development during the British Mandate 1918-1948*. His Majesty's Stationary Office: London 1948.

Kenyon, Kathleen M. *The Architecture of Islamic Jerusalem*. British School of Archaeology: Jerusalem, 1976.

Kollek, Teddy, and Abraham Rabinovich. "Decade of United Jerusalem," *Encyclopedia Judaica Yearbook 1977-78*. Keter Publishing House: Jerusalem, 1979.

Kroyanker, David. *Developing Jerusalem 1967-1975*. Jerusalem Committee, with the Jerusalem Foundation: Jerusalem, 1975.

—-. *Jerusalem Planning and Development 1978-79*. Jerusalem Committee, with the Jerusalem Foundation: Jerusalem, 1979.

—-. *Jerusalem Planning and Development 1979-82*. Jerusalem Institute for Israel Studies for the Jerusalem Committee: Jerusalem, 1982.

—-. *Jerusalem Planning and Development 1982-1985: New Trends*. Jerusalem Committee, with the Jerusalem Foundation in conjunction with the Jerusalem Institute for Israel Studies: Jerusalem, 1985.

—-, and Yael Guiladi. *Jerusalem 1978: Between Two Decades*. Jerusalem Committee, with the Jerusalem Foundation: Jerusalem, 1978.

—-, and Dror Wahrman. *Jerusalem Architecture: Periods and Styles: The Jewish Quarters and Public Buildings Outside the Old City Walls 1860-1914*. Jerusalem Institute for Israel Studies and Domino Press: Jerusalem, 1983.

Kutcher, Arthur. *The New Jerusalem: Planning and Politics*. Thames and Hudson: London, 1973.

Levin, Michael. "The Stones of Jerusalem," *Journal of Jewish Art*, Vol. 2. Spertus College of Judaica Press: Chicago, 1975.

—-. "Public Art in Jerusalem," *Ariel*, No. 52, 1982.

Lichfield, Nathaniel. "Planning and Development of Jerusalem," *Encyclopedia Judaica Yearbook 1974*. Keter Publishing House: Jerusalem, 1974.

Michell, George (ed.). *Architecture of the Islamic World*. Thames and Hudson: London, 1978.

"Moshe Safdie: Building in Context," *Process: Architecture*, No. 56. Process Architecture: Tokyo, March 1985.

Pedersen, Kirsten. *The History of the Ethiopian Community in the Holy Land from the Time of Emperor Tewodros II till 1974*. Ecumenical Institute for Theological Research: Tantur, 1983.

Peters, Paulhans. "Die Altstadt," *Baumeister: Zeitschift für Architektur Planung*. Unwelt: Munich, March 1985.

Pierotti, Ermete. *Plan de l'Église de la Résurrection*. Lemercier: Paris, [c. 1860].

—-. *Plan de Jérusalem ancienne & moderne*. Paris, [1861].

—-. *Jerusalem Explored*, being a description of the ancient and modern city, with numerous plans and sections (2 vols). Bell and Daldy: London, 1864.

Pothorn, Herbert. *A Guide to Architectural Styles*. Phaidon: Oxford, 1983.

Prawer, J. "Jerusalem in Crusader Days," *Jerusalem Revealed, Archaeology in the Holy City 1968-1974* (Yigael Yadin, ed.). Israel Exploration Society, Jerusalem: 1976.

Rosen-Ayalon, Miriam. "Murals in the Moslem Quarter of Jerusalem," *Ariel*, No. 31, 1972.

—-. "The Islamic Architecture of Jerusalem," *Jerusalem Revealed, Archaeology in the Holy City 1968-1974* (Yigael Yadin, ed.). Israel Exploration Society: Jerusalem, 1976.

—-. "The Early Islamic Monuments of al-Haram al-Sharif: An Iconographic Study," *QEDEM*, No. 28. Jerusalem, 1989.

—-. "On Suleiman's Sabils in Jerusalem," *The Islamic World, from Classical to Modern Times: Essays in Honor of Bernard Lewis* (C.E. Bosworth, et al., eds.). Darwin Press: Princeton, 1989.

Safdie, Moshe. *The Harvard Jerusalem Studio*. MIT Press: Cambridge, Mass., 1986.

—-. *Jerusalem: The Future of the Past*. Houghton Mifflin: Boston, 1989.

Sauer, Paul. *Uns rief das Heilige Land: Die Tempelgesellschaft im Wandel der Zeit*. Theiss: Stuttgart, 1985.

Saylor, Henry H. *Dictionary of Architecture*. John Wiley: New York, 1963.

Schick, C. "Notes from Jerusalem," *PEFQSt*, pp.213-214. London, 1887.

—-. "The Stones of Jerusalem," *PEFQSt*, pp. 50-51. London, 1887.

—-. "Arabic Building Terms," *PEFQSt*, pp. 194-201. London, 1893.

—-. "Die Baugeschichte der Stadt Jerusalem," *Zeitschrift des Deutschen Palästina-Vereins*, No. 17, 1894-1895, pp. 261-276.

Schmelz, U.O. "The Evolution of Jerusalem's Population," *Urban*

Geography of Jerusalem, companion vol. to *Atlas of Jerusalem*. Massada Press: Jerusalem, 1973.

Shachar, Arie. "The Functional Structure of Jerusalem," *Urban Geography of Jerusalem*, companion vol. to *Atlas of Jerusalem*. Massada Press: Jerusalem, 1973.

—-. "The Hebrew University on Mount Scopus," *Ariel*, No. 58, 1984.

Shapiro, Shachar. "Planning Jerusalem, the First Generation 1917-1968," *Urban Geography of Jerusalem*, companion vol. to *Atlas of Jerusalem*. Massada Press: Jerusalem, 1973.

Sharon, Arieh. *Planning Jerusalem: The Old City and its Environs*. Weidenfeld and Nicolson: Jerusalem, 1973.

Tanai, D. "The Ben-Zakkai Synagogue: Reconstruction and Restoration," *Jerusalem Revealed, Archaeology in the Holy City 1968-1974* (Yigael Yadin, ed.). Israel Exploration Society: Jerusalem, 1976.

Wager, Eliyahu. *Illustrated Guide to Jerusalem*. Jerusalem Publishing House and Keter Publishing House: Jerusalem, 1988.

Zago, Manreque (ed.), Michael Levin and Tamar Goldschmidt (text and selection of art), Garo H. Nalbadian (photography). *Sculptures in Jerusalem*. Buenos Aires, Jerusalem, 1983.

In addition to the works in English cited above for David Kroyanker, the author has written extensively in Hebrew on the architecture, town planning, and physical development of Jerusalem. These writings have appeared not only in book form but also as articles for both magazines and newspapers. The books are listed below, in English translation and in chronological order.

Jerusalem Architecture: Periods and Styles, Arab Buildings Outside the Old City Walls. Keter Publishing House and Jerusalem Institute for Israel Studies: Jerusalem: 1985.

Jerusalem Architecture: Periods and Styles, European-Christian Buildings Outside the Old City Walls. Keter Publishing House and Jerusalem Institute for Israel Studies: Jerusalem, 1987.

Jerusalem Openings: Gates, Doors, Windows and Grills. Zmora, Bitan Publishers: Tel-Aviv, 1987.

Jerusalem: Conflicts Over the City's Physical and Visual Form. Zmora, Bitan Publishers and Jerusalem Institute for Israel Studies: Tel-Aviv, 1988.

Jerusalem Architecture: Periods and Styles: The Period of the British Mandate 1918-1948. Keter Publishing House and Jerusalem Institute for Israel Studies: Jerusalem, 1989.

Zoltan Shimshon Harmat, Architect (1900-1985), 60 Years of Creative Work. The Built Heritage—Research and Documentation: Jerusalem, 1990.

Jerusalem Architecture: Periods and Styles: Modern Architecture Outside the Old City Walls 1948-1990. Maxwell-Macmillan-Keter Publishing and Jerusalem Institute for Israel Studies: Jerusalem, 1991.

Jerusalem Architecture: The Old City. Keter Publishing House and Jerusalem Institute for Israel Studies: Jerusalem, 1993.

Dreamscapes: Unbuilt Jerusalem, Tower of David. Museum of the History of Jerusalem: 1993.

The Making of City Hall Complex, Jerusalem. Ariel Publishing House: Jerusalem, 1993.

Glossary

The terms cited here are, for the most part, defined according to their use in the present book, as well as in the context of Jerusalem architecture.

ablaq: Arabic for stones of different hues, particularly white and red, combined in masonry construction. Widely used, especially in Mamluk and Moorish architecture, *ablaq* had considerable stylistic influence on several of the finest buildings erected in the Arab neighborhoods outside the Old City walls, notably during the Mandate Period, but also at the new City Hall inaugurated in 1993.

acanthus: A plant of the Mediterranean region whose serrated leaves have provided a decorative motif for stone architecture since Classical times. The motif appears quite often in the wrought-iron doors of shops erected in Jewish neighborhoods during the late 19th century.

aisle: In a church, a passage running parallel to the nave and separated from it by a colonnade.

ambulatorium, ambulatory: An enclosed passageway around the apse of a church or around a shrine; also the covered passage around a cloister.

apse: The semicircular end of a church, beyond the nave, crossing, sanctuary, and choir.

arabesque: Intricately woven, decorative patterns consisting of abstract curvilinear forms or stylized plants, endlessly repeated. Very widespread in Muslim art and architecture, arabesque patterns are ubiquitous in Jerusalem's buildings surviving from the Mamluk Period.

arcade: A regular series of arches borne upon piers or columns, sometimes forming a covered walkway. Widely present in public buildings erected in Jerusalem by European Christians during the 19th century, as well as in luxurious Arab building.

Armenian ceramic tiles: Glazed ceramic tiles decorated with geometric and floral patterns, often in shades of blue and turquoise. Produced by Armenian craftsmen brought to Palestine from Turkey at the beginning of the British Mandate, the tiles were used to embellish a variety of structures put up during the Mandate Period, notably in affluent Arab neighborhoods, but also in such British-sponsored institutional buildings as Rockefeller Museum and Government House.

Art Deco: A decorative style canonized by Paris' 1925 Exposition Internationale des Arts Décoratifs et Industriels Modernes and widely adopted in Western architecture throughout the 1930s. Sleekly glamorous, streamlined, sometimes angular, and sometimes cursive, Art Deco made its presence felt in Jerusalem in the rounded wings of buildings and in the iron gates and window grilles of the International Style houses built by both Jews and Arabs during the 1930s and 1940s.

Art Nouveau: A decorative style notable for its flame-like organic forms and dynamic, whiplash lines, Art Nouveau was all the rage in the architecture and applied arts of Europe and the Americas from about 1890 until the early years of the 20th century. Perhaps because of the features it shared with Arabesque, Art Nouveau did not become very common in Jerusalem, although it does appear in some wrought-iron gates of affluent Arab homes. *See also* Jugendstil.

Ashkenazi, Ashkenazim (pl.): Jews from Germany and Eastern Europe, as contrasted with the Sephardi(m) from Spain.

atrium: The main inner room, shaped as an open court, in a Roman house; also the forecourt, often surrounded by a colonnade, at the front of a church. A familiar feature in Jerusalem, especially in public buildings erected by European Christians during the late 19th century.

Awqaf (plural of Waqf): The Muslim Religious Endowments, whose real-estate holdings cannot be sold, only leased for a number of years.

Ayyubids: Led by Saladin, the Islamic Ayyubids conquered Jerusalem in 1187, after which they ruled it intermittently until 1250.

Baroque Style: A style of art and architecture dominant in Europe during the 17th and 18th centuries, the Baroque is characterized by exuberantly curving or arabesque lines and surfaces, a Classical vocabulary of forms and motifs, full-bodied plasticity creating a dynamic play of light and dark, oval interior spaces, and symmetrical compositions enlivened by occult balances. In Jerusalem, the Neo-Baroque made its appearance in a number of institutional buildings erected by European Christians in the 19th century.

barrel or tunnel vault: A semi-cylindrical vault, which could also be described as a round-headed arch extended to something like tunnel length. *See also* vault.

basilica: In Christian architecture, a longitudinal church with a central nave flanked by side aisles and concluding in one or more apses.

Bauhaus: A school of design established in Weimar, Germany, by Walter Gropius in 1919. Subsequently, the term "Bauhaus" became virtually synonymous with "modernism" in the fine and applied arts, between which the Bauhaus did not make qualitative distinctions. Stressing form as a product of function, the Bauhaus cultivated a minimalist aesthetic of pure geometry, the better to make the visual arts, most especially architecture, reflect the needs and materials of the industrial age. However, since the Bauhaus also held a Utopian belief in the power of the arts to improve the human lot, it also challenged industrial methods by teaching and honoring the crafts, such as weaving and potting. But even here the aesthetic favored by the school proved to be the essence of modernism, in all its abstraction. With the advent of Nazism in 1933, the Bauhaus closed, which prompted many of its teachers and students to emigrate, some of them to Palestine, where they introduced the school's celebrated values. The results can be seen in the center of Jerusalem and in the Rehavia neighborhood. In architecture, the Bauhaus is all but synonymous with the International Style.

bougainvillea: A climbing ornamental plant with brightly colored blossoms, mainly purple, often found decorating the entrances to Arab houses in such neighborhoods as Talbiyeh, Katamon, and Baka, built in the 1930s and 1940s.

brise-soleil: From the French meaning "sun break," a *brise-soleil* is a fixed or movable device, such as louvers or screens, attached to windows or doors for the purpose of blocking the entry of direct sunlight. A common feature in Jerusalem, especially on the International Style buildings of the 1950s and 1960s.

Brutalism, Brutalistic Style: International Style architecture in its rawest, most reductive form, often characterized by rough, exposed concrete surfaces and equally exposed painted-steel structures. After emerging in the 1950s, Brutalism went on to dovetail, in the 1960s, with the attempts of local architects to endow Jerusalem with an authentic, original style of building, notable for its "nervous" assemblages of angular or sloping surfaces, "periscopes," recesses, and projections.

buttress: Traditionally, an external mass of masonry built against, or at an angle to, an external wall to strengthen it and thus resist outward thrust, especially when generated by an arch or a vault rising above the wall on the other side. Found not only in the Romanesque structures that survive in Jerusalem, but also in some of the Christian buildings erected during the 19th century.

Byzantine Style: Developed under the Byzantine Empire, beginning in the 4th century AD, the Byzantine Style in church architecture takes the form of square or rectangular naves crowned by circular domes set upon corner pendentives and sheathed within by brilliantly colorful programs of symbolic imagery, both abstract and representational, executed in glittering mosaic. Also featured are round-headed arches and colonnades fashioned of rich marbles and stone capitals relief-carved in intricate, lacelike designs. In Jerusalem, the Byzantine Style manifests itself in a ubiquitous assortment of cubic, dome-vaulted stone structures. Most of the synagogues built in the Old City, especially during the 19th century, are in a Neo-Byzantine style.

caliph: Title for a religious or civil head of an Islamic state.

capital: The culminating member of a column, pillar, or pier, and the cushion upon which an entablature rests or the base from which an arch springs.

capitulations: Treaties signed between the Ottoman Sultans and the Christian states of Europe concerning the extraterritorial rights to be enjoyed by the subjects of a signatory power while in the state of the other.

cardo: A transversing street in a Roman town. In Jerusalem the Cardo runs north and south, beginning at Damascus Gate.

"carpet" tiling: *See* tiles, carpet.

Classicism: In architecture, a formal and structural language developed in the Greco-Roman world, a mode of designing and building that generally involved exploitation of the Doric, Ionic, Corinthian, Composite, and Tuscan orders, individually or in combination. With its columns, pediments, and domes, its harmonious, human-derived proportions, classicizing architecture usually connotes European humanism in its most august and dignified state. However, it could also be dramatic as in Renaissance/Baroque buildings or even light and playful as in those of the 18th century. In Jerusalem, Classicism frequently reflected a dependence on Renaissance Italy, especially as reinterpreted for the institutional buildings erected by European Christians during the 19th century.

Classic Revival: In reaction to the elaborations of Baroque and Rococo design, an architectural movement whose purpose was to reintroduce sobriety and gravitas in the use of Greco-Roman models. A frequent characteristic of the institutional architecture erected in Jerusalem by European Christians during the 19th century. *See also* Neo-Classicism.

cloister: Adjacent to a church or within a monastic complex, an open, square court surrounded by an ambulatory that is often arcaded. Common in institutional architecture erected in Jerusalem by European Christians during the 19th century.

colonnade: A row of columns set at regular intervals, usually for the purpose of supporting the superstructure of a masonry building.

column: A cylindrical upright structural member, generally composed in Classical architecture of base, shaft, and capital. More than any other feature, it is the capital and its style that determine the order of the architecture—Doric, Ionic, Corinthian, Composite, Tuscan, etc.

concrete: A structural material, made by mixing sand, gravel, and cement powder with water. Used as bonding in brick and stone masonry, or as artificial stone once poured into molds and hardened. Common in Jerusalem architecture since the 1920s.

Corinthian: The most ornate of the Classical orders invented by the Greeks, with a fluted shaft rising from a base, formed like a series of graduated rings, and culminating in a tall capital embellished with two rows of acanthus leaves and large corner volutes. Favored by affluent Arabs for homes erected in Jerusalem from the late 19th century to the 1940s.

cornerstone: A foundation stone; a stone forming the corner of a building, especially in the architecture of 19th-century Jerusalem; a stone prominently situated on the main façade and engraved to record the dedicatory ceremonies.

corridor effect: A type of urban layout notable for streets flanked by continuous façades, as in many European town centers or in that part of Jerusalem's downtown erected under the British Mandate.

cross vault: Two barrel or tunnel vaults intersected at right angles, thereby forming a groin vault. *See also* barrel vault *and* vault.

Crusaders: Europeans who besieged Jerusalem, held by Muslims since 638, and conquered it in 1099, when they established the Latin Kingdom of Jerusalem. The Crusaders maintained their power in the city until the Ayyubid conquest in 1187, and then again briefly in 1229-44, this time ceding Jerusalem to the Mamluks. It was the Crusaders who imported Europe's Romanesque architecture to Jerusalem.

crypt: In a Christian church, a vaulted subterranean chamber, usually situated under the choir, for the reception of tombs and the housing of relics in a chapel.

Cultural Mile: A term coined by Mayor Teddy Kollek to describe the cultural and public facilities built outside the Old City wall as part of the 1970s "green revolution." Running from Jaffa Gate and Sultan's Pool to the Jerusalem Theater, the Cultural Mile includes many old structures renovated through the Jerusalem Foundation to house such recreational centers as the Cinémathèque, Mishkenot Sha'ananim, Liberty Bell Park, and Bloomfield Park. It is a southwestern extension of the National Park that surrounds the Old City.

cupola: The Italian word often used as a synonym for "dome."

curtain wall: In modern architecture an exterior wall that serves no structural purpose. Characteristically made of glass, steel, or aluminum panels, it hangs in front the building's structural frame and seals the interior against the outside elements. Along with the International Style, a modest version of the curtain wall appeared in Jerusalem as early as the 1930s, especially in stairwell façades.

Decumanus: The main artery of a Roman town, the Decumanus survives in the Old City of Jerusalem, where it runs west-east, starting at Jaffa Gate.

drum: A cylindrical or polygonal wall rising above the main part of the building below and supporting a dome above. Common in ecclesiastical architecture built in Jerusalem during the 19th century.

Eclecticism: An architectural style in which features from various earlier styles, often remote in both time and place, are combined to create something new. An important characteristic of Christian and Arab structures built in Jerusalem as well as in the West during the late 19th century and the early 20th.

Effendi(s): A former Ottoman title of respect, especially for government officials, but also for the well educated, the well-off, and the aristocratic.

entablature: The upper, horizontal members of a Classical order—architrave, frieze, and cornice.

Eretz Israel: Hebrew for the "Land of Israel" or Palestine.

Erker: From the German, a bay window or oriel. *See also* kösk *and* oriel.

façade: The face of a building, usually the main one or architectural front, which is most often distinguished from the other faces by the elaboration of its architectural or ornamental detailing.

Fatimids: Muslim rulers of Jerusalem from the time of their conquest in 969 until the Crusaders took the city in 1099. The Fatimids had their capital in Cairo.

firman: An edict or administrative order issued by or in the name of a Middle Eastern sovereign (formerly the Turkish Sultan).

gable: A triangular wall segment formed by the sloping sides of a pitched roof or the peaking sides of a Gothic window or portal. In Classical architecture, called a "pediment."

garden neighborhoods: A system of expansive urban planning undertaken during the 1920s in Jerusalem's New City, where most houses were one- or two-family structures, each of them surrounded by a garden. A number of such neighborhoods came into being, among them Rehavia, Beit Hakerem, and Talpiot.

gentrification: Physical and social renovation in old, core-city neighborhoods, usually at the initiative of middle-class citizens seeking distinctively urban but lively places of residence in lieu of the suburbs. Widespread in Jerusalem outside the Old City walls, particularly since the late 1970s.

Gothic Style: The great period of European art and architecture that stretched from the mid-12th century to the end of the Middle Ages. Taking light to be the supreme symbol of divine presence on earth, Gothic builders strove for a dematerialized architecture of soaring, luminous spaces quite unlike the mass and bulk of the Romanesque precedent. Gothic is thus readily identifiable by its ogive or pointed arches, high cross rib vaults, tall or "rose" stained-glass windows, and flying buttresses. During the 19th century, Neo-Gothic appeared in Jerusalem, owing to construction undertaken there by European Christians.

groin vault: *See* cross vault *and* vault.

hajj: Arabic meaning the pilgrimage to Mecca that all devout Muslims are supposed to make at least once in their lifetimes.
See also painting, *hajj*.

halukka. Hebrew signifying the system, largely pre-Zionist, for raising funds abroad to finance the construction and maintenance of Jewish communities in the holy cities of Eretz Israel. Halukka funds helped underwrite most Jewish neighborhoods built in Jerusalem during the 19th century. *See also* kolel.

hammam: The Arabic word for a public or private bathhouse. Two public baths dating from the Mamluk Period survived in the Old City until recent times.

hamsah: Arabic for a handcrafted ornament meant to bring good luck and thwart the evil eye. A *hamsah* often adorns entrances to Muslim dwellings in villages and in the Old City's Muslim Quarter, but it can also be found on the houses of Jews from the "Oriental" communities, especially those built in the late 19th century.

Haram al-Sharif: The Arabic term, meaning "the Noble Enclosure," for the Temple Mount, or Mount Moriah, the great esplanade where formerly the Jewish Temple stood and now the site of the Dome of the Rock, Al-Aqsa Mosque, and other sanctuaries. The third holiest place for Muslims, after Mecca and Medina, and the most significant architectural space in Jerusalem.

hosh: The word for the inner courtyard of a traditional Arab home, usually a village dwelling or a house in the Old City.

hyperbolic-paraboloid roof: A large, sail-shaped dome constructed of concrete no thicker than a few centimeters and designed to span or cover large, open spaces. Common all over the world in the 1950s for sports facilities, churches, and convention centers, this roof system can be found in Jerusalem on the sports building and on the synagogue of the Hebrew University's Givat Ram campus.

industrialized building: Construction in which various components (wall sections, ceilings, stairs, windows, etc.) are manufactured in a factory and then installed in the building. In Jerusalem, common mainly in public housing projects since the early 1970s.

International Style: In architecture, the signature style of the 20th century, which took hold in the 1920s and 1930s before climaxing in the first two decades following World War II. For International Style practitioners, architecture means space rather than mass and form in the service of function, to the detriment of ornament for its own sake. In Jerusalem, the International Style went far toward satisfying the practical need for housing produced with absolute economy. The local result has been a minimalist, functional, even industrialized architecture of broken and stepped boxlike forms, semicircular and curved elements, flat roofs, and horizontal strip windows. *See also* Art Deco, Bauhaus, Moderne, *and* strip window.

Ionic: One of the five Classical orders of architecture, this one characterized by its slender fluted shaft, voluted capital, dentilled cornice, and continuously ornamented frieze.

iwan: In an Arab dwelling, a large vaulted hall with one side left open, often giving access to an interior court.

Jerusalem Foundation: An association established in 1966 by Jerusalem's Mayor Teddy Kollek to initiate, support, and manage all manner of special projects—cultural, social, health, educational, religious, charitable. Among its successes, the Jerusalem Foundation has brought into being Bloomfield and Liberty Bell parks, renovated structures along the Cultural Mile (Cinémathèque, Khan Theater), built health centers (in East Jerusalem, for example), and sited dozens of sculptures in public spaces throughout the city.

Jugendstil: German for "Youth Style," signifying the Middle European version of Art Nouveau and its aesthetic of dynamic, curvilinear organicism. *See also* Art Nouveau.

Karaites: A Jewish sect, dating back to the 8th century, whose members rejected rabbinic Judaism and accepted only the Scriptures as authoritative.

keystone: The structurally imperative central stone, or voussoir, at the apex of an arch. In Jerusalem, the wedge-shaped keystones above many 19th-century doorways are lavishly decorated.

khan: Arabic for "caravansarai," a Persian term signifying an edifice, usually two-storied, with vaulted shelters ranged about an interior courtyard, or series of courtyards, for the accommodation of travelers along a trade route. While guests slept upstairs, their animals were stabled on the ground floor. Some khans were built in the Old City, mainly during the Mamluk Period.

khanaqah: A small *khan* or hostel for Sufi mystics, built in the Old City during the Mamluk Period.

kibbutz: *See* urban kibbutz.

kizan: Arabic for hollow clay pipes of a sort usually arranged in a triangle and placed in the balustrades of roofs and porches. They allow air to gain the interior while ensuring privacy; they also permit residents to see without being seen. Widespread in the Old City.

kolel: Hebrew for 1) an Eretz Israel community of people from a particular country or locality, often supported by their compatriots in the diaspora; 2) an institution for higher Torah learning. During the 19th century, kolels built many Jewish neighborhoods in Jerusalem.

kösk: Turkish and Arabic for a closed bay window, balcony, or oriel projecting from the façade of an Arab house and latticed so that women could, without revealing themselves, observe passersby in the lane below. Common in the Muslim Quarter of the Old City. *See also* Erker *and* oriel.

lantern: The latticed or fenestrated turret or small tower crowning a dome and admitting light as well as air into the interior below.

lintel: The horizontal stone or wood beam spanning the gap between the upright structural posts on either side of a door or window.

liwan: In an Arab dwelling, the all-important central room giving access to other, lesser rooms on either side.

loopholes: In a fortification, vertical slits, usually widening inward, through which archers or riflemen could take aim at their approaching adversaries. Built into the 16th-century wall surrounding the Old City.

machicolation: Along the top of a fortification, an overhanging defensive structure notched to permit safe firing at the enemy and punctured below to allow arrows, molten lead, and/or boiling oil to be dropped on besiegers. Built into the Old City's 16th-century rampart but never used for its intended purpose.

madafah: In Arab villages, a special house or room within a house reserved for guests.

madrasa: A Muslim religious or theological school, composed of a mosque, study rooms, and living quarters for students, all ranged about an inner courtyard. During the Mamluk Period, numerous madrasas were built in Jerusalem near the Haram al-Sharif.

Mamluks: Muslim rulers of Jerusalem from 1260 until 1517, the Mamluks were a caste of Asian slaves who converted to Islam and governed from Damascus and Cairo.

Mamluk Style: One of Jerusalem's most beautiful and striking features, Mamluk Style is notable for its calligraphy, *muqarnas* stalactites, and colorful *ablaq* masonry. These elements often appear in affluent Arab homes of the Mandate Period.

megastructure: A massive multipurpose structure incorporating most of the functions and requirements of a complete city. Much favored in Jerusalem during the late 1950s and throughout the 1960s, megastructure provided the governing concept for the rebuilt Mount Scopus campus of Hebrew University.

mesamsam: Arabic for delicate stone dressing, more refined than *taltish*, common in traditional Jerusalem architecture, particularly on the lintels of doors and windows.

mihrab: In the *qibla* wall of a mosque, the prayer niche indicating the direction of Mecca, which in Jerusalem is south.

mikveh: A Jewish ritual bathhouse common in the traditional neighborhoods built by Orthodox Jews outside the Old City walls, beginning in the mid-19th century.

minaret: A tall, slender tower, with one or more encircling balconies, from which the muezzin calls Muslims to prayer five times a day. The most beautiful minarets in the Old City survive from the Mamluk Period.

Moderne: A common style of architectural design incorporating decorative elements characteristic of the era since World War I, but without the great formal innovations of International Style modernism.

Moorish Style: An Islamic style from Spain, known for its horseshoe arch and relatively rare in Jerusalem.

mosque: A Muslim house of prayer and public worship.

muezzin: The Muslim crier who, from a minaret or other part of a mosque, summons the faithful to prayer at stated hours five times a day.

muqarnas: Decorative stalactite work fashioned of stone or plaster and commonly found in Mamluk architecture. In Jerusalem, muqarnas graces the Mamluk buildings near the Haram al-Sharif, certain Mandate buildings, such as the Palace Hotel, and some affluent Arab villas.

mushrabiyya: A kind of lattice cover for windows on the street façade of a Muslim home. A modern version, executed in metal, is used as a decorative element in the new Jerusalem City Hall complex.

National Park: The ring of gardens created around the Old City walls, a project begun in 1967 and now extended to 600 acres of green areas, plantings, historic structures, and roads. It sets the Old City apart within the overall urban fabric of Jerusalem.

nave: The main central space in a church, often flanked by side aisles and extending longitudinally from the entrance to the transept or crossing.

Neo-Baroque Style: *See* Baroque Style.

Neo-Byzantine Style: *See* Byzantine Style.

Neo-Classical Style, Neo-Classicism: A late-18th-century and early-19th-century revival of the Greco-Roman orders introduced for the sake of reclaiming the tradition from Baroque elaboration or Rococo overrefinement and rendering it purer, graver, and more monumental. Very common in the architecture erected in Jerusalem by European Christians during the 19th century. *See also* Classic Revival.

Neo-Gothic Style: *See* Gothic Style.

Neo-Oriental Style: Widespread in Jerusalem, a local architectural style developed in reaction against the anonymous, standardized boxes erected during the 1950s and 1960s. The style takes its inspiration primarily from the Old City and the Jewish neighborhoods built in the late 19th century. Characteristic are small, "broken," and staggered masses with recessed and projecting elements, slopes and angles, gates, arcades, and, above all, a great variety of arches, as well as window structures made of precast concrete. Salient examples can be found in such new neighborhoods as Gilo and Ramot.

Neo-Renaissance Style: *See* Renaissance Style.

Neo-Romanesque: *See* Romanesque Style.

no-man's-land: Following the 1948 war, the area between the ceasefire lines that divided Jerusalem into two cities, Israeli-Jewish and Jordanian-Arab. This area, fenced in by barbed wire and strewn with mines, served as a buffer zone. It was redeveloped after the 1967 Six-Day War.

ogive arch: A pointed arch with ogee or ogival curves on either side.

"Old Yishuv": The pre-Zionist Jewish community in Palestine, with many of its members concentrated in the Old City's Jewish Quarter.

onion dome: A bulbous dome tapering upward to terminate in a point or spire. Common in the church architecture of Russia as well as that of Middle and Eastern Europe, but also found in some of Jerusalem's Neo-Baroque buildings.

oriel: A bay window projected from the wall of an upper story to form an extension of the room within. Locally called "erker" or "kösk." Very common in the Muslim Quarter as well as in the Neo-Oriental architecture erected in Jerusalem since the 1970s. *See also* kösk.

Orientalism: In Jerusalem, an historically evocative or nostalgic architectural style derived from local Near Eastern traditions and quite fashionable during the 1920s. Viewed by its advocates as the foundation of an authentic "Jewish-Hebraic" architecture, and by its opponents as a relic of 19th-century Eclecticism.

Ottomans: The dynasty that ruled the Turkish Empire, including Palestine, from their capital in Constantinople (Istanbul) for four hundred years, beginning in 1517.

paintings, hajj: Vivid paintings commemorating a pilgrim's return from Mecca and hung at the entrance to a Muslim home. The pictures usually depict the Black Stone at Mecca, the Dome of the Rock shrine in Jerusalem, and colorful flowers. *See also* hajj.

palmette: Ornamental motif derived from the palm leaf and popular among the most ancient civilizations of Asia Minor. Also found in some 19th-century Greek Orthodox buildings in the Old City.

parvis: The open square leading to a large church, such as that in front of Jerusalem's Church of the Holy Sepulcher.

pediment: In Classical architecture, the triangular gable formed by the slopes of a low-pitched roof and often decorated with relief sculpture. Also, any similarly shaped architectural member built over a door, window, or niche.

pendentive: Inverted concave triangle that springs from each corner of a square structure to provide the continuous base for a circular dome above.

pergola: A light structure generally made of parallel wood colonnades supporting an overhead series of wood beams or rafters. Common in Jerusalem (especially in the Rehavia neighborhood) from the late 1920s through the 1940s, when it was used in International Style buildings to define open spaces in gardens or on balconies and roofs.

piazza: An open public space or square surrounded by buildings.

pier: Any upright mass of masonry designed to support the superstructure of a building. A pier differs from a column by the rectangularity of its plan.

pilaster: A vertical, usually flat half-column engaged with a wall rather than freestanding, thus frequently more decorative than structural in purpose.

pillar: Any vertical, shaftlike structural member, such as a pier, a column, or a pilaster.

pilotis: Popularized by Le Corbusier, a French term for stilts used to support a building above the ground and thus free the space below for some nonstructural purpose. In Jerusalem, pilotis can be found in International Style buildings erected during the 1950s and 1960s, notably on the Hebrew University's Givat Ram campus.

portal: An impressive or monumental, often elaborated entrance, gate, or door.

portico: A roofed porch, frequently colonnaded and approached by a broad flight of steps. Common in the institutional architecture erected in Jerusalem by European Christians during the 19th-century.

Post-Modernism: A mixed, revivalist mode developed in the 1970s and 1980s by American and European architects reacting to the banal oversimplifications of the International Style as practiced in the 1960s. Post-Modernists attempted to combine advanced technology with traditional forms reinterpreted in a highly idiosyncratic and decorative manner. In Jerusalem, the Neo-Oriental style became the local version of Post-Modernism. See also Neo-Oriental Style.

precast concrete: Concrete units shaped by casting in molds prior to their introduction into a building. In Jerusalem, often used for domestic architecture built since the 1970s.

Pro-Jerusalem Society: A public association founded in 1918 by Ronald Storrs, the British Military Governor of Jerusalem, for the purpose of safeguarding the Holy City. The Society undertook to restore the great 16th-century walls and to revive local popular crafts.

qibla: In a mosque, the wall oriented toward Mecca, which in Jerusalem is the south wall.

rails: Iron beams, similar to those used in train tracks, appropriated in Jerusalem for ceilings and balconies, particularly after the city received rail service in 1892, which allowed heavy construction materials to be imported in large quantities.

reinforced concrete: Concrete strengthened with steel rods or mesh introduced into the material before it has hardened in the mold.

Renaissance Style: Born and defined in 15th-century Italy, the Renaissance revived the humanistic world of Greece and Rome, in reaction against the otherworldliness of the Middle Ages, even while endowing humanism with near-medieval religious content. In architecture, the Renaissance masters—Brunelleschi, Alberti, Bramante, Michelangelo, Sangallo, Sansovino, Palladio—did not merely copy Classical models; they also reinterpreted them in highly imaginative, independent ways, always with harmony, balance, and a keen sense of the monumental. In Jerusalem, the Renaissance arrived in the mid-19th century as the Neo-Renaissance Style, much favored by European Christians when they undertook their local building campaigns. Some elements of this revivalist style, such as grand staircases, pilasters, and capitals, can also be found in affluent Arab homes erected during the Mandate Period.

"rising sun" motif: A theme, common in Art Deco buildings dating from the 1920s and 1930s, that symbolized the dynamism, vision, thrust, and hope of the technologically advanced modern world. It appears mainly on gates in Jewish neighborhoods built during the period.

Romanesque Style: With Gothic, which Romanesque preceded, one of the two great styles of Europe's High Middle Ages, lasting from 9th century to the 12th and characterized by round-headed arches, massive masonry, groin- and barrel-vaulted interiors, an early version of structural ribs, modest fenestration, and lavish, richly imaginative sculpture. The Crusaders brought Romanesque to Jerusalem, where it still triumphs in the Church of the Holy Sepulcher and the Church of St. Anne. Come the late 19th century, Neo-Romanesque would be favored in buildings, such as the Lutheran Church of the Redeemer, erected by European Christians active in Jerusalem.

Romanticism: An early 19th-century European movement that reacted against 18th-century rationalism by reviving the Middle Ages, complete with their spirituality and love of nature, while also purifying Classicism of what was thought to have been Rococo over-refinement. Romanticism prepared the way for the Eclecticism that would distinguish so many buildings erected in Jerusalem in the modern era, right through the Mandate Period of the 1920s and 1930s, which produced the Eclectic but splendid Government House.

rose window: A large, circular window filled with stone tracery and stained glass and characteristically found above the main doors on the west front of Romanesque and Gothic churches.

rotunda: A building circular or "central" in plan and usually domed. The most famous rotunda in Jerusalem forms part of the Church of the Holy Sepulcher.

rustication: Masonry with deeply recessed joints between stones that are often rough-hewn. In Jerusalem, found mainly in Neo-Renaissance buildings erected by European Christians during the 19th-century.

sabil: Arabic for a public fountain. Most of the sabils of Old Jerusalem were built by order of Sultan Suleiman the Magnificent in 1536-37.

satellite neighborhoods: Built around the inner city of Jerusalem after the reunification in 1967, these neighborhoods, such as Neveh Ya'akov, Ramot, Gilo, and East Talpiot, were intended to create political-physical facts and thus limit the expansion of Arab building.

Sephardi, Sephardim (pl.): The term for Jews with roots in Spain and Portugal, wherever resident, as contrasted with the Ashkenazi(m) from Middle and Eastern Europe.

Six-Day War: The brief war that broke out in June 1967 when Israel reacted to Arab threats and blockade by defeating the Egyptian, Jordanian, and Syrian armies. An important outcome was the reunification of Jerusalem.

spandrel: The triangular section of wall on either side of an arch.

squinch: A small arch or vault built into the upper interior angles of a square or polygonal structure to form the base for a circular drum or dome.

stalactites: See muqarnas.

Strassendorf: German for the kind of "street village" that served as the model for the Templer Colony built in Jerusalem in the late 19th century. Also known as the "German Colony," it comprises a row of houses, surrounded by spacious gardens and trees, arrayed along a main street, with side streets branching therefrom. See also Templers.

streamline: Common in the International Style but even more in Art Deco and Moderne, streamlining, by virtue of its sweeping attenuations and periodic curling into sleek, rolling waves, connotes the dynamism and thrusting progress so prized by the modern world. In Jerusalem it can be seen in the semicircular wings, curved balconies, and balustrades of Jewish buildings constructed in the city center during the 1930s.

strip window: A key characteristic of the International Style, the strip window is a relatively low, horizontally elongated aperture deep-set within a concrete framework and shaded by a thin, overhanging concrete roof.

Sufi: Member of a deeply ascetic Muslim order dating back to 11th-century Persia.

Sultan: Primarily the sovereign of the Ottoman or Turkish Empire, which, before it broke up during World War I, ruled much of Balkan Europe as well as most of the Middle East, including Palestine.

suq: A marketplace in the Islamic world. The most picturesque and colorful suqs of Jerusalem are in the Old City.

synagogue: Jewish house of prayer and worship.

taltish: Arabic for stone dressed with a surface of medium coarseness, thus more refined than tubze. Most of the buildings erected in Jerusalem during the Mandate Period were faced with taltish stone.

Taphos: Greek for "sepulcher" and the monogram of the Greek Orthodox Patriarchate. Composed of the Greek letters *Tau* and *Phi*, the *Taphos* sign appears on the front of most Greek Orthodox buildings.

Temple Mount: The walled-in, elevated, trapezoid area in Jerusalem's Old City, where the First and Second Temples once stood. This was the largest sacred enclosure in the Greco-Roman world. See also Haram al-Sharif.

Templers: An independent sect of Christians from South Germany that established several agricultural settlements in Palestine during the late 19th century. In Jerusalem the Templers founded the German Colony, whose houses recall those of the villages they came from.

tiles, carpet: Colorful floor tiling decorated mainly with geometrical forms, flowers, and foliage. Especially common in the affluent Arab neighborhoods built during the Mandate Period.

Torah: The Pentateuch, which contains the five books of Moses; in a wider sense, also the entire body of traditional Jewish teaching and literature.

tracery: A decorative screen of stonework, used as mullions in stained-glass windows—especially rose windows—and the arched sections of Gothic windows—or as patterned relief on a stone wall. Typical of Romanesque and Gothic architecture.

transept: In a basilican-plan church, wings or arms set at right angles to the nave, thus forming a cross-plan building.

tubze: Arabic term signifying the coarsest form of rusticated stone.

tunnel vault: See barrel vault and vault.

turba: Arabic for "mausoleum," a building erected over a tomb. The Old City contains many such structures, especially from the Mamluk Period.

turret: A small defensive tower, often projected from the corner of a castle or a fortified wall.

tympanum: The pediment in Classical architecture; in medieval architecture, the triangular wall formed by the lintel of a doorway and the arch above it.

Umayyads: The Muslim dynasty that conquered Jerusalem in 634 and ruled it until 750, when the city fell to the Abbasids. The Umayyads, whose capital was Damascus, endowed Jerusalem with the Dome of the Rock, completed in 691. Most of their buildings, such as the palace complex south of the Haram al-Sharif, were destroyed in the earthquake of 748.

urban kibbutz: A communal housing project with a physical form and rural atmosphere similar to those of the classic kibbutz (collective settlement) but without the collective way of life normally practiced in kibbutzim. Two such projects emerged in Jerusalem during the 1930s: Me'onot Ovdim A and B, both established in the Rehavia neighborhood.

vault: An arched ceiling fashioned of masonry or concrete. See also barrel vault and cross vault.

veranda: A covered porch or balcony, generally used for leisure, especially in affluent Arab homes built outside the Old City during the 1920s and 1930s.

vernacular architecture: A mode of building indigenous to a region, which in the Jerusalem area is typified by such Arab villages as Silwan and Lifta. Since 1967 a number of quasi-vernacular housing projects have been erected in the new Jewish neighborhoods of south Jerusalem.

Via Dolorosa: For Christians, the holiest street on earth, along which Jesus walked, bearing the cross from the trial before Pontius Pilate to the crucifixion on Golgotha. Along this "Street of Sorrow" are nine Stations of the Cross, marking the progression of agony suffered by Christ. The remaining five Stations are within the Church of the Holy Sepulcher. During the 19th century, European Christians erected many institutional buildings along the Via Dolorosa.

volute: A spiral or scroll-like form found most frequently in architecture, as in Ionic and Corinthian capitals.

Western Wall: Popularly called the "Wailing Wall," this is all that remains of the Temple, which makes it one of Judaism's holiest places. Actually, the Western Wall is part of the retaining rampart of the Temple Mount enclosure.

wildbau: Masonry fashioned of rough stones laid without regard to parallel courses. Used in Jerusalem mostly for public housing built in the 1950s.

Wilhelmine Style: Architectural style developed in Germany during the reign of Kaiser Wilhelm II (1888-1918). Representational and imperial in character, the Wilhelmine Style combined various "neo" modes according to the Eclectic fashion of the time. It is monumental, lavish, expensive, and best seen in Jerusalem at Augusta Victoria Hospital on Mount Scopus.

wrought-iron work: Hammered or forged into shape, wrought iron makes a frequent appearance in Jerusalem as decorative gates and window grilles at or on Arab buildings.

Yad Vashem: An Israeli national institution dedicated to commemorating those who perished in the Holocaust. Composed of a museum, archives, memorials, offices, and a Hall of Remembrance, the Yad Vashem complex, opened to the public in 1957, stands on a hill in west Jerusalem.

yeshiva: A traditional Jewish academy devoted primarily to studying the Talmud and rabbinic literature. In the 19th century, yeshivas were among the most important and imposing buildings erected in Jewish Jerusalem outside the Old City walls, and in the restored Jewish Quarter after 1967.

Index

A

Abdul Aziz, Sultan: 73
Abdul Hamid II, Sultan: 60, 119
Absalom's Tomb: 11, 15, 16, 152, 177
Aelia Capitolina: 14, 28, 99
Aftimos Market: 68, 72
Aghion Villa: 160, 163
Agrippa I, King of Judea: 27
Alexander the Great: 13
Allenby, General Edmund: 143, 144, 152
Allenby Camp: 143
Alwalid, Caliph: 32
American Colony: 118, 119
Antonia Fortress: 14
Architects:
    Adamson: 151
    Adler, Friedrich: 24, 80
    Amisar, Micha: 194, 199
    Aronson, Shlomo: 83, 197
    Azrieli, David: 195
    Barluzzi, Antonio: 140, 176, 178
    Bartaud: 131
    Bartos, Armand: 169
    Ben-Dor, Dan and Raphael: 157
    Best, David: 94, 98
    Blum, Moshe: 194
    Boubet, Etienne: 128
    Broid, Pasqual: 194
    Bugod, Peter: 93, 99
    Chaikin, Benjamin: 148, 161
    Cherniak, Abraham and Zippora: 157
    Diamond, A.J.: 189, 192
    Ehmann, Friedrich: 120
    Elhanani, Abba: 172
    Elhanani, Arye: 176, 177
    Eppinger, Martin, Ivanovitch: 132
    Favier, M.: 155, 163, 167
    Ferguson, Franklin T.: 186, 187
    Figueiredo, Eunice: 99
    Frankel, Eliezer: 94
    Friedman, Alexander: 156, 177, 178
    Gad, Dora: 169, 178
    Gierlich, Vendelin: 194
    Gil, Ya'akov: 183
    Goeritz, Mathias: 194, 199
    Goraly, Nehemia: 182
    Greim, D.: 135
    Guillemot and Planche: 128
    Harrison, Austen St. Barbe: 146-148, 150
    Halprin, Lawrence: 197
    Harmat, Zoltan S.: 158, 163
    Harmon, Arthur Loomis: 143, 150
    Hecker, Wilhelm: 159
    Hecker, Zvi: 180
    Holliday, Clifford: 146, 148
    Houris, Spyro: 146, 148, 163-166
    Idelson, Binyamin: 177
    Jeffrey, George: 136
    Johns, J.W.: 73, 80
    Karmi, Ram: 186, 192
    Karmi-Melamed Ada: 192
    Katseff, Haim: 186
    Kaufmann, Richard: 146, 157, 158, 160
    Katz, Kalman: 98
    Kendall, Henry: 144
    Kertesz, Gabriel: 196
    Kiesler, Frederick: 169
    Klachko, Louis: 182
    Klarwin, Joseph: 170
    Kornberg, Fritz: 148, 158
    Krakauer, Leopold: 161
    Kutchinsky, Dov: 157
    Leibnitz, Robert: 126, 127
    Levi, Meir: 183
    Mandel, Sa'adia: 94, 196
    Mansfeld, Al.: 169, 178
    Meltzer, Nahum: 98, 182
    Mendelsohn, Erich: 145, 146, 159-161
    Miller, Zvi: 194
    Nahas Bey: 153
    Neufeld, Joseph: 173, 179
    Niv-Krendel, Esther: 93
    Palmer, Ferdinand: 122
    Petasis: 146, 148, 164
    Piacenini, Marcello: 147
    Pite, A. Beresford: 138
    Plessner, Ulrich: 195
    Rahamimoff, Arie: 99, 196
    Rattner, Yohanan (Eugen): 146, 147
    Rau, Heinz: 159, 173-175
    Rechter, Ya'aKov: 147, 182, 191
    Renard, Heinrich: 125, 126
    Reznik, David: 173, 174, 177, 185-187, 190, 199
    Richmond, Ernest: 92
    Rubin, Meir: 156
    Safdie, Moshe: 95, 96, 99, 190, 191, 193, 197
    Sandel, Theodor: 122
    Sansur: 131
    Schick, Conrad: 77, 106, 122-124, 140
    Schoenberg, Ze'ev: 180
    Shaked, Shmuel: 186
    Sharon, Arieh: 170, 177, 180
    Sharon, Eldar: 170, 180
    Sivan, Joseph: 194
    Spector, Arthur: 183, 194, 199
    T'lil, Daoud: 146
    Tabatchnik, I.Z.: 152
    Tanai, Dan: 94
    Vogt, Emile: 154
    Winter, Percy: 147
    Yahalom, Lipa: 177
    Yaski, Avraham: 183, 194, 195
    Yellin, Eliezer: 159
    Zarhi, Moshe: 182
    Zippor, Gershon: 185
    Zur, Dan: 177
Architectural firms
    Ahrens-Burton-Koralek: 99
    Alexandroni-Arnon-Yaski-Hebron-Nadler-Nadler-Powsner: 175
    Bugod-Figueiredo-Niv-Krendel: 189, 192
    Karmi-Karmi-Meltzer: 174
    Kolker-Kolker-Epstein: 189, 192
    Meltzer-Igra: 189, 192, 197
    Nadler-Nadler-Bixon-Gil: 176
Armenian Quarter: 66, 76, 140
Armenian Tiles: 92, 148, 150, 165, 166
Augusta Victoria Hospice: 119, 126-128, 146
Austrian Hospice: 66, 73, 76, 80
Avigad, Nachman: 93
Avi-Yonah, Michael: 14
Awqaf (Muslim Endowments): 50, 99
Ayyubid Period: 22, 32, 43, 44

B

Bank Leumi: 147
Batei Mahseh: 21, 91, 94, 96, 98
Bar Kokhba, Shimon: 14
Beit Hama'alot: 155
Bloomfield Park: 195, 198
British Mandate Period: 17, 91, 143-164
"Broad Wall": 27, 94
Bukharan Quarter: 102, 107-111
Byzantine Period: 15, 28, 32

C

Calder, Alexander: 199
Cardo: 19, 28, 92, 93, 96, see also Decumanus
Casa Nova: 147
Cathedrals: see Churches
Central Post Office: 147
Chagall, Marc: 173
Chapel: see Churches
Christian Quarter: 68, 76, 119
Churches, Cathedrals, and Chapels:
    Alexander Nevsky: 76, 77
    Christ: 68, 73, 74, 77, 78, 80, 81
    Condemnation: 78
    Dominus Flevit: 176
    Dormition: 119, 125, 126
    Ecce Homo: 78
    Ethiopian: 144
    Flagellation: 76
    Holy Sepulcher: 15, 16, 17, 19, 20, 28, 34, 37, 38, 40, 66, 68, 76-78, 85, 118, 128, 132
    Holy Trinity: 119, 132, 133
    Latin Patriarchate: 76
    Maria Latina: 24, 41, 80
    Mary Magdalene: 135
    Redeemer: 24, 41, 73, 75, 76, 78, 80, 119
    St. Agnes: 37
    St. Andrew's: 148
    St. Anne: 37, 38, 40, 41, 44
    St. George the Martyr: 138
    St. James: 68, 78
    St. John the Baptist: 76, 87
    San Salvatore: see Monasteries
Citadel/Tower of David: 11, 13, 21, 41, 42, 58, 60, 73, 92, 195
City Hall: 140, 147, 189, 191, 192
Collège de Terre Sainte: 68
Collège des Frères: 68, 81
Constantine, Roman Emperor: 15, 38
Convents: see Monasteries and Convents
Cotton Merchants Market: 48, 50, 51, 92
Crusader Period: 16, 22, 24, 37-43
Custodia di Terra Santa: 128
Cyrus, King of Persia: 12

D

Damascus Gate: 19, 27, 60, 62, 99, 115, 126, 136, 144
Danziger, Yitzhak: 199
David, King of Israel: 11, 27, 125
David's Tower: see Citadel/Tower of David
David, City of: 11, 24
Decumanus: 19, 28, see also Cardo
Deutsche Platz: 91, 94
Diskin, Orphanage: 152
Dome of the Chain: 30
Dome of the Rock: 16, 20, 27, 28, 30, 32, 37, 58, 92, 148
Dome of Learning: 44
Dung Gate: 60, 99

E

Ein Karem: 119, 128, 135, 172
English Mission Hospital: 136, 138
Ethiopian Quarter: 115, 117, 140, 164

F

Fatimids: 12, 44
Finn, James: 119, 136, 138, 155

Franciscan Orphanage: 80
Frank, Matthaus: 121
Franz Josef, Austrian Emperor: 73

G

Garden neighborhoods: 157-161
Gates: see specific names
Gate of Mercy (Golden Gate): 30, 201
Gate of the Chain: 19, 44, 47, 64
Generali Building: 147
German Colony: 119-124, 198
Goliath's (or Tancred's) Tower: 42
Government House: 148, 149, 197
Greek Orthodox Patriarchate/
 Church: 34, 76, 77, 132, 139, 140, 157

H

Haas Promenade: 197
Hadassah Hospital: 146, 172, 173, 179
Hadrian, Roman Emperor: 14, 16, 99
Haram al-Sharif: 16, 17, 19, 20, 28, 32, 36, 40, 42, 44, 45, 47, 64, 92, 99, 116; see also Temple Mount
Hasmoneans: 13
Hassenfeld Amphitheater: 196
Hebrew Union College: 172, 175, 191, 193
Hebrew University: 145, 146, 170, 172, 173, 185, 186, 190
Heichal, Shlomo: 177
Herod, King of Judea: 12-14, 20, 27
Herod's Gate: 60
Hezekiah, King: 11, 12
Hospices: see specific names
Hospitals: see specific names
Hotels
 American Colony: 117
 Grand New: 68, 81
 Hilton (Holiday Inn Crown Plaza): 182
 Hyatt Hotel: 179, 190
 King David: 150, 153, 154, 172
 King Solomon: 182
 Laromme: 191
 New Imperial: see Grand New
 Palace: 147, 153
Husseini, al- family: 114, 117, 118

I

Israel Museum: 169-171, 176

J

Jaffa Gate: 19, 58, 60, 76, 92, 98, 99, 115, 140, 179, 195, 197
Jerusalem Foundation: 98, 196

Jerusalem Music Center: 196
Jerusalem Shopping Mall: 194
Jesus Hilfe Leprosarium: 121, 123, 124
Jewish Quarter: 21, 23, 24, 27, 32, 47, 85, 88, 90, 92-96, 98, 99, 164
John of Smyrna: 76
Josephus Flavius: 14

K

Kadishman, Menashe: 199
Khan al-Sultan: 48, 50
Khan Theater: 196
Khutzot Hayotzer: 196
Kidron Valley Tombs: 152, 177, 192
 see also Absalom's Tomb and Zechariah's Tomb
Kirya: 170
Knesset, 170, 171, 177
Kollek, Teddy (Mayor of Jerusalem): 17, 98, 195

L

Liberman, Alexander: 198
Liberty Bell Park: 191, 195
Lifta: 111, 112, 122
Lions' Gate (St. Stephen's): 19, 40, 60, 61, 64, 98
Lipchitz, Jacques: 199

M

Mamluk Period: 14, 16, 22-24, 45-57, 85, 96
Madrasa:
 al-Ashrafiyya: 45, 47, 51, 52, 99
 Is'ardiyya: 55
 Tankiziyya: 45, 47, 52
 'Uthmaniyya: 54
Mausoleum of:
 Al-Kilaniyya: 55
 Barka Khan: 47
 Turkan Khatoun: 47
Maxmillian of Bavaria, Duke: 76
Mclean, William: 144
Minaret: 48
Monasteries and convents:
 Cross: 139
 Deir al-Sultan: 78
 Greek Orthodox: 66, 68, 77, 139
 Moskobiyeh: 135
 Ratisbonne: 131, 132, 152
 St. Anne: see Churches
 St. Claire: 128
 San Salvatore: 66, 70, 73, 76, 78, 81
 Sisters of the Rosary: 131
 Sisters of Zion: 21, 77, 78
 Soeurs Réparatrices: 128
 Montefiore, Moses: 101, 102, 104, 109, 196

Moore, Henry: 199
Mosques:
 Al-Aqsa: 16, 17, 19, 20, 27, 32, 34, 37, 41, 44, 47
 Al-Maulawiyya: 37
 Nabi Daoud: 125
 Omar: 48
Mount Herzl: 170
Mount Moriah: 27
Mount of Olives: 119, 176
Mount Scopus: 126, 145, 146, 148, 179, 185, 187
Mount Zion: 28, 60, 119, 125
Muhammad: 16, 28, 32
Muristan: 37, 68, 73, 77
Muslim Quarter: 23, 24, 82, 83, 90, 96, 114-116

N

Nashashibi family and villa: 116, 117, 163, 198
National Institutions: 147, 157
National Library: 146, 148, 173
National Park: 21, 195, 196
Nebuchadnezzar, King of Babylon: 12
Neighborhoods (New Jerusalem):
 Abu-Tor: 155, 182
 Baka: 115, 162, 164
 Batei Neitin: 106, 107
 Batei Ungarn: 101, 102, 105-107
 Bayit Vegan: 157
 Beit Hakerem: 157, 169
 Beit Hanina: 183
 Bukharan Quarter: see specific entry
 Ethiopian Quarter: see specific entry
 German Colony: see specific entry
 Geula: 155
 Gilo: 179, 180, 183
 Givat Ram: 170, 172, 173, 186, 192
 Ir Ganim: 180
 Katamon: 155, 162, 164, 169
 Kiryat Hayovel: 169, 179, 198
 Kiryat Menahem: 169
 Kiryat Moshe: 109, 157
 Mahaneh Yisrael: 102
 Makor Baruch: 155
 Makor Hayim: 157
 Mamilla: 115, 162, 179, 196
 Manahat: 193, 194
 Mazkeret Moshe: 104, 109
 Me'ah She'arim: 101, 102, 106, 107, 132
 Mishkenot Sha'ananim: 91, 101, 102
 Mishkenot Yisrael: 103
 Musrara: 115, 169
 Nahalat Shiva: 110, 111, 132, 159, 197, 198
 Ohel Moshe: 104, 109
 Pisgat Ze'ev: 179
 Ramot: 179, 180, 182
 Ramot Eshkol: 157, 180
 Rehavia: 111, 132, 139, 147, 155-163, 169, 171
 Sanhedriya: 155
 Sha'arei Hessed: 110, 111
 Sheikh Jarah: 148, 164
 Shmuel Hanavi: 169
 Shuafat: 183
 Talbiyeh: 148, 155, 162-165, 171, 195
 Talpiot: 157, 169, 179, 183
 Yemin Moshe: 102, 109, 196
 Zichron Moshe: 106, 109, 111, 159
New Gate: 60, 98, 119
Noguchi, Isamu: 171
Notre Dame de France Hospice: 128, 131, 132

O

Ohanessian, David: 148, 150, 166
Old Yishuv: 85
Omar Ibn Khattab, Caliph: 15, 16
Ophel: 11, 14
Orient House: 114
Orphanages: see specific names
Ottoman Period: 14, 17, 58-83

P

Phasael's Tower: 13
Piellat, Marie Paul Amédée, Baron de: 130
Pompey, Roman General: 13
Pontius Pilate: 14
Psephinus Tower: 42
Ptolemies: 13

Q

Qayt Bay, Sultan and Sabil of: 47, 51, 52
Quarter: see specific names

R

Ramparts: 12, 17, 58, 60, 92, 98
Ratisbonne: see Monasteries
Rockefeller Museum: 147, 150, 192
Rumpf, Gernot: 198
Rothschild House: 90, 91, 94
Russian Compound: 111, 119, 131-133, 147

S

St. Étienne Biblical Research Institute: 128, 131
St. George's College: 136
St. John's Ophtalmic Hospital: 136

St. Louis Hospital: 128, 130
St. Paul's Hospice: 126
St. Stephen's Gate: see Lions' Gate
St. Vincent de Paul School and
    Orphanage: 128
Saint-Phalle, Niki de: 198
Saladin (Salah al-Din): 16, 37, 44
Salameh Villa: 163, 167
Salomon, Yoel Moshe: 111
San Salvatore Church: see Monasteries
Schneller Syrian Orphanage: 104, 119, 122, 138, 155
Schocken Library: 160
Schocken, Salman: 160, 161
Seleucids: 13
Sennacherib, King of Assyria: 12
Sergei, Grand Duke Hostel: 133, 135
Shemi, Yehiel: 176
Sherover Promenade: 197
Siloam Pool and Tunnel: 11, 12
Silwan: 111, 112, 149
Solomon, King of Israel: 11, 27
Solomon's Stables: 12, 27
Solomon's Temple: see Temple, First
Storrs, Ronald: 92, 143, 144
Styles:
    Art Deco: 146, 152, 163
    Art Nouveau: 126
    Baroque: 122, 130, 132
    Brutalist: 185
    Eclectic: 145, 153
    International: 45, 145-147, 159, 163, 172, 173, 185
    Mamluk: 50, 147
    Moderne: 145, 147, 163
    Neo-Baroque: 80, 128, 139
    Neo-Byzantine: 68, 80, 86, 87
    Neo-Classical: 80, 118, 147, 163
    Neo-Gothic: 76, 80, 108, 130, 131
    Neo-Moorish: 108
    Neo-Oriental: 24, 96, 179, 183, 185, 190-192, 197
    Neo-Renaissance: 80, 108
    Neo-Romanesque: 41, 80, 126, 130
    Post-modern: 185, 190, 191, 195
    Renaissance: 118, 130-133
    Romanesque: 37, 38, 43, 125, 131
Suleiman the Magnificent, Sultan: 17, 23, 24, 30, 58, 60, 64, 96
Sultan's Pool: 64, 196
Supreme Court Building: 192, 193
Synagogues:
    Eliyahu Hanavi: 86
    Great Synagogue: 177
    Hurvah: 21, 47, 85, 86, 95
    Istanbuli: 86
    Johannan Ben Zakai: 86, 88
    Kehilat Tsion (Middle): 86, 87
    Porat Yosef: 86
    Tiferet Yisrael: 85, 86, 95

T

Talitha Kumi Orphanage: 123
Teddy Stadium: 194
Temple Mount: 11, 12, 14, 16, 19, 20, 24, 27, 30, 32, 37, 85, 111, see also Haram al-Sharif
Temple, First: 11, 12, 27, 151
    First Temple Period: 85, 94, 98
Temple, Second: 12, 14, 20, 22, 27
    Second Temple Period: 14, 27, 58, 93, 94, 177
Templers, German 19th-century: 119-121, see also German Colony
Templar Knights, Order of: 12, 37
Thabor House: 124
Ticho House: 116, 198
Titus: 14
Tower of David, see Citadel/Tower of David
Tumarkin, Yigal: 199

U

Umayyad Period: 17, 23, 28-36

V

Via Dolorosa: 19, 21, 40, 66, 76, 99

W

Wailing Wall: see Western Wall
Wauchope, Arthur: 149
Western Wall: 14, 20, 27, 85, 93, 95, 96
Wilhelm II, Kaiser: 24, 73, 119, 126, 127
Wohl Archaeological Museum: 94

Y

Yad Lebanim: 177, 199
Yad Vashem: 170, 176, 177
Yannai, Jacob: 98
Yeshiva:
    Etz Hayyim: 88
    Hakotel: 94, 95
    Porat Yosef: 95, 96
YMCA: 143, 147, 150, 151, 197

Z

Zechariah's Tomb: 15, 177
Zion Gate: 19, 60, 64
Zoo (Tisch Family Zoological Garden): 194

Picture Credits

Numbers refer to pages, except those numbers in parentheses, which refer to illustrations on the pages cited.

Albatross Ltd. (Dubi Tal, Moni Haramati): 27, 65, 70(3), 71, 72(2), 86(3), 97, 126(3), 128(1),135(2), 140(4), 150(3), 154(3), 169, 177(5), 179, 181(4,6), 182(4), 186(1), 189(3), 191(3), 192(2), 194(4), 195(7), 196(1,3), 197, 198(2);
Ben-Dov, Meir: 43(3);
Cleave, Richard: 31;
Folberg, Neil: 26, 39, 41(5), 62(3), 72(1), 88(3), 96(2), 105, 112, 115(5), 125, 129, 137, 142;
Gross, Paul: 183(5);
Harris, David: 10, 12, 14, 15, 18, 20, 21, 25, 28, 29, 30(2), 32(1,4), 34(4), 35, 36(3,4), 38(3), 42(1, 2), 43(3), 44(4), 46, 48, 49, 50, 51, 53, 54, 56, 57(3), 58, 59, 61, 64(3), 66, 67(4), 68, 69, 70(2), 74(3,4), 75, 76, 77(3), 78, 79, 84, 86(1), 90, 92, 93, 94, 95, 96(1), 98(1), 99(4), 102, 103(4), 110(1), 113(3), 117(4), 119, 121(5), 123(5), 131(5), 134, 138, 139(3), 141, 145, 146, 151, 152(3), 153(5), 157, 159, 161, 164, 168, 170(3,4), 171, 172, 173, 174, 175, 176, 177(3,4), 178(2), 180(2), 184, 186(2), 191(4), 192(1), 193, 195(5,6), 196(2), 198(1,3), 199(5), 200, 201;
Israel Museum: 86(1);
Kahan, Norberto: 41(6);
Kroyanker, David: 34(1,3), 36(1), 38(1), 40, 44(5), 47, 52(2), 55, 57(2), 60, 64(1), 67(6,7), 70(4), 73, 74(1), 77(4,5), 82, 83, 86(2), 93(3), 101, 103(5,6), 104(1,2), 106, 107, 108, 109, 110(2), 111, 113(2), 115(4), 116, 118, 120, 121(4), 122, 123(6), 124, 126(2), 127(4), 128(3), 130, 131(3,4), 132, 133(3,5), 135(4), 139(4,5), 140(1,2), 143, 147, 148, 149, 150(1,2,4), 152(1), 153(4,6), 154(2), 155, 156, 158, 160(2), 162, 163, 165, 166, 167, 170(2), 174(1), 180(1,3), 181(5,7,8), 182(1,2,3), 183(6), 185(3), 186(3,4), 189(2), 190, 194(1,2,3), 199(4);
Lehmann, Yoram: 62(1,2);
Milon, Reuven: 30(1), 177(2), 178(1), 185(4), 188(1), 196(2);
Ofek Aerial Photography Ltd.: 6;
Radovan, Zev: 41(4), 100;
Suchowolski, Meidad: 22;
Tower of David/The Museum of the History of Jerusalem: 11(2,3), 13, 16, 17(2,3), 22, 30(1), 41(6), 62(1,2).

ADDITIONAL PICTURE CREDITS
Ben-Dov, Meir, *Atlas Carta, Jerusalem*, Jerusalem, 1991 (Hebrew), p. 37(5,6);
Burgoyne, Michael, *Mamluk Jerusalem*, London, 1987, p. 51(3);
Central Zionist Archives, Jerusalem, p.160(1);
Hirschfeld, Yizhar, *The Eretz Israel Home*, Jerusalem, 1987 (Hebrew), p.111(3);
Sharon, Arieh, *Planning Jerusalem*, Jerusalem, 1973, p. 60(2);
Wilson, Charles, *Picturesque Palestine*, London, 1880, p. 64(3).

Chronology of Jerusalem

Canaanite Period .... Until c. 1000 BC

First Temple Period .... 1000 BC—586 BC
    King David conquers Jerusalem .... 996 BC
    King Solomon builds Temple .... c.950 BC

Second Temple Period .... 538 BC—70 AD
    Completion of Second Temple .... 515 BC
    Reign of King Herod the Great .... 37—4 BC
    Third Wall built by Agrippa I .... 44 AD
    Destruction of Jerusalem .... 70 AD

Roman Period (Aelia Capitolina) .... 135—324

Byzantine Period .... 324—638

Early Muslim Period .... 638—1099
    Umayyad Dynasties .... 660—750
    Dome of the Rock built 691
    Abbasid Dynasties .... 750—969
    Fatimid Rule .... 969—1099

Crusader Period .... 1099—1187
    Holy Sepulcher inaugurated 1149

Ayyubid Period .... 1187—1250
    Saladin conquers Jerusalem 1187

Mamluk Period .... 1260—1517

Ottoman Period .... 1517—1917
    Sultan Suleiman the Magnificent .... 1520—1566
    Sultan Abdul Hamid II .... 1876—1909

British Mandate Period .... 1917—1948
    Military Government .... 1917—1920
    British High Commissioners .... 1920—1948
    War of Independence 1948

Divided Jerusalem .... 1948—1967
    Teddy Kollek elected mayor 1965
    Six-Day War .... June 1967

Unified Jerusalem .... 1967—present

Acknowledgments

I offer sincerest gratitude to all those who assisted me, over the past fifteen years, in my research on the architecture, town planning, and physical development of Jerusalem, and thus also in the preparation of this book. Most particularly I wish to acknowledge the following:

The Jerusalem Institute for Israel Studies, where Ms Ora Ahimeir and Professor Abraham Friedman lent their professional and organizational assistance, abetting both my research efforts and the publication process;

Teddy Kollek, former Mayor of Jerusalem, who supported my research work for over 12 years;

Professor David Amiran, who, during the past twelve years, assisted me academically in my research;

Ralph Mandel, for writing a fine historical introduction to the book, as well as for editing and translating my Hebrew text into readable English.

Jana Burshtein, who applied her goodwill, talent, and skill in preparing most of the line drawings and maps;

Photographer David Harris, who deserves special thanks for many of the most illuminating photographs in the book;

Ruth Cheshin, Mendel Kaplan, Amy S. Cohen, Uzi Wexler, Amos Mar-Chayim, Amnon Niv, Ya'akov Efrati, Avraham Havilio, and Father Emanuel Jacobs, who assisted in obtaining financial support throughout the years, at the various stages of research;

The Jerusalem Municipality, the Jerusalem Foundation, the Kaplan-Kushlick Foundation, the Revson Foundation, the National Academy of Science and Humanities, the S.H. and Helen Scheuer Family Foundation, the Ministry of Education and Culture, and the Embassy of the Federal Republic of Germany, who supported my research with a number of grants.

The librarians and archivists at the Jewish National and University Library, the Central Zionist Archives, the Historical Archives of the Jerusalem Municipality, and the Tower of David/Museum of the History of Jerusalem, all of which helped in the gathering of material;

Marc Walter, for the skill, imagination, good taste, and labor he devoted to the layout and design of the book;

To my mother Edith and my daughters Michal and Tamar, I wish to express my love and appreciation for their devoted support.

Last but not least, I acknowledge deep gratitude to my beloved wife Leorah, who was a full-time partner at every stage of the project, from research all the way through editing and proofreading.

David Kroyanker
Jerusalem May 1994

Copyright © The Jerusalem Institute for Israel Studies